Billy Clah.

This book unites speech act theory and conversation analysis to advance a theory of conversational competence. It is predicated on the assumption that speech act theory, if it is to be of genuine empirical and theoretical significance, must be embedded within a general theory of conversational competence capable of accounting for how we do things with words in naturally occurring conversation, and it can usefully be seen as a synthesis of traditional speech act theory, conversation analysis, and artificial intelligence research in natural language processing. Michael L. Geis analyzes a variety of naturally occurring conversations, presenting them within a framework of computational interest and within Discourse Representation Theory. In particular, he offers an explicit mapping of semantic and pragmatic (i.e. speech-act-theoretic) meaning features and politeness features into so-called conventionalized indirect speech act forms.

# Speech acts
# and conversational
# interaction

# Speech acts and conversational interaction

MICHAEL L. GEIS

*Department of Linguistics*
*The Ohio State University*

**CAMBRIDGE**
UNIVERSITY PRESS

Published by the Press Syndicate of the University of Cambridge
The Pitt Building, Trumpington Street, Cambridge CB2 1RP
40 West 20th Street, New York, NY 10011-4211, USA
10 Stamford Road, Oakleigh, Melbourne 3166, Australia

First published 1995
Reprinted 1997

Printed in Great Britain by Antony Rowe Ltd, Chippenham, Wilts.

*A catalogue record for this book is available from the British Library*

*Library of Congress cataloguing in publication data*
Geis, Michael L.
Speech acts and conversational interaction / by Michael L. Geis.
p.   cm.
Includes bibliographical references.
1. Speech acts (Linguistics). 2. Conversation analysis.
3. Communicative competence. 4. Psycholinguistics.
5. Social interaction. 6. Pragmatics. I. Title.
P95.55.G38   1995
401'.41 – dc20   94–48352 CIP

ISBN 0 521 46499 4 hardback

*For Jonnie*

# Contents

*Contents*

# Preface

In this study, I propose and defend a new theory of speech acts predicated on the assumption that speech act theory, if it is to be of genuine empirical and theoretical significance, must be embedded within a general theory of conversational competence capable of accounting for how we do things with words in naturally occurring conversation. The theory I shall propose, Dynamic Speech Act Theory (DSAT), can usefully be seen as a synthesis of traditional speech act theory (cf., especially, Searle 1969, 1975, 1979), conversation analysis (cf., especially, the references to Schegloff, Sacks, and Levinson in the bibliography), and artificial intelligence research in natural language processing (cf., especially, the citations in the bibliography to the work of Allen, Cohen, Litman, and Perrault, also Patten, Geis, and Becker (1992)). Important additional influences are the work of Brown and Levinson (1987) on politeness and Halliday and Hasan (1989) on register.

I shall take the position here that the goal of a theory of conversational competence should be specification of the properties of devices capable of engaging in conversational interactions – devices that we might call "conversation machines." As such, the theory would be a theory of the conversational competence that underlies our ability to engage in goal-achievement and goal-recognition in conversation and our ability to produce and understand utterances (and nonverbal behaviors) appropriate to the context. I shall argue in these pages that correctly conceived, speech-act-theoretic structures will play a critical role in accounting for these abilities.

From conversation analysis, I draw the thesis that the actions participants engage in in conversation – actions like requesting, offering, promising, making assessments, and the like – are social **as opposed to** linguistic actions. This is a significant departure from speech act theory. Though Austin, Searle, and others noted that there is a social dimension to actions like these, they were – and still are – viewed by speech act theorists as actions we perform "in saying something" (Austin 1962: 91). The importance of this step lies in the fact that once it is recognized that so-called speech acts are social, as opposed to linguistic acts, the temptation to associate the performance of particular speech acts with the uttering of sentences having particular linguistic forms diminishes greatly.

From conversation analysis, I also draw the thesis that the fundamental unit of investigation for speech act theory should be naturally occurring conversational sequences, not the individual, constructed utterances, isolated from actual or even explicitly imagined conversational contexts that traditional speech act theory has been based on. I argue that the focus of our research should be less on how we might make a request or issue an invitation in uttering a single sentence, and more on how we do requesting and inviting in multiturn conversational interactions.

The strength of speech act theory is that it offers a relatively explicit theory of communicative actions, something conversation analysts have resolutely refused to do. Searle (1969), for instance, explicitly connected speech acts and the goals (his "essential conditions") they are intended to achieve – an essential feature of any theory of action – and laid out sets of necessary and sufficient conditions on the felicitous and successful performance of such acts. What it does not offer is an explicit means of mapping utterances into speech acts. In order to accomplish this goal, I shall argue that Searle's speech act structures must be revised and we must move from the view that utterances should be mapped into speech acts to the view that utterances should be mapped into elements of speech act structures – into the conditions and domain predicates of such structures. This is the single most important step in the development of a speech-act-theoretic account of conversational interaction.

One of the major flaws of virtually all research on conversation – on discourse generally – is its lack of explicitness. Though I cannot claim that what I offer here is fully explicit, an earlier version of this theory has been partially implemented computationally in work with Terry

Patten and Barbara Becker (Patten, Geis, and Becker 1992). This paper reported on an effort to simulate the travel agent side of an interaction with a client. Our simulation covers little conversational ground, but does demonstrate that a speech-act-theoretic approach to conversational interaction of the sort I shall advance here is sufficiently precise to be implementable and is computationally attractive in other respects.

There is one important exception to the claim that approaches to discourse are inexplicit and this is Discourse Representation Theory (DRT) (Kamp and Reyle 1993) and other similar semantic approaches. A signal virtue of Discourse Representation Theory is that it allows inclusion of pragmatic information. In chapters 6 and 7, I show how the present theory of speech acts can be implemented in Discourse Representation Theory.

In chapter 1, I provide a brief survey and critique of traditional speech act theory, including the argument that so-called speech acts are social as opposed to linguistic acts. In chapter 2, I argue that we must turn our attention away from the actions we perform in uttering single sentences to the examination of multiturn interactions in which we do requesting, inviting, and the like. I shall argue that we should concern ourselves not with what action is performed in uttering individual sentences but with what utterances contribute to the work of interactions, that is, with what they contribute to the satisfaction of speech act conditions and instantiation of domain predicates. In chapter 3, I sketch the architecture of DSAT, show how it is like and different from the speech act structures posited by Searle, and illustrate how it applies to the analysis of request and invitation routines in conversation. In chapter 4, I discuss the interactional effects of acts, developing in the process a variant of Brown and Levinson's (1987) theory of politeness. In chapter 5, I provide a critique of a number of theories of indirect speech acts, arguing that the focus on how we (imagine that we) use single utterances in constructed contexts to perform speech acts has led to an over-simple view of the nature of conventions of use and of the conditions in which individual utterances can be used to do such things as make requests, give invitations, make offers, etc. In chapter 6, I provide an alternative treatment of conventions of use that accounts for a variety of colloquial English request forms, including typical indirect speech act forms, that is based on the thesis that the colloquial forms of interest are pragmatically compositional. In chapter 7, I contrast two views of the structure of conversation – the largely text-oriented approach of conversation analysis and the cognitive approach of DSAT. It is in this chapter, that I demonstrate how DSAT can be incorporated in DRT. And, in chapter 8, I offer a sketch of utterance generation from the perspective of DSAT.

This work owes a very great deal to my former collaborator, Terry Patten, with whom I have worked on the computational implementation of my views. I am also greatly indebted to William Lycan (philosopher), Georgia Green (linguist), David Good (psycholinguist), and Ken Turner (linguist), and two anonymous Cambridge University Press reviewers for comments on earlier drafts. I am also indebted to a number of students who have provided very useful criticisms of earlier views, including, in particular, Kate Welker (especially), Lindsay Amthor, Barbara Becker, Charles Miracle, Jay Moody, Jack Rouser, Nicole Schrickel, Michela Shigley-Giusti, and Todd Yampol.

# 1

## The nature of speech acts

### Introduction

In this study, I propose and defend a new theory of speech acts predicated on the assumption that speech act theory, if it is to be of genuine empirical and theoretical interest, must be embedded in a theory of conversational competence that is grounded in naturally occurring and experimentally derived conversational data. My approach is therefore quite different from that of traditional speech act theorists, who have focused almost exclusively on intuitive assessments of isolated, constructed examples like those in (1), as opposed to analysis of naturally occurring multiturn request sequences like (2).

(1) a. I request that you give me hot chocolate with whipped cream.
    b. Please give me hot chocolate with whipped cream.
    c. Can I have hot chocolate with whipped cream?

(2) Merritt (1976: 337)

|  |  |  |
|---|---|---|
| CUSTOMER: | Do you have hot chocolate? | $T_1$ |
| CLERK: | mmhmm | $T_2$ |
| CUSTOMER: | Can I have hot chocolate with whipped cream? | $T_3$ |
| CLERK: | Sure ((leaves to get)). | $T_4$ |

Interestingly, Searle (1992: 7), the originator and principal

1

proponent of traditional speech act theory[1] has recently taken a pessimistic view of the possibility of giving "an account of conversations parallel to our account of speech acts," claiming that there cannot be "constitutive rules for conversations in a way that we have constitutive rules of speech acts." I would concede that traditional speech act theory does not provide a particularly promising platform for development of a theory of conversational competence. However, if modified in certain critical respects, speech act theory can, in fact, provide constitutive rules for conversation – not for conversations as a whole, of course, but for specific types of multiturn interactions – that facilitate identification of actions and account for how actions are performed in multiturn interactions.

The weaknesses of speech act theory as an approach to the analysis of conversation have been recognized by others, most notably by the conversation analysts, Schegloff (1984, 1988) and Levinson (1981, 1983). Levinson (1981: 475) argues correctly, for instance, that "speech act types are not the relevant categories over which to define the regularities of conversation" and (Levinson 1983: 289) challenges the twin theses that there is some specifiable function from utterances to speech acts and that sequences of utterances in conversation can usefully be described in terms of sequences of speech act types.[2] Before considering the conversation analytic criticisms of speech act theory,[3] and those of my own, let us first briefly review those features of speech act theory that will be of greatest interest here.

[1] The idea of a speech act goes back to Austin's (1962) concept of an illocutionary act. Speech act theory itself – the theory of the constitutive rules for speech acts – must be credited to Searle.

[2] He associates these theses with Labov (1972), Sinclair and Coulthard (1975), Longacre (1967), Labov and Fanshel (1977), Coulthard and Brazil (1979), and Edmondson (1981). Searle (1992) himself is skeptical about the possibility of accounting for conversational sequences as sequences of speech act types, as was just noted in the text.

[3] Conversation analysts view actions like requesting, offering, inviting, and the like as communicative social actions, not speech acts, if what is meant by the term "speech act" is an act necessarily performed "in saying something," to use Austin's (1962) phrase. In this, they are clearly correct. However, their criticisms of speech act theory ring hollow, for they have themselves offered no theory of communicative actions at all, much less one that is comparable in sophistication to speech act theory, nor have they even addressed the issue of constructing a mapping from communicative actions to utterances. Their notion of an "action in interaction" is therefore ultimately no better founded than the notion of a speech act.

2

## A brief sketch of speech act theory

In his very influential book, *How to Do Things with Words*, the philosopher, John Austin (1962), observed that in **saying** something that has a certain sense and reference, one is normally also **doing** something other than just saying something – making a request, as in the case of the sentences of (1), or making a promise or offer, or an apology, etc.

According to Austin, in uttering a sentence like (1a) the speaker performs the **locutionary act** of vocalizing a sentence with a certain sense and reference, and also, of necessity, performs an **illocutionary act** (or what has come more commonly to be called a "speech act") as well, in this case the act of making a request. Austin also noted that uttering a sentence to perform a particular illocutionary act will normally have some sort of effect on the addressee. He writes that "saying something will often, or even normally, produce certain consequential effects upon the feelings, thoughts, or actions of the audience, or of the speaker, or of other persons: and it may be done with the design, intention, or purpose of producing them" (p. 101). Acts of this sort Austin called **perlocutionary acts**. Austin provides the following example, illustrating these three types of acts (p. 102):

(3)  Act (A) or Locution
      He said to me, "You can't do that."
     Act (B) or Illocution
      He protested against my doing it.
     Act (C.a) or Perlocution
      He pulled me up, checked me.
     Act (C.b)
      He stopped me, he brought me to my senses, &c.
      He annoyed me.

It is clear from this that Austin recognized that illocutionary acts can have a variety of effects ranging from what might be called their "transactional effects" (cf. (C.a) and "He stopped me" in (3)), which is the usual ostensible goal of an act, to what might be called their "interactional effects" (cf. "He annoyed me" in (C.b)).[4]

---

[4]  The interactional effects of an act include threats to the addressee's negative face (the addressee's desire not to have her freedom of action restricted) and positive face (the addressee's desire to be valued and to have what she values valued), among other things. See Brown and Levinson (1978) and chapter 4 below for a discussion of positive and negative face, of the notion of a face threat, and for a discussion of how participants redress face threats.

3

Austin (1962) focused a good deal of his attention on what he called performative sentences – sentences like (1a), utterance of which normally counts as performing the action named by the verb. Such sentences typically are nonnegative, present tense, auxiliariless sentences containing a performative verb, first person subject, a sometimes optional second person direct or indirect object, and a clausal or infinitival verbal complement of some sort. Other examples are

(4)  a. I order you to turn out the lights.
     b. I promise to turn out the lights.
     c. I bet you five dollars that Bill will turn out the lights.
     d. I propose that we get someone else to turn out the lights.

Austin argued that sentences like (1a) and (4) do not have truth-values and are therefore not subject to truth-conditions.[5] However, he noted that utterances can misfire or go wrong in ways other than being false. Thus, were I to see a new boat about to be launched into a lake, run up to it as it is being lowered into the water, and smash a bottle of champagne over its bow and say, *I hereby christen thee, "The Albatross,"* the boat would not thereby be christened "The Albatross," for I did not have the authority to christen this boat. However, what I said was not false. Austin would have said that my attempt to christen this boat was "infelicitous," and, since then, conditions on the successful and appropriate performance of an act have usually been referred to as "felicity conditions."[6]

[5]  There is a vast literature on the question whether performative sentences have truth-values. Some of this literature was prompted by the claim of R. Lakoff (1968), Ross (1970), Sadock (1974) and others, who worked within the framework of Generative Semantics, that every sentence must be assigned a "performative prefix" in underlying structure. According to this hypothesis, pairs like *Bill Clinton is President* and *I declare that Bill Clinton is President* have the same underlying linguistic representation. One of the great difficulties with this analysis is that it entails that a sentence that manifestly does have a truth-value (e.g., *Bill Clinton is President*) might be semantically identical to one that does not (*I declare that Bill Clinton is President*). See Lycan (1984) and references therein for a discussion of what he and his colleague Boër (Boër and Lycan 1976) call the "performadox." See also Recanati (1987) for a useful discussion of these issues.

[6]  There are two types of conditions, constitutive conditions and regulative conditions. Constitutive conditions are necessary conditions on successful performance of an act; if they are not satisfied, the act simply does not get performed. Regulative conditions are not conditions on the successful performance of an act, but are concerned with how happily or how well it is performed. If I say, *Let me make you a sandwich*, to you, I will have made an offer even if you do not need food and I know that you do not need food and will not accept my offer. It is a defective offer, in that it is insincere, but is an offer nevertheless.

4

Performative sentences can go wrong because someone does not have the status required to perform the act (only certain persons can say, *I hereby pronounce you husband and wife* and thereby marry others), does not have a necessary belief (as when someone says, *Sandy has gotten married to Terry*, while believing that Sandy has not gotten married to Terry),[7] or does not have a necessary intention (as when someone says, *I'll be there*, when he has no intention of being at the place in question), or some precondition on initiation of the act is not met (as would be true if a landlord were to demand a rent payment from someone who is merely visiting a tenant in her building), among other things.

Austin made a distinction between what he called "explicit" performatives and "implicit" or "primitive" performatives. Compare the explicitly performative *a*-forms of (5)-(6) with their more collo- quial implicitly performative counterparts.

(5) a. I order you to turn out the lights.
  b. Turn out the lights.
(6) a. I promise to be there.
  b. I'll be there.

Austin notes (p. 33) that an implicit performative like (6b) "may or may not be a promise," whereas it would be difficult to maintain that (6a) is not. Promises are normally uttered in contexts in which the promisor believes that the addressee has some need or desire that she wishes the promisor specifically to satisfy. Suppose, in this light, that someone, who has not been invited to a particular party, idly asks me who is going to be at this party and I provide her a list of names, ending with *...and I'll be there as well*. In this context, this utterance would not count as a promise to my addressee to be at this party because she has no need or desire for me to be there that I am proposing to satisfy. On the other hand, should my interlocutor have been invited to the party and say to me that she will go to the party if and only if I go and I say (6b), then I will have made a promise to her to go to the party, for she has expressed a desire for me to go to this party. Unlike explicit performatives, then, the force that utterance of a declarative sentence like (6b) has depends critically on context; in this case, whether it has been established, not just that the addressee has

---

[7]  In such a circumstance it could be that Sandy and Terry are actually married and that the sentence is therefore true.

some need or desire, but that the addressee wishes the speaker specifically to satisfy it.

## Searlean felicity conditions

One of Searle's (1969) most important contributions to speech act theory was his development of the Austinian concept of felicity. Searle argued that speech acts, which is the term he preferred for Austin's illocutionary acts, are subject to four types of felicity conditions: preparatory conditions, sincerity conditions, propositional content conditions, and essential conditions. The felicity conditions he gave for requests are given in (7).

(7) Searle's conditions on requests (H is the hearer and S is the speaker)

Propositional content: Future act A of H.

Preparatory:

H is able to do A. S believes H is able to do A.[8]

It is not obvious to both S and H that H will do A in the normal course of events of his own accord.

Sincerity: S wants H to do A.

Essential: Counts as an attempt to get H to do A.

In this formulation, what Searle calls the "essential condition" corresponds to what I shall be calling the "transactional effect." What is missing from this account (but not from Austin's treatment) is reference to possible interactional effects of making a request.[9]

## Indirect speech acts

In discussions of speech acts, it is common to make a distinction between direct and indirect speech acts. As Austin noted, a request to turn out the lights can be communicated **directly**, not only by using an explicit performative sentence like (4a), but also by employing an implicit performative sentence such as (8).

---

[8] Searle's providing alternate characterizations of this condition – one in "objective" terms and one in terms of speaker beliefs – will not do. In this study, I shall argue that conditions should be stated objectively, with the issue of speaker beliefs arising in utterance planning.

[9] Searle (1969) seems to have accepted Austin's views on perlocutions. Nevertheless his speech act structures do not reflect this.

(8)   Please turn out the lights.

However, a number of scholars (Sadock 1970, 1972, Gordon and Lakoff 1971, Green 1975, and Searle 1975) have noted that essentially the same request can be communicated **indirectly** through the use of questions like those in (9):

(9)   a.  Could you turn out the lights?
      b.  Would you mind turning out the lights?
      c.  Why don't you turn out the lights?

or an assertion like (10):

(10)   I'd like for you to turn out the lights.

A case like (8) illustrates the very important point that certain literal speech acts can be performed directly using the sentence type "dedicated" to the performance of that act. Thus, we can use a declarative sentence in a literal way to make an assertion (*Bill Clinton is President*) or use an interrogative sentence literally to ask a question (*Is Bill Clinton President?*) or use an imperative sentence literally to give a directive (*Vote for Bill Clinton!*). In these cases, the relationship between the utterance's form and literal meaning and the act that is performed must be said to be wholly conventional because it is arbitrarily linked to a particular syntactic form and cannot therefore be inferred.[10] Such acts are called "literal acts" by Searle (1975) and I will follow his terminology in the pages that follow. However, cases like (9) and (10) suggest that we can use these linguistic constructions to perform speech acts other than or in addition to those that they are conventionally associated with.

Searle (1975) took the line that there are basically two types of indirect speech acts. One type **must** be "calculated," to use Grice's (1975) term. The other type involves cases in which Searle claims their force **can** be calculated, but is not. Instead, he argues that their illocutionary force is conventionally associated with particular

---

[10]   Sadock and Zwicky (1985) argue that a sentence type is defined by a pairing of a syntactic form and a conventionalized (and therefore "literal") illocutionary force. I will adopt their view in the pages to follow.

sentence patterns.[11] Searle (p. 61) offers (11) as an example of the first type.

(11)   Student X: Let's go to the movies tonight.
       Student Y: I have to study for an exam.

Searle argues that Y's utterance performs two illocutionary acts, a **primary** act of rejecting X's proposal and a **secondary** act of asserting that he has to study for an exam. According to Searle, Y performs the secondary illocutionary act of asserting something by uttering a sentence which on its literal meaning has the conventional force of an assertion and he refers to this act as the **literal act**. The primary illocutionary act in this sort of case, on the other hand, is conveyed indirectly via common sense reasoning of a Gricean sort based on the literal meaning of Y's utterance, felicity conditions on proposals, and contextual and general background information.

The second type of indirect speech act involves data like (9) and (10). Speech acts performed employing sentences like these are said to be indirect because they are used to perform an action other than that which is most immediately suggested by their literal meanings. Thus, taking the utterances of (9) and (10) at face value, we might say, for instance, that the speaker of (9a) is requesting information about the ability of the addressee to perform an action, whereas the speaker of (10) is asserting a proposition predicating a desire of the speaker that the addressee perform some action. In each of these cases, therefore, the speaker's intended illocutionary point – that the speaker means to cause the addressee to turn out the lights – must be inferred. The inferences in question are a species of conversational implicature (Grice 1975), for as Searle (1975) showed, it is possible for the addressee to calculate the speaker's illocutionary point in cases such as these by employing common-sense reasoning based on Grice's (1975) "Cooperative Principle."

Although the illocutionary points of utterances like (9) and (10) are calculable, Searle and other early writers such as Sadock (1970, 1972), Gordon and Lakoff (1971), Morgan (1978), and Green (1975) took the position that we do not actually calculate them but

---

[11]   Who exactly first identified the class of indirect speech acts Searle referred to as being conventionalized is not completely clear. Sadock (1970) certainly noted them, as did Gordon and Lakoff (1971), who referred to Sadock's paper, as well as to an unpublished paper by Georgia Green on a similar topic.

instead (a) associate underlying linguistic representations (logical forms) with them that directly account for their request forces (Sadock and Green), or (b) apply conversational postulates to their logical forms from which their request forces can be derived in one inferential step (Gordon and Lakoff), or (c) through the application of conventions of use that short-circuit the implicature (Searle and Morgan). In each of these cases, the authors treated the implicatures as conventionalized in some manner – as a convention of meaning (Sadock and Green, and, but in a different way, Gordon and Lakoff) or a convention of use (Searle and Morgan). I shall examine the theories of Gordon and Lakoff and of Searle and Morgan in chapter 5.

## Dynamic Speech Act Theory

In this and the chapters that follow, I provide an alternative account of speech act theory that differs from the theory just sketched in a number of critical respects. The basic theses of this theory are:

I.  **In uttering any sentence, a speaker necessarily performs a literal act which is conventionally associated with the type of sentence uttered.** I shall follow Sadock and Zwicky (1985), who argue that a sentence type results from a pairing of a syntactic form with a conventional conversational use. Thus, in uttering a declarative sentence, one conventionally performs the literal act of asserting something; in uttering an interrogative sentence, one conventionally performs the literal act of asking a question; and in uttering an imperative sentence, one conventionally performs the literal act of directing someone to do something. We may reasonably refer to this literal act as a speech act, for it is performed "in saying something." In this respect, I believe that DSAT is in full agreement with Searle.

II. **Searlean primary speech acts (e.g., offering, promising, requesting, inviting, suggesting, etc.), which are, of course, the acts that have most interested pragmaticians and others, are social as opposed to linguistic in nature and are therefore better viewed as communicative actions than as speech acts.** Both Austin and Searle recognized that there is a social dimension to any illocutionary act or speech act. However, I shall argue that none of the differentia of

9

speech acts is linguistic in nature and, further, that there is nothing to be gained, and much to be lost, if we continue to think of speech acts or illocutionary acts as acts performed in saying something. I give this argument in the present chapter.

III. **The thesis that there exists or should exist a mapping from individual utterances to primary speech acts must be abandoned.** As Searle (1992) has himself noted, his speech act theory does not provide a promising foundation for an account of conversation. Describing a given interaction (for instance, a service encounter in which one person tries to cause another to provide him with something) as a sequence of primary speech acts inevitably requires arbitrary choices, as Levinson (1983: 289) has noted, and the resulting descriptions are uninsightful. Only if we abandon the thesis that there is a direct association with primary speech acts and individual utterances can we provide an interesting, empirically satisfactory speech-act-theoretic account of conversation. I make this argument in the present chapter.

IV. **What we do within any interaction (specifically, any communicative interaction) is constrained by the properties of the type of interaction in which we are engaged.** As a consequence, the focus of speech act theory must shift from the actions we perform in uttering specific sentences to the properties of interactions and to what utterances contribute to the interactions in which they occur.

V. **Searle's view of the structure of speech acts must be revised in several respects, including adding an interactional effect or goal, for doing so is central to understanding politeness phenomena in conversation.** Associated with any interaction is an interaction structure that specifies the initial state from which the act is launched, which is often, but not always the same as Searle's sincerity condition, the transactional effect of the act, which is normally the equivalent of Searle's essential condition, a set of interactional effects[12] of the act (which constitute the face-threats associated with the act), a set of satisfaction conditions on

---

[12] I am employing Cheepen's (1988) distinction between transactional and interactional goals, but I shall sometimes use the term "effects," rather than "goals" for reasons that will become clear. I take a somewhat different view of interactional effects than does Cheepen.

10

successful accomplishment of the transactional effect (which are quite similar to Searlean preparatory conditions), and a domain, which consists of a specification of what the interaction is about (e.g., the properties of the thing the speaker desires the addressee to provide to the speaker). There is no propositional content condition per se; the domain predicates do the work of the propositional content condition, and more. I discuss these revisions and the motivations for them in chapters 3 and 4.

VI.   **Each utterance may have a transactional significance (as opposed to an illocutionary force) that reflects what the utterance contributes to satisfaction of the conditions of interaction structures and instantiation of their domain predicates or an interactional significance that reflects what it contributes to face-work (Goffman 1967) or both.** On this view, rather than associating a Searlean speech act with each utterance, we associate one or more elements of the interaction structure associated with the interaction that represents the contextual meaning of the utterance in the context in which it occurs. This specific assumption makes a theory of the constitutive rules of conversational sequences possible. This is discussed in chapters 3 and 4.

VII.  **There exists a device, the pragmatic stratum, that maps elements of interaction structures (i.e., conditions and domain predicates), which may be thought of as pragmatic "meaning" features of a certain type, semantic features, and certain features of the social and discourse context, specifically style, politeness, register, and discourse features, into utterances of the sort that occur in colloquial interactions.** It is the pragmatic stratum that allows us to account for conventions of use in a fully formal manner. This is discussed in chapter 6.

VIII. **Speech act theory must be dynamic in that interaction structures must be incorporatable in a computational model of utterance generation and utterance understanding or a dynamic semantic theory (or both).** The present theory, in an early incarnation, played a central role in the computational model of utterance generation of Patten, Geis, and Becker (1992). In chapter 7, I show how interaction

11

structures can be employed in DRT by way of accounting for how we achieve goals (more precisely, transactional effects) in interaction.

These revisions of speech act theory are substantial, to be sure. Indeed, I am sure that many, if not most, adherents of traditional speech act will find it very difficult to abandon the thesis that individual utterances have primary illocutionary force – it seems to be a powerfully seductive view. However, it is the architecture of speech act theory – the theory of the structure of speech acts – that is its defining characteristic and my interaction structures are not different in kind from Searle's speech act structures even if they are somewhat different in detail and in how they are employed.

## A critique of speech act theory

I would like to turn now to consider two flaws in speech act theory that preclude an empirically and theoretically credible account of how we do things in conversation. These are, first, the thesis that a defining characteristic of actions like requesting, offering, and the like is that they are actions performed "in saying something" (as Austin put it), and, second, that individual utterances have primary illocutionary force (in addition to literal force), that is, that in uttering a sentence, a speaker performs not only a literal act (an assertion, question, or directive) but also a primary act (a request, offer, promise, bet, or threat, etc).

### Speech acts as communicative actions

Whether to call actions like making requests, making offers and promises, conveying and requesting information, giving warnings, and making bets "speech acts" or "communicative actions" is not merely a terminological question, for as in any other area of investigation, our pretheoretic characterizations of the phenomena we study can considerably influence what sorts of analyses we are likely to give. If we see these acts as being speech acts (linguistic acts), for instance, we will be strongly inclined (incorrectly) to associate them with the use of particular linguistic constructions. Two phenomena particularly encourage this way of thinking about speech acts. Performative sentences, which played a major role in the development of Austin's (1962) views, especially encourage such a view,[13] as do cases of indirect speech acts like those performed in uttering sentences like (9) and (10), for in both cases it has seemed to many that the act performed is at least partially determined by the linguistic form of the sentence uttered.

The thesis that there is a direct mapping of primary speech acts into linguistic forms is largely a consequence of the methodology employed by speech act theorists. Austin, Searle, and most others have based their work almost exclusively on their intuitions as to how single, constructed sentences isolated from real or (usually) even explicitly constructed contexts might be used. Obviously, if one should ask oneself how one might be able to use sentences like (9) and (10), one will almost certainly answer that one can use them to make requests. And, it is powerfully attractive to go on and associate the apparent potential request forces of these sentences with the sentences them-selves, or (a slight improvement) with the uttering of these sentences, **for that is all that one is considering.** In failing to examine how we actually do things with words in conversation, speech act theorists have failed to appreciate the absolutely critical contribution of context in circumstances in which we find single utterances being used to do things like make requests, invitations, and offers, etc.

My argument that communicative actions are social, as opposed to speech (linguistic) acts is based on three main facts. The first is that many such acts can be performed nonverbally and that even in cases when a communicative action must be performed verbally, it does not follow from this fact alone that it must therefore be a speech (linguistic) act. The second is that none of the differentia of communicative actions is linguistic. Rather, they involve particular factual states, social relationships between participants, psychological states and attitudes, among other nonlinguistic things. Third, social features of context play a critical role in the differentiation of communicative actions.

## NONVERBAL PERFORMANCES OF SPEECH ACTS

Suppose a company captain has called for volunteers to reconnoiter behind enemy lines and that a soldier is interested in volunteering for this mission. She might volunteer by taking a step forward or raising

[13]    But see Bach and Harnish's (1979) very different treatment of performatives.

an arm, or by saying, *I'll do it*, or, *I volunteer*. Clearly, in stepping forward or in raising an arm, the soldier performs essentially the same act as she would perform in saying *I'll do it* or *I volunteer*. Now, we can either say that the soldier was not doing volunteering in stepping forward or in raising her arm or we can say that volunteering is an action that can be performed nonverbally, as well as verbally, and is therefore not a **speech** act. There are other actions that can be performed nonverbally. One can request something by reaching for it, or offer something by extending it to someone who has an evident need for it. And, on being asked a *Yes-No-*Question, one can answer it (in some cultures) by nodding one's head (for "Yes") or shaking it back and forth (for "No"), or with a shrug of the shoulders (which might communicate an inability to answer the question). One can point something out to someone by simply pointing to it or by saying, *Look at that!* There are other acts, of course, which are more difficult to perform nonverbally, to which I shall return shortly.

If we define the notion "illocutionary act" or "speech act" in such a way as to insist that it be an act performed **in** saying something, we shall obviously not be able to say that stepping forward or raising an arm performs the **illocutionary** act or **speech** act of volunteering in the scenario I sketched above.[14] The fact is, however, that, from the captain's perspective, the soldier who steps forward to signal a willingness to go on the mission and the soldier who says, *I will*, to signal a willingness to go will have done the same thing, and it is this action – a communicative action – that speech act theorists should be concerned with.

Austin (1962) seems to be responsible for the view that illocutionary acts are necessarily verbal acts. He has said (p. 119) that "stating, informing (as distinct from showing), arguing, giving estimates, reckoning, and finding (in the legal sense)" cannot be performed except by saying something. The same is true, he says, of "the great majority" of verdictives (*I take it that you are saying. . ., I find for the plaintiff*) and expositives (*I deny that I did it, swear that I didn't do it*, etc.). However, it does not follow from the fact that one might have to use language to perform some action that what is most important about it is that it is performed verbally. One cannot kiss another

---

[14] It has been suggested (by an anonymous publisher's reviewer) that there may be no harm in this in that stepping forward does not predicate a future act of the speaker in the way that saying, *I will*, or, *I volunteer*, does. However, this would be a question-begging response, for the propositional content condition is itself an artifact of Searle's claim that speech acts are to be associated with the uttering of individual sentences.

person without closing one's lips together, drawing air into one's lungs, thereby creating a partial vacuum, and then releasing the bilabial constriction, but if we follow the suggested line of reasoning of Austin we will have to conclude that kissing is primarily, and most importantly, a bilabial, ingressive pulmonary act. It is a bilabial, ingressive pulmonary act, even sometimes a reciprocal bilabial, ingressive pulmonary act, but it is also, and more importantly, a social action, ranging in significance from signaling sexual interest to showing affection, to communicating a greeting (the kissing that is done between celebrities on television shows), to communicating respect (as when someone kisses the hand of some royal woman). Kissing is, in short, a social action, even if it necessarily requires performance of a physical action. Precisely the same is true of requesting, offering, making threats, giving warnings, conveying information, requesting information, or uttering verdictives and expositives, etc. These are social actions even if they sometimes require some sort of linguistic action – talking, writing, signing, etc. And, once one has recognized that communicative actions are social actions and that many types of communicative actions can be performed nonverbally, the temptation to associate these actions with particular linguistic forms diminishes greatly.

## THE DIFFERENTIA OF SPEECH ACTS

Perhaps the most compelling argument one can give in support of the thesis that speech acts are social actions, as opposed to speech acts, is that the differentia of the various different classes of speech acts involve particular factual states, psychological states – beliefs, desires, attitudes, and feelings, and social relations among participants, not linguistic properties of utterances. Recall, for instance, Searle's felicity conditions on requesting, given above in (7). Of these conditions, the only one that could possibly be said to be linguistic in character is the propositional content condition. However, this is not, in fact, a **linguistic** condition for it makes no reference to the necessary occurrence of some particular sound, morpheme, word, phrase, or syntactic property (e.g., word order), but to what the sentence is about and would be the same if one were speaking German, Swahili, or Chinese.

Searle's propositional content condition is an artifact of his problematic methodology. If one is only considering how one might do

15

requesting with a single utterance, as Searle normally did, then it might make sense to insist that the propositional content of the utterance be this or that. However, multiturn conversational sequences do not, as a whole, express a proposition. Nor need a multiturn conversational sequence of some particular type even contain a specific utterance expressing the propositional content Searle associates with that act-type. The hot chocolate example cited on page 1 above contained no such example – indeed, the propositional content of the final turn of the requester in this interaction predicated a **future state** of the **requester**, not a **future action** of the **requestee**.

Speech act taxonomies generally support the thesis that speech acts are social, as opposed to linguistic, acts. Searle (1979: 2–8) provides a taxonomy of speech acts based on a wide variety of factors, including

- differences in the illocutionary point or purpose of the act
- differences in what he calls "direction of fit" of words to the world (i.e., do the words purport to correspond to the world, as in the case of garden-variety assertions or is the point to try to get the world to match the words, as in the case of directives?)
- differences in expressed psychological states
- differences in the force with which the illocutionary point is made
- differences in the relative status of the speaker and hearer and whose interests are served
- differences in preferred or required discourse positions
- differences in propositional content that are determined by illocutionary force indicating devices
- differences as to whether the act must be performed as a speech act (i. e., through saying something)
- differences in regard to whether or not an action is a part of some extra-linguistic institution (e. g., a wedding ceremony)
- differences in regard to whether or not the verb that "names" the act can be used performatively (e. g., *threat* cannot be used performatively)

Many of these factors, and they are some of the most important ones, are totally nonlinguistic, such as differences in illocutionary point or purpose, differences in expressed psychological states, differences in force, and differences in regard to whether an action is a part of some ceremony. None of the others turns out to be all and only linguistic.

It is clear that differences in illocutionary point represent differences in "real world" goals and are in no way linguistic. There are several factors that are semantic or, at least, quasi-semantic. The thesis that there are differences in the "direction of fit" between worlds and words sounds semantic. Certainly differences in propositional content are semantic differences. However, though semantics is clearly a part of linguistics, propositional content *per se* is not linguistic. The sentences, *I love you*, and, *Ich liebe dich*, express the same proposition, but this proposition is no more a part of English than of German or any other language.

Those who have assumed that speech acts other than literal acts are in some special way linguistic acts have rested their case on instances in which utterances are said to contain "some syntactical feature which, given the rest of the sentence and a certain context of utterance, expresses an illocutionary force" (Searle 1985: 2). Searle's best examples of this involve performatives and alleged cases of conventionalized indirect speech acts. In the former case, literal meaning (with context), not the linguistic form of the sentence, determines its force. If *I promise you to leave* counts as a promise but *He promises you to leave* and *I promised you to leave* do not, this is due to the meanings of these sentences (to which syntax makes a contribution, of course), not just their syntactic forms. I shall argue against the thesis that alleged cases of conventionalized indirect speech acts have conventional force in the sense meant by Searle in chapter 5.

One particular alleged marker of illocutionary force, namely, *please*, is worth special comment. If I say, *A large pineapple, please*, in a frozen yoghurt store, it might be said that *please* marks the utterance as a request. Note, however, that saying, *A large pineapple*, would also count as a request in such a store, so it is the context, not the appearance of *please* that determines that *A large pineapple* is a request. *Please* is better viewed as a politeness marker redressing the face-threat associated with making a request. In fact, the word *please* occurs in offers (e.g., *Please have another cookie*) and invitations (*I'm giving a come as you are party tonight. Please come*), as well as requests, from which it follows that it is not an illocutionary force marker of just requests. What it seems to do is redress the face-threat associated with acts that presuppose the willingness of the addressee to agree to the act.

The only other factor that might be said to be linguistic concerns differences in preferred or required discourse position. Certainly, how an utterance is interpreted will normally depend on its discourse position. Notice, for instance, that if the sentence, *You saw John?*, occurs after *I saw John yesterday* in a conversation, it will be interpreted as a request for confirmation or clarification or an expression of surprise, depending on how it is intoned, rather than as a straightforward request for information. But this is just to say that context plays a critical role in utterance interpretation, with discourse position making one sort of contribution to the context.

Bach and Harnish (1979: 41) identify four classes of "Communicative Illocutionary Acts": constatives, directives, commissives, and acknowledgments, and claim that

> For us, **constatives** express the speaker's **belief** and his **intention** or **desire** that the hearer have or form a like belief. **Directives** express the speaker's **attitude** toward some prospective action by the hearer and his intention that his utterance, or the attitude it expresses, be taken as a **reason** for the hearer's action. **Commissives** express the speaker's intention and belief that his utterance **obligates** him to do something (perhaps under certain conditions). And **acknowledgments** express **feelings** regarding the hearer or, in cases where the utterance is clearly perfunctory or formal, the speaker's intention that his utterance satisfy a **social expectation** to express certain feelings and his belief that it does. (emphasis mine)

If Bach and Harnish are correct, the differentia of the major classes of illocutionary acts involve distinctions between the expression of beliefs, of attitudes, of intentions or desires to act or to cause others to act, and of feelings. Such differentia are characteristic of social actions, but not of linguistic (speech) acts.

Bach and Harnish note that in the case of certain directives (e.g., orders, prohibitions, grants of permission), the speaker acts on the belief that he or she has sufficient authority over the addressee that simply expressing his or her desires should be sufficient to guarantee compliance, whereas in the case of others (requests and questions) this is not true. If Bach and Harnish are correct, the differentia for these two subclasses of illocutionary acts involve relative social standing.[15] Nowhere do Bach and Harnish (or anyone else, so far as I know) distinguish two different types of illocutionary acts or two different

[15] Searle (1969: 66) makes essentially the same point.

subtypes of some type of illocutionary act on the basis of phonological, lexical, morphological, or syntactic properties of utterances.

A more careful look at the properties that differentiate different types of illocutionary acts makes all the clearer the social nature of such acts. Promising and offering are felicitously done only in circumstances in which the person making the promise/offer believes that the person to whom the promise/offer is being made has some need or desire which the promise/offer is intended to satisfy. Indeed, promises do not even constitute an independently performable act, for they are response items, restricted to conversational contexts in which the person to whom the promise is addressed has indicated not just that he has a need or desire, but that he specifically wishes the promisor to satisfy that need or desire.[16] However, when in doubt whether someone wishes us specifically to satisfy a need, we make offers instead. Moreover, the essential difference between an invitation (*Would you like to come over for lunch?*) and a proposal for joint action (*Let's go get some lunch!*) lies in whether or not the person initiating this interaction is to serve as host. This, again, is scarcely a linguistic matter.

I think we must conclude that if we take such actions as volunteering, making complaints, giving warnings, making requests, making promises or offers, and issuing invitations or proposals for joint action as being exemplars of illocutionary acts, then illocutionary acts must be seen as communicative actions, rather than linguistic acts with a social dimension. However, there are certain types of actions that we perform in using language that might be said to be speech acts, namely Searle's literal acts: making assertions through using declarative sentences, asking questions using interrogative sentences, and issuing directives using imperative sentences. I see no harm in calling these acts speech acts, but, as we shall see, very little hangs on this point.

---

[16] This dependence on some indication by the addressee that he specifically wants the speaker to satisfy his need or desire is what distinguishes promises from offers and is the explanation for why promises are normally found in response to requests. In the movie, *Jurassic Park*, there was a promise that might seem to have been *sui generis* in that it was not prompted by someone's making a request. In that movie, an adult who is trying to save two children from hungry dinosaurs makes an unsolicited promise, namely, *I'll be back soon, I promise*, but it is clear that the children would very much want him to return soon. This illustrates the point that facts true in a context can serve to satisfy conditions on communicative actions.

## THE ROLE OF CONTEXT

The thesis that speech acts are social in nature accords well with the fact that what illocutionary act a sentence can be used to perform depends on nonreferential, social aspects of context.[17] I might say, *It's going to rain today*, by way of **making a complaint** if the fact that it is going to rain presents a problem for me (I have planned a picnic) or I might say this to you by way of **issuing a warning** to you if the fact that it is going to rain presents a problem for you (you have planned a picnic), but if I were a TV weather announcer, I might say this simply to **convey information** to people about what sort of weather they will have, expecting some to take the news well (gardeners) and others to take it badly (picnickers). Clearly participants' knowledge of their own and others' plans (the complaint and warning cases) and participants' social statuses and roles (the weather announcer case) are critical to determining what communicative action the initiator means to engage the responder in.

Similarly, *Can you solve this sort of quadratic equation?* might be said by a university professor to a student in a context in which she is attempting to decide whether or not to place him in an advanced mathematics course, or be said by a desperate student to another student in an attempt to get the latter to help him with his homework. In the first case, the professor's saying *Can you solve this sort of quadratic equation?* counts as a request for information; in the second, it counts as making a request for action (i.e., for help). Clearly, the social context (academic interview vs. homework session) and the relationship between the speaker and interlocutor (professor-student vs. student-student) play a decisive role in determining what communicative action is being performed by the speaker in uttering the sentence and these are social, not linguistic factors. Examples like these abound where identical utterances will have different illocutionary forces in different contexts.

### Do utterances have primary illocutionary force?

A central tenet of traditional speech act theory is that both a literal act and a primary act must be associated with the utterance of any

---

[17] There is one possible class of counter-examples to the claim that the illocutionary force of an utterance depends on context and this is the class of performative utterances, which, normally, have what force they have solely as a function of their literal meanings. However, see Bach and Harnish (1979) for another view rather closer in spirit to my approach than to Austin's. See also Recanati (1987).

sentence. I have conceded that it is reasonable to assume that individual utterances have a literal force. Indeed, such an assumption is necessary to understand the literal meanings of utterances. However, there are three fundamental difficulties with the thesis that individual utterances have primary illocutionary force. First, it fails to appreciate the critical contribution of context to the illocutionary force of utterances. Second, the claim is conceptually flawed in that it involves the reification of actions. And third, when we turn to apply speech act theory to multiturn conversational sequences, we find that there are inevitable, unresolvable uncertainties in the assignment of primary illocutionary force to individual utterances, and that even were it possible to provide credible mappings of the utterances of multiturn exchanges into Searlean primary speech acts, doing so would provide little insight into such exchanges.

### CONTEXT AND ILLOCUTIONARY FORCE

Though anyone who works in pragmatics must take at least the ritual stance that context plays a critical role in utterance interpretation, it is remarkable the degree to which pragmatic analyses either ignore or, at least, fail fully to exploit context. In the case of those indirect speech acts that must be calculated, Searle assumed that context must play a critical role in the determination (calculation) of what action the speaker intends to be performing. However, though Searle acknowledged that context plays a role in the interpretation of even those indirect speech acts that have become conventionalized, he provided no systematic treatment of context nor said precisely what this role is. The same is true as well of Morgan (1968), who provided the most explicit treatment of so-called "conventionalized indirect speech acts."

I demonstrated that context is critical to the interpretation of the illocutionary force of indirect speech act forms in our discussion immediately above of the example *Can you solve this sort of quadratic equation?* To drive this point home, it will be useful to consider the following additional data:

(12)  a. Can you reach that book?
   b. Can you eat more cake?
   c. Can you clean and jerk as much as Sandy?
   d. Can you come over tonight?
   e. Can you get off my fucking foot?

21

Sentence (12a), uttered by a short person to a tall person, would surely be heard as a request. Sentence (12b), if uttered by a host holding a piece of cake over a guest's plate, would surely be heard as an offer. Sentence (12c) sounds like an information question pure and simple. Sentence (12d) sounds a lot like an invitation. Sentence (12e) is hardly a request. It might be an indirect order or even an indirect threat. Obviously, both context and the literal meanings of the sentences are important in determining how they are interpreted. What is not important is the form of the sentence uttered except for what it contributes to determination of the literal meanings of the sentences. Certainly we would not want to say, as Searle and Morgan did, that utterances of the form, *Can you VP*, where "VP" contains an action predicate, are conventionalized request forms.

Lycan (p. 163) has noted, in connection with Searle's view that speaker-meaning and reasoning based on Gricean principles, speech act principles, and background information will suffice to provide an account of illocutionary forces of utterances, that "naturally, Searle intends 'context' to help the hearer make this selection, but that is a vacuous truism, and pointing it out contributes nothing to our superficial account of the hearer's reasoning." The thesis that the fact that context might play a role in how we construe utterances is a "vacuous truism" is a rather startling one. However, I think what Lycan is saying is that appeals to context are vacuous unless we can provide a systematic, principled role for context, and in that I would agree.

Suppose (if I may speak in traditional speech-act-theoretic terms) that we were to say that an utterance U can be employed with primary illocutionary force F in a context C, where C consists of some set of propositions reflecting the context-relevant beliefs of the speaker, if U and C collectively entail or implicate (henceforth **specify**) satisfaction of the full set of felicity conditions on F.[18] This comes down to saying that context contributes premises in a speech-act-theoretic argument supporting a particular illocutionary interpretation. Relevant premises of the context will consist of those factual considerations that bear on satisfaction of felicity conditions. In the case of an utterance like *Can you pass the salt?*, such premises would normally include the speaker's belief that the addressee can

---

[18] Let us say that a proposition $p$ **implicates** another proposition $q$ if, in a normal utterance, a speaker who tokened just a sentence expressing $p$ would thereby conversationally implicate $q$ in the sense of Grice.

see that the speaker cannot reach the salt, that the addressee is able to pass the salt (the salt is near the addressee and the addressee is physically able to engage in salt passing), and that the addressee is willing to pass the salt (a condition on agreeing to dine with someone). In short, **every condition on requesting is satisfied by the context but for one**: identification of the desired thing and implicating or asserting a desire for it. All that is required of the speaker in such a context is to make some sort of affirmative reference to salt consistent with a desire for it, such as by saying, *Can you pass the salt?*, *Could I have the salt?*, *I need the salt*, *Mind passing the salt?*, *Would you pass the salt?*, *Is that the salt next you to?*, or *The salt, please*. I trust that this is not a vacuous use of context.

Suppose, then, that we have a context C which consists of the propositions that the speaker can be expected to want condiments and edibles while dining with the addressee, that the addressee is willing to pass salt to the speaker, and that the addressee is in all respects able to pass salt to the speaker. The question arises: in virtue of what properties of utterances like *Can you pass the salt?*, *Could I have the salt?*, *I need the salt*, *Mind passing the salt?*, *Would you pass the salt?*, *Is that the salt next to you?*, or *The salt, please* does requesting get done in context C? The answer would seem to be their meanings: it is the fact that they contain an affirmative reference to salt, i.e., a reference to salt consistent with a desire for it. It is manifestly not the linguistic form *per se* that determines that the utterance is a request. However, this is not to say that the sorts of sentences used in making requests (if I may continue my use of traditional speech-act-theoretic language) will not exhibit the conventionalization of form characteristic of colloquial language. In fact, a point that Searle and Morgan missed is that conventionalization of form for function is a general characteristic of colloquial language, rather than a special feature of the forms used to perform so-called "indirect speech acts."[19]

It is clear from this exercise that indirect speech act forms provide no evidence that primary illocutionary force is a property *simpliciter* of particular sentence or utterance forms. The primary illocutionary force of any utterance is a product of the meaning of the utterance and the context in which it occurs. However, before this argument can be fully accepted, it will be necessary to say what

---

[19] I will demonstrate this for register phenomena in chapter 2.

is meant by the term "meaning" here. I turn to that question in the next chapter.

## THE REIFICATION OF ILLOCUTIONARY FORCE

Some speech act theorists have held that primary illocutionary force is a property of **sentences,** as opposed to utterances. This is true of the abstract-performative treatment of the speech acts. Ross (1970) and Sadock (1974), for instance, argued that the illocutionary force of utterances is a function of the literal meanings of the sentences uttered. According to them, a sentence like (13a) has the same underlying semantic structure as (13b) and (14a) has the same underlying semantic structure as (14b).

(13)  a. John Austin was an English philosopher.
      b. I assert that John Austin was an English philosopher.
(14)  a. Pick up that cigarette butt!
      b. I order you to pick up that cigarette butt!

Sadock wrote (p. 16) that "within a semantically based grammar, the underlying syntactic representation (i.e., the logical representation) of a sentence whose illocutionary force is not directly represented in surface structure in terms of a performative formula will still have to contain the semantic correspondent of a higher performative clause defining the illocutionary force of the sentence" and went on to say (p. 19) that "we may say that **illocutionary force is that part of the meaning of a sentence which corresponds to the highest clause in its semantic representation** [emphasis his]." This is the famous "abstract-performative hypothesis."[20]

More commonly, I think, people have supposed that primary illocutionary force is a property of **utterances.** Austin (1962: 71) seems to be taking this point of view when he says of the imperative mood of a sentence like *Shut it!*, that it "makes the utterance a 'command' (or an exhortation or permission or concession or what not!)." Searle (1969: 161) uses locutions like (p. 161) "ask the question, *Is the king of France bald?*," which suggests that uttering the sentence *Is the king of France bald?* counts as asking a question. In later work, Searle and Vanderveken (1985: 7) claim that "a

[20] This theory is a dead horse I shall not trouble to beat again. For very useful critiques, see Boër and Lycan (1976), Lycan (1984), and Recanati (1987).

materially adequate semantics of a natural language must recursively assign illocutionary acts (elementary or complex) to each sentence for each possible context of use." On this view, illocutionary acts are properties not of sentences *simpliciter*, but of sentence-context pairs. Since many have held that utterances are pairings of sentences with contexts, Searle could be taken here as holding to the view that it is utterances, not sentences, that have illocutionary force.

The thesis that illocutionary force is a property either of sentences or utterances (or, if this is different, sentence-context pairs) is to reify what are essentially actions. This shows up in the widespread use of nouns to refer to what are clearly acts. Searle (1969) not only talks about asserting, questioning, ordering, and promising, but also (p. 160) of assertions, questions, commands, and promises. This reificationist view of illocutionary acts reaches full flower in the taxonomy of Bach and Harnish (1979) in which they employ nominal forms (some of which are nominal uses of adjectivalized verbs) such as "assertives," "concessives," "requestives," "questions," "promises," and "offers" to identify types of illocutionary acts (except interestingly for the class of "acknowledgments" where verb forms like "apologize," "congratulate," "reject," and the like are used). This way of talking about illocutionary acts encourages thinking of them as things and thus as properties – as properties of utterances or even of sentences.

In a conversation in which a single utterance suffices to make a request or offer or promise (say using, *Could I have a cup of hot chocolate with whipped cream?*, in doing requesting) it would be fair to say that the speaker made a request in saying, *Could I have a cup of hot chocolate with whipped cream?*, but it would not follow from this that the utterance (to say nothing of the sentence employed in making the utterance) **is** a request. As Stampe (1975) pointed out years ago, it is people, not sentences or utterances, that do things. Saying of a specific instance of uttering, *Could I have a cup of hot chocolate with whipped cream?*, in a certain context C, that *Could I have a cup of hot chocolate with whipped cream?* **was** a request in context C may be appealing, but it isn't accurate. We could say that the speaker meant to be making a request in uttering this sentence in this context or that the hearer took the speaker to be making a request when the speaker uttered this sentence in that context, or both.

25

## *The mapping problem*

Concerning speech act theory, Schegloff (1988: 61) argues that "what a rudimentary speech act theoretic analysis misses, and I suspect a sophisticated one will miss as well, is that parties to real conversations are always talking in some sequential context," where a "sequential context" is taken by him (p. 61) to be the "more or less proximately preceding and projectably ensuing talk." He then goes on to say that "the outlook is not hopeful, for speech act theory has inherited from traditional philosophy the single act or utterance as its fundamental unit." In this, Schegloff is clearly correct, for any attempt to map Searlean primary acts into the utterances that comprise multi-turn conversational sequences cannot succeed.

Anyone who tries to apply traditional speech act theory to natural conversations will discover, as Levinson (1981) has pointed out, that multiple, inconsistent assignments of force to the utterances of conversations can normally be given that are fully consistent with the theory. Consider, for instance, what assignments of force might be given to the first and third turns of conversation (15).

(15)   Merritt (1976: 337)
      CUSTOMER: Do you have hot chocolate?              $T_1$
      CLERK:       mmhmm                                 $T_2$
      CUSTOMER: Can I have hot chocolate with whipped cream? $T_3$
      CLERK:       Sure ((leaves to get)).                   $T_4$

Since the literature (Merritt 1976) contains evidence that speakers do sometimes mean to be making requests in uttering sentences like, *Do you have hot chocolate?*, we must entertain the possibility that this utterance is being used to make a request in this case that is later amplified. However, it is equally possible that the speaker is asking a literal act question by way of performing the primary act of requesting information in this conversation. The same options are available in the case of *Can I have hot chocolate with whipped cream?* Is this a literal act question being used to request information or is it a literal act question being used to make a request for hot chocolate? The difficulty with traditional speech act theory is that at least as good an argument can be given for the one analysis as for the other. The response item *sure* provides no support for the thesis that the speaker was heard as making a request. *Sure* commonly occurs in exchanges in which the speaker is reassuring the addressee about something and occurs after requests for information (A: *Is Mary going to come to your party?*, B: *Sure*), as well as requests for things or the performance of actions. Thus, there is nothing in what is said by the clerk that decides the issue whether this question is a request for information or a thing-request.

There is a more perspicacious view of what the customer in this interaction is doing. The fact is that what an utterance is intended to do in any given circumstance depends on the state of knowledge of the speaker. If the speaker of *Can I have hot chocolate?* knows or believes that the clerk has hot chocolate, then she presumably would not be using the utterance to request information, but rather to provide information – to signal a desire for hot chocolate. Similarly, if the customer believes to a moral certainty that anyone who offers hot chocolate will offer it with whipped cream, then, clearly, this utterance would not be intended to request information, but rather to provide it – to signal that she wants the hot chocolate with a dollop of whipped cream. However, if she is in doubt about the availability of whipped cream, then she will clearly mean to be requesting information. In the first instance, I will say that the utterance is "value-positing" (information providing) in that the point of the utterance is to communicate a desire for a dollop of whipped cream on her hot chocolate and the interrogative form is intended to display deference to the addressee. In the latter case, the utterance is value-requesting (information requesting) and the interrogative form derives from this fact. In my view, it is whether an utterance is value-positing or value-requesting and what speech-act-theoretic condition it addresses, not what primary speech act might be said to be being performed in uttering it, that is of greatest importance in understanding what we do with utterances in conversation.

As a second example, consider in connection with conversation (16) whether Carl should be said to be requesting information or making a request at turn $T_1$ when he said, *Are you going to be free from 1: 30 to 2: 30?*, and whether Debbie should be said to be requesting confirmation of a discourse presupposition that Carl wanted her to watch his child or was actually offering to watch the child at turn $T_2$.

(16)  Jacobs and Jackson (1983b: 299)
      Carl is standing in the hallway of the speech department, holding the hand of his 15-month-old son, Curtis.
      CARL:   Hey Debbie. Are you going to be free from

| | |
|---|---|
| 1: 30 to 2: 30? | $T_1$ |
| DEBBIE: Yeah, I think so. You want me to watch him? | $T_2$ |
| CARL: Yeah | $T_3$ |
| DEBBIE: I'd love to. It'd be a pleasure. | $T_4$ |
| CARL: Okay. Thanks. I'll bring him around then. | $T_5$ |

Again, the opening question, *Are you going to be free from 1: 30 to 2: 30?*, would, in traditional speech-act-theoretic terms, be said to be a literal act question and a primary act request for information. The question arises as to what *You want me to watch him?* is doing in this conversation. There are two possibilities – that Debbie is requesting confirmation of her discourse presupposition that Carl wants her to watch his child and implicating a willingness to do so or is making an offer. In fact, in conversations like this one which are initiated by addressee-availability questions (e.g., *Whatcha doin?*, *Doin' anything tonight?*, etc.), we often find replies consisting of some sort of affirmative response followed by a question like, *Why do you ask?*, that is, by an inquiry about the prior speaker's purpose in asking the question. In light of this fact, it seems reasonable to say that *You want me to watch him?* is also an inquiry about the prior speaker's goal (i.e., is value-requesting in nature) that implicates a willingness to watch the child.

As these examples illustrate, applying traditional speech act theory to naturally occurring conversations is fraught with uncertainty, for alternative analyses equally consistent with speech act theory can commonly be given for the individual utterances that comprise such conversations. In my view, this uncertainty is irremediable as long as it is assumed that in uttering sentences speakers necessarily perform both a literal act and a primary act. As we shall see in the next two chapters, what is critical about any transactionally significant utterance in a conversation is whether it is value-positing or value-requesting and what interaction structure condition or domain predicate (or both) it posits or requests a value for. In short it is the work the utterance does in the interaction, not what Searlean primary act it performs, that is of interest.

If we adopt Searle's view that utterances have both a literal and a primary illocutionary force and were we to apply this view to multiturn interactions, we would be forced to say that an interaction like (16) consists of the following initial sequence of literal act/primary act pairs (if we ignore the initial greeting and assuming that we could agree that Debbie is making an offer at Turn 2):

28

Turn 1: Carl/literal act question/primary act request for information

Turn 2: Debbie/literal act assertion/primary act of conveying information

followed by

Debbie/literal act question/primary act offer

Turn 3: Carl/literal act assertion/primary act of accepting the offer

We might then go on to say that this is one of a very large set of possible "sequence sets" employed in requesting, i.e., sequences of triples consisting of a specification of the speaker, the literal act being performed and the primary act being performed. The difficulty with this sort of approach is that it has no explanatory power whatever. It would be the worst sort of taxonomic analysis.

### *Interactional generation of communicative actions*

In conversation (16), Carl does not actually say anything that can reasonably be said to **be** a request, nor does Debbie say anything that can definitely be said to **be** an offer even if we adopt the Searlean speech-act-theoretic way of talking about actions. We have requesting and offering without requests and offers. If we wish to say that Carl was doing requesting and Debbie was doing offering in this interaction, as is perfectly reasonable, we must say that these actions are in some sense trans-sentential, emergent properties of the interaction.

By way of illustrating, rather than proving this point, let me contrast excerpts from two hypothetical telephone conversations.

(17)   SANDY: Are you free tonight?
       TERRY: Yeah.
       SANDY: Ya wanta go to a movie?
       TERRY: Yeah.
(18)   TERRY: I'm sure bored.
       SANDY: Me too. Why don't we go to a movie?
       TERRY: Okay.

Though I have no attested cases just like these,[21] they illustrate two types of possible interactions, one (cf. (17)) in which the initiator

---

21   We shall consider an invitation sequence in chapter 4 that is arguably a case like (18).

29

comes to the interaction with the intention to invite the other party to come along to a movie and another (cf. (18)) in which the intention to issue an invitation emerges within the interaction. In both cases, we have inviting going on, but the invitation arises very differently in the two cases.

Isaacs and Clark (1990)[22] report on a class of conversational sequences they call "ostensible invitations," in which one speaker B attempts to induce another speaker A into proffering an invitation to an event E, the result of which is that A insincerely invites B to E. According to Isaacs and Clark, there are seven features to ostensible invitations, to wit (p. 498):

(19)   a.  A makes B's presence at E implausible.
      b.  A extends invitation only after it has been solicited.
      c.  A doesn't motivate invitation beyond social courtesy.
      d.  A doesn't persist or insist on the invitation.
      e.  A is vague about arrangements for event E.
      f.  A hedges the invitation.
      g.  A delivers the invitation with inappropriate cues.

They give (20) as an example of such a conversation.

(20)   Issacs and Clark (1990: 500)
    PETER: Guys, let's get going! We're gonna miss the preview before "Pee Wee's Big Adventure."
    DAN: Where are you guys going? I mean, are you guys going somewhere?
    PETER: Yeah, I'm going to University [Avenue] to check out the Pee Wee Herman flick.
    DAN: Is everyone else going, too?
    PETER: Well, not everyone. Paul, Phil, and Matt are.
    DAN: I've heard it's great! I'd like to see it sometime. Anyway . . .
    PETER: Well, uh, do you want to . . . uh, if *you* want to *you* can come. I mean it really doesn't matter.

It is clear in this case that Peter's invitation to Dan to come along with

---

[22]   The data employed in this paper are problematic, as the authors note, for they are based almost entirely on recollected conversations. However, conversation (54) in chapter 3 comes very close to being an ostensible invitation.

him and his friends was generated primarily through Dan's drawing attention to the fact that he seems to have been excluded from some set of people (which is an affront to his positive face) and his expressed desire to see the movie. From this it is clear that he is willing to go along with the other guys. He takes pains not to say explicitly that he is able to go at the time of the conversation, though this is clearly implicated. I suspect that this omission may be deliberate in such cases for it gives the excluded person a face-saving way to back out of the exchange if no invitation is forthcoming. In any event, the invitation proffered was the product of an interaction.

As a final point, it must be noted that there are certain kinds of communicative action that cannot be construed as performable by a single speaker. A particularly nice case involves bets, as was pointed out to me by Ken Turner. If I say to you, *I'll bet you $5 that Clinton wins reelection*, I have not made a bet, I have simply proposed one. It is only if you accept the proposal that a bet has been made. Similarly, one cannot make a bargain (e.g., a trade of one thing for another) with someone without their agreement. And, as we have noted, we virtually never make promises without it being made clear by the person to whom we make the promise that this person specifically wants us to perform the act in question.

## Psychological reality

Those who have worked on speech act theory appear to have taken the position that the association of primarily illocutionary force with particular utterances has a certain psychological reality. Good (MS) has argued, however, that there is no empirical evidence that speech-act-theoretic illocutionary descriptions play an actual role in comprehension – that it is necessary to see an utterance like *Could you give me a ride home after work today* as a request in order properly to understand it. Note that the addressee could describe her "up take" in any of the following ways:

(21)   a. I took the speaker to be requesting me to give him a ride home after work.
       b. I took the speaker to be trying to get me to take him home after work.
       c. I took the speaker to need a ride home after work and to want me to provide it.

Clearly, any one of these accounts of what the speaker of *Could you give me a ride home after work today?* was doing is as good as any other, but only the first employs an illocutionary description. The second makes reference to what I am calling the transactional effect of the interaction the speaker initiated (Searle's essential condition) and the third makes reference to the initial state condition of the interaction (Searle's sincerity condition) and to the problem (the speaker's ridelessness) that caused him to come to have a desire that the addressee provide this ride. The specifically illocutionary description of the speaker's action has no privileged status. Good's point is sound: there is no empirical evidence supporting the thesis that associating an illocutionary force with an utterance has any psychological consequences.

## Conclusion

In this chapter I have argued that speech acts – rather, communicative actions – are social actions, as opposed to linguistic actions, and that we should not associate communicative actions with the uttering of individual sentences or utterances. In the next two chapters, I shall argue that what is important about an utterance is what it contributes to the work of the interaction in which it occurs, not what action is performed in uttering it. In the next chapter, I provide a theory of meaning that lays the foundation for this different conception of the role of individual utterances in speech act theory according to which utterances have a transactional and/or interactional significance (as opposed to force) that reflects the contribution they make to the work of the sequence.

# 2

$\approx$

# *Meaning and force*

## Introduction

In chapter 1, I argued that it is a mistake to associate illocutionary force or illocutionary force potential with individual sentences or utterances. In this chapter, I shall argue instead that utterances have a **significance** in context that derives from what the utterance contributes to the work of the interaction in which it occurs. I shall argue, in particular, that any utterance that occurs in an interaction will have a **transactional significance** that reflects what it contributes to achievement of the transactional effect of the interaction (i.e., Searle's essential condition) or an **interactional significance** that reflects the "face-work" (Goffman 1967) the utterance does or both.[1] In this chapter, I shall discuss what I mean by the notion of significance, and go on to argue that utterance significance constitutes an actual level of meaning in conversation.

## The meaning of "meaning"

There are at least three senses of the word "meaning"[2] that are relevant to a theory of conversational interactions. These three senses are illustrated by the following sentences.

[1] By "face-work," I mean (among other things) the work the utterance does by way of redressing or mitigating the face-threats (Brown and Levinson 1978) associated with what people say.

[2] See Lyons (1977: 1f) for a discussion of the many meanings of "meaning."

(1)  a. What is the meaning of "Ich liebe dich"?
   b. I didn't mean to upset you when I said I loved you.
   c. When you say you love me it doesn't mean anything to me.

In the case of (1a), the word *meaning* corresponds to the notion of literal or conventional meaning (*L*-Meaning), and is captured in part by the truth-conditional approach to meaning. The second use of the word *mean* in the examples of (1) involves the notion of speaker intention (*I*-Meaning). The sentence *I didn't mean to upset you when I said I loved you* is well-paraphrased by *I didn't intend to upset you when I said I loved you*. The third use involves the notion of utterance significance (*S*-Meaning). The speaker of (1c) is saying that the addressee's professing to love the speaker is of no significance to the speaker. In this chapter, I shall discuss each of these senses of the term "meaning," and in the process show how each is relevant to the theory of conversational competence, in general, and to the theory of conversational interactions, in particular.

## *I-Meaning*

The importance of speaker intentions in understanding communication was forcefully advanced in Grice's (1957) influential paper "Meaning". In that paper, he distinguished what he called "natural meaning" (cf. the use of "mean" in (2a)) from 'non-natural meaning' or 'meaning$_{NN}$' (cf. the use of "meant" in (2b)).

(2)  a. Those spots mean measles.
   b. Sandy's saying that the garbage hadn't been taken out yet meant that she wanted me to take out the garbage.

In the latter case, as Grice noted, there must be an intention on the part of the speaker in saying what was said to cause some response in the addressee, where this response is at least partially determined by the addressee's recognition of the speaker's intention to produce this response in saying what was said.

As I shall use the term, *I*-Meaning can be equated with the goals of participants, that is, with the intended effects of what they say and do. The initiator of a given interaction will normally have (at least) two

34

goals,[3] an intended transactional effect and an intended interactional effect. The importance of the former type of goal (intended effect) has long been recognized in speech act theory – it corresponds to Searle's essential condition. And, though Austin and others did recognize that illocutionary acts have interactional effects, there has been little concern with this type of effect. This is an unfortunate omission, for the interactional effects of any act are as important as the transactional effect in any speaker's deciding both what to say at any point in an interaction and how to say it.

The point just made is worth repeating: a speaker's interactional goals can influence **both what** the speaker says and **how** the speaker says what he has decided to say. Recall conversation (16) on page 27 of chapter 1 in which Debbie replies to Carl's question *Are you going to be free from 1:30 to 2:30?* by saying *Yeah, I think so. You want me to watch him?* In saying *You want me to watch him?*, Debbie implicates that she is willing to watch Carl's child if that is what he wants her to do, and this very much advances the conversation forward. The question is why does Debbie trouble herself to say this given that simply saying, *Yeah, I think so,* would have constituted a fully cooperative response in that it provides precisely the information Carl's question requests. The answer to this question is that in saying, *You want me to watch him?*, Debbie is inviting the imposition on her that Carl's wanting her to watch his child entails. That is, she says what she says, rather than nothing, to achieve an interactional goal, namely to pay respect to Carl's positive face.

Debbie's response, *I'd love to. It'd be a pleasure,* to Carl's, *Yeah,* is also quite unnecessary transactionally. Indeed, for all practical

---

3   The speaker who initiates an interaction will normally have a transactional goal (to cause someone to do something, to persuade someone of something, etc.), as well as interactional goals. However, associated with the utterance of each sentence are also transactional and interactional goals. Thus, for instance, if I mean to cause you to give me a ride home from work, my transactional goal will be to cause you to give me this ride. My interactional goal might be to mitigate as much as possible the threat to your negative face-need not to have your freedom of action restricted and the potential threat to my positive face-need to be valued (which would very much be threatened by a bald rejection). Suppose, then, that I choose to initiate this request in saying, *Do you live anywhere near Henderson and High?* I will argue that the transactional goal in uttering this sentence is to determine whether a precondition on your willingness to give me this ride is met, namely your finding the destination of this ride not to be inconvenient. My intended interactional goal is to mitigate these threats to face by providing you with an "easy out" (which substantially mitigates the threat to your negative face) that also provides a way for you to reject the request that does not greatly threaten my positive face. I will refer to these two types of goals as interaction-specific and utterance-specific goals.

purposes, with the exception of identifying where Carl will surrender his child to Debbie, the transactional work of the interaction is accomplished once Carl says, *Yeah.* Thus, again, we must explain why Debbie troubles herself to say what she says, and, again, the explanation must be that she does so in an attempt to achieve the interactional goal of paying respect to Carl's positive face.

How a speaker says what he says can be influenced by his interactional goals as well. As we shall see below in this chapter, a speaker who wishes to achieve some particular transactional effect in uttering a sentence will normally have available a variety of utterances he might employ, associated with each of which is a different interactional effect. The speaker who wants his dining partner to pass the salt might say, *Could you pass the salt?, Can I have the salt?, I need the salt, Gimme the salt,* among a variety of other possibilities, and choosing one utterance over another will normally have interactional consequences.

## L-Meaning

I shall take the position here that the truth-conditions of the sentence uttered in an interaction must be part of what we understood to be the *L*-Meaning or conventional or literal meaning of an utterance.[4] However, it is necessary to include a bit more than truth-conditions in what we understand by *L*-meaning. Note that if sentence (3a) is true, then (3b) must be true as well.

(3)   a. I have spoken to Sandy again.
     b. I have spoken to Sandy before.

Though (3a) may seem to entail (3b), the truth of (3a) does not seem to depend on the truth of (3b). Instead, it is argued that (3b) is a presupposition (or conventional implicature) of (3a) and that (3a) cannot have a truth-value unless (3b) is true.[5] Clearly this presupposition (conventional implicature) is due to the conventional meaning of *again* and must therefore be a part of what we understand by *L*-Meaning. Additionally, since the truth-conditions of sentences

---

[4]   This approach to the analysis of linguistic meaning goes back to Davidson (1967b). The notion of a truth-condition goes back to Tarski (1956).
[5]   See Levinson (1983: 67ff) for a discussion of these issues, as well as for pertinent references.

36

containing deictic forms like *I, you, here, now* depend on the reference of such forms, deixis of this sort must also be a part of what is involved in the study of *L*-Meaning.

In some contemporary semantic theories, such as Discourse Representation Theory (DRT), it is argued (Kamp and Reyle 1993) that the Davidsonian view that sentences/utterances have determinate truth-conditions is not generally true. Utterances containing deictic forms are an obvious case in point, for their referents can only be determined at utterance time. So also are utterances containing anaphoric elements (e.g., pronouns) and definite noun phrases, as research in DRT has made clear (Roberts MS, Kadmon 1987, 1990). These sorts of facts have led to theories in which truth-conditions of utterances are assigned dynamically with respect to the context in which they occur. As we shall see in this and the next chapter, dynamic theories of meaning are necessary not only to account for the *L*-Meanings of utterances but also, and even more critically, for their *S*-Meanings.

### *S-Meaning*

It should be clear that someone's uttering a sentence is an event and that just as we seek out the meaning (significance) of physical events (a concern of natural scientists and others) or political events (a concern of journalists and others), we, as language users, seek out the meaning (significance) of people's uttering sentences to us (utterance events). I would like to argue that what pragmatics ought to be about – what speech act theory ought to be about certainly – is meaning in the sense of utterance significance and thus that semantics, which is about *L*-Meaning, and pragmatics, which is about *S*-Meaning, are about meaning in radically different senses of the term. This is not a wholly new idea. It is implicit in Grice's (1975) work, as well as that of Searle's. What is different about my proposal is that I shall argue that *S*-Meaning is an actual level of meaning in conversation.

An utterance event, like any other event, takes on significance for us to the degree that it somehow "fits in" with some body of antecedently held beliefs from which it receives some sort of explanation, which is to say that determining the significance of an event, including an utterance event, is the result of abduction (Peirce 1955: 151ff). While on the moon, an American astronaut once dropped two objects of different masses from the same height and found, not surprisingly, that they hit the surface of the moon at the same time. Consider what significance this event would have for someone who does not know or understand the law of gravity. The naive view of objects falling in space is that how fast an object falls is determined wholly by properties of the object – by its weight. Given this view, two objects having different weights must fall at different rates, and someone holding this view would simply not understand the astronaut's demonstration, for it does not fit in with his body of antecedently held beliefs. Such a person might experience surprise or wonder or might doubt that he had correctly seen what was presented or he might reject it as a trick. The significance of this event for such a person, if it has any significance at all, is that it contradicts what he believes to be true.

On the other hand, this event would be perfectly understandable to anyone who understands the law of gravity, for this law speaks to the mutual gravitational attraction between each object and the moon. For such a person, the event in question would have a significance that is derived from her knowledge of physics, her belief that this was an honest experiment, etc. In short, we understand events and events have significance for us to the degree that we can bring antecedently held beliefs to bear in explaining how the events came to be (or conjure up new beliefs that combine with antecedently held beliefs in explaining how they came to be).

Interestingly the parallel between "the meaning of a sentence" (*L*-Meaning) and the "meaning of an event" (*S*-Meaning) extends to how we use the word "understand," for we can talk about "understanding a sentence" and "understanding an event." We can say that a speaker of English understands the *L*-meaning of the sentence *The two objects hit the surface of the moon at the same time* if he knows **what** circumstances or events the sentence is **true of** and the physicist understands the significance of the event described by this sentence if she understands **why** it is that what the sentence describes is true. The distinction is between understanding **what event a sentence is about** and understanding **why an event has occurred**. Understanding an utterance – an utterance event – requires understanding why the utterance was produced, that is, what the goal or intended effect(s) of the speaker was in producing the utterance.

"Utterance significance," as I shall use the term, is **public** and can be **calculated** in a manner made familiar by Grice (1975).[6] It includes "transactional significance" and "interactional significance," as I am employing these notions. It might also be extended to include other aspects of utterance significance. What I shall argue here is that the significance of an utterance occurring in a given interaction results from mapping the utterance into elements of the interaction structures associated with the interaction the parties to a conversation are engaged in, the transactional significance of an utterance deriving from what it contributes to achievement of the transactional effect of the act and an interactional significance deriving from the face-work that it does.

## Arguments for a level of S-Meaning

In what remains in this chapter, I shall provide three arguments in support of the thesis that *S*-Meaning constitutes an actual level of meaning in conversation. The first argument is that we cannot account for politeness and register variation in conversation unless we postulate the existence of a level of transactional significance. The second is that there is substantial evidence that this level of meaning is psychologically real. The third is that we simply cannot account for utterance generation without such a level of meaning.

### *Sociopragmatic variation*

Typically, any speaker will have available a wide variety of ways of saying what he has to say at any given point in a conversation. Suppose Terry goes to a "widget" store, where he encounters Sandy, who is a clerk, and conversation (4) ensues.[7]

(4)  TERRY: *Ya have any widgets?*                      $T_1$
     SANDY: Just got a shipment in yesterday.           $T_2$
     TERRY: *I'd like three.*                           $T_3$
     SANDY: Sure.                                       $T_4$

---

[6]  This is not to say that significance is always calculated. A significant amount of short-circuiting (Morgan 1978) is involved in implicature-drawing – much more than has generally been recognized as we shall see in this chapter and in chapter 6.

[7]  I don't wish to be taken as suggesting that this hypothetical example proves anything. It is being used to facilitate exposition of the theory. Actual examples will be employed at later points in this study to support particular claims about similar phenomena.

It is clear that at turn $T_1$, Terry could have said any of the utterances of (5) or of (6) by way of determining whether or not Sandy has widgets for sale.

(5)  a. Do you have any widgets?
     b. Ya have any widgets?
     c. Have any widgets?

(6)  a. Have you got any widgets?
     b. Ya got any widgets?
     c. Got any widgets?

What was said of turn $T_1$ applies equally to turn $T_3$. Terry could have uttered any of the following sentences (among many others) by way of placing an order for three widgets:

(7)  a. I'd like three.
     b. Can I have three?
     c. I'll take three.
     d. Gimme three.
     e. Could you gimme three?
     f. Can you gimme three?

The syntactic variation we have in the case of (7) is quite striking. All three sentence types are represented and there is variation in what the subject is, what auxiliary verb occurs if any, and what main verb occurs.

Clearly, a major problem for the theory of conversational competence is to account for variation of this sort. We need to understand, in particular, how the different linguistic choices available to a speaker at any given point in a conversation differ interactionally and we need to understand how interactional choices are realized linguistically, that is, how politeness, style, and other sociopragmatic features are mapped into rules of grammar.

In order to say that we have a set of variants – dialect variants, style variants, politeness variants, or register variants – we must have something that varies and something that stays the same. In what follows, I will argue that what stays the same in the case of dialect and style variation is *L*-Meaning (unless, of course, we are speaking about semantic variation itself, in which case it is form that stays constant) but that what stays the same in the case of politeness and register variation is *S*-Meaning.

In the case of dialect variation, perhaps the best understood kind of variation, we have variation in linguistic form (except for semantic variation itself), with *L*-Meaning held constant. Thus, in SE Ohio, high lax vowels are made tense before [š], giving [fiš] ("fish"), where most Ohioans have [fɪš], and [puš] ("push") instead of [pʊš]. Of course, [fiš] and [fɪš] have the same *L*-Meaning, as do [puš] and [pʊš]. Similarly, the syntactic variants *I didn't do anything* (Standard American English) and *I didn't do nothin'* (numerous American dialects) *L*-Mean the same thing, as do *He isn't going* (SAE) and *He ain't going* (numerous American dialects) or *He is sick* (SAE) and *He sick* (African-American English Vernacular).[8]

The utterances of (5) and those of (6) constitute paradigmatic cases of syntactic stylistic variation, as do instances of contraction (e.g. *He'd go if you asked* versus *He would go if you asked*). Paradigmatic instances of phonological stylistic variation are cases like [takŋ] and [takn] ("talking"), where, in casual speech, the more marked velar nasal is replaced by the less marked alveolar nasal or [ɪnvayt] and [ɪmvayt] ("invite"), where the alveolar nasal assimilates to the labiodental fricative [v] in casual speech in the latter form. In both types of cases, what is held constant is *L*-Meaning.

Zwicky and Zwicky (1982) take the line that stylistic variation concerns variation associated with "relationships between speakers" and includes variation along such dimensions as "intimacy/distance, casualness/formality, deference/dominance, peremptoriness/politeness, attention/inattention, and perhaps others." This characterization is consistent with the position that stylistic variation reflects what Halliday and Hasan (1989) would call "tenor conditions." I shall argue though that Zwicky and Zwicky's characterization of the

---

8    There appear to be instances of dialect differences in which a dialect may have some means of expressing something not readily available in another dialect. Thus, there is no completely straightforward Standard American English equivalent to African-American Vernacular English habitual *be* or remote past *been*. Here, I think we want to say that we have dialect differences without dialect variation.

dimensions of stylistic variation is overbroad, for it includes variation such as we find in (5) in which it appears that *L*-Meaning is held constant (cf. the casualness/formality dimension) and variation such as we find in (7) in which the variants clearly differ in *L*-Meaning (cf. the deference/dominance and peremptoriness/politeness dimensions).

In this study, stylistic variation will be understood as linguistic variation that reflects variation in social power and/or social distance of speaker and addressee (and between speakers and spoken-of third parties in the case of languages like Japanese) in which the variants have the same (or virtually the same) *L*-Meanings. On this view, the variation between *do + have* and *have + got* in the sentences of (5) and (6) constitutes style variation. The same would be true of the familiar and polite forms for "you" found in a number of European languages (e.g., *tu-vous* in French and *du-Sie* in German) which once reflected power differences, and now tend to reflect social distance relationships, and the alternate lexical choices of some East-Asian languages that reflect power relationships. In Japanese and Javanese, for instance, when someone of lower status speaks to someone of higher status, he or she will "elevate" his or her lexical choices.[9] These lexical variants seem to be referentially identical.

## POLITENESS VARIATION

The utterances of (7) constitute paradigmatic instances of **politeness variation** and involve what Zwicky and Zwicky referred to as the deference/dominance and the peremptoriness/politeness contrasts, as well as what we might call "orientation" contrasts. Utterances (7a)–(7c) are speaker-oriented (their subjects are *I*), whereas (7d)–(7f) are addressee-oriented (their subjects are *You*). This distinction shows up linguistically in subject position: speaker-oriented utterances have first person subjects and addressee-oriented utterances have second person subjects. All other things being equal, addressee-oriented utterances are more polite than speaker-oriented utterances.[10]

Utterances (7b) and (7e)–(7f) show deference to the addressee. The distinction between utterances that do and do not show deference

---

[9] This phenomenon is not unknown in English. A young person might say, *I gotta go get my wheels and run back to my pad,* to a peer, but, *I have to go get my car and go back to my apartment,* to a social superior.

[10] See Fraser and Nolen (1981) for an experimental study evaluating people's politeness judgments. The most polite form they observed was *I'd appreciate it if you'd do that,* but from that point on, the observation in the text holds true.

is manifested syntactically through sentence type. If an utterance is speaker-oriented and shows no deference it is declarative in form (cf. (7a)); if it is speaker-oriented and shows deference, it is interrogative (cf. (7b)). If an utterance is addressee-oriented and shows no deference, it is imperative (cf. (7d)) or declarative (cf. *You can give me three*) in form; if it is addressee-oriented and shows deference, it is interrogative (cf. (7e)). All other things being equal, it is more polite to show deference than not to show it.

These data also exhibit a good deal of variation in the verb and auxiliary. This seems to reflect what condition the utterance specifies. Forms (7a)–(7c) specify what Searle called the sincerity condition of requests, (7d) and (7e) specify the willingness condition on requests, and (7f) specifies the ability condition. These features constitute (some of) the pragmatic meaning features relevant to politeness.[11] All other things being equal, specification of the willingness condition (*Would you gimme three?*) is more polite than specification of the ability condition (*Could you gimme three?*).[12]

As this brief discussion suggests, there seem to be systematic relationships between the forms of utterances and the politeness choices speakers make in choosing to use them. In chapter 6, I shall provide and defend a formal mapping of certain meaning features and politeness (and, to a lesser extent, style, and register) features into linguistic features that determines the forms of utterances. The device that effects this mapping is the "pragmatic stratum," a component of our conversational competence, as opposed to linguistic competence *per se*, or, put somewhat differently, a level of cognitive, as opposed to linguistic structure.

Unlike cases of dialect and style variation we discussed, the variants in (7) clearly do not have the same *L*-Meanings. But if we are to say that they are variants, it is imperative that we say what it is about them that is the same. I would argue that they would each do precisely the same transactional work should they occur at turn $T_3$ in conversation (4) in that each would communicate that the number of

---

[11] I say, "pragmatic," for the meaning features involve predicates of conditions on communicative acts.

[12] Interestingly, though imperative forms like *Gimme three!* are relatively impolite in English, they are less so in other languages. In an experiment run by Linda Harlow and me (Geis and Harlow forthcoming), we found that French speakers employ them much more frequently than do English speakers in the same experimental context. We would prefer to say that the French do not find this form particularly impolite, rather than saying that the French are less polite than English speakers.

widgets desired is three. Let us say, then, that while these variants differ in *L*-Meaning, they have the same transactional significance or *S*-Meaning in this context.

As we have seen, the existence of politeness variation provides a powerful argument in support of the assumption that *S*-Meaning is a level of discourse meaning. The same is true of register variation. Returning again to conversation (4), note that Terry could have initiated the conversation with either of the sentences of (8).

(8)  a. Do you carry widgets?
     b. Do you stock widgets?

The sentences of (8) differ from each other (and from (5)) in *L*-Meaning. The fact that one can say, *We carry, but don't stock widgets* demonstrates this. Sentence (8a) could get a *Yes*-answer if asked of a clerk in a furniture store that stocks samples of what it sells (on special order), but does not sell what it stocks. Sentence (8b) could not. In a retail store in which one is able to purchase only what is in stock, the *L*-Meaning difference between (8a) and (8b) would not be functional and the utterances would have the same meaning in context, that is, the same *S*-Meaning. Similarly, in that context, the sentences of (8) would have the same *S*-Meaning as (5) and (6).

Now, *carry* and *stock* occur in the retail register in virtue of their *L*-Meanings. This is not true of *have*. Instead, *have* has come to have a context-specific meaning as "have for sale" in the retail sales register. If one goes into a retail store that uses light bulbs to illuminate the store but does not sell them and says, *You have any light bulbs?*, to a clerk, one will (I did) get a range of responses from *Do you mean ever?* (a Sony electronics store) to *No* (various stores) despite the fact that there are light bulbs in the store providing illumination. In order to account for this, we must say that *have* is being taken to mean "have-for-sale" in this case, rather than "possess" *simpliciter*. It seems that there are (at least) four uses of *have* in play in a retail store: "possess" (for simple possession), "possess-for-sale" (*stock*), "possess-for-use," and "select." In a hardware store, for instance, an utterance like *Do you have any change?* would be heard as "Do you possess any change?," *Do you have any light bulbs?* would be heard as "Do you possess-for-sale light bulbs?," *Do you have a bathroom?* would be heard as "Do you possess-for-use a bathroom?," and *Can I have four light bulbs?* would be heard as "Can I select four light bulbs?"[13] In order to account for the "have-for-sale" interpretation, we must conclude that in the retail sales register, the *L*-Meaning difference between *stock* and *carry,* on the one hand, and *have,* on the other, is normally neutralized. The forms have the same *S*-Meaning (significance in context).

I shall take the position here that *have L*-Means "possess" in the possess-for-sale and possess-for-use cases. How it is taken depends on the nature of the object of *have.* If the object refers to a sellable, it will be heard as possess-for-sale. If it refers to a useable, it will be heard as possess-for-use.

In a study of the travel agent register, I have found that travel agents routinely use the verb *put* as in (9), an utterance that seems to *L*-Mean "I can book you on a flight that arrives in Miami at noon."

(9)    I can put you in Miami at noon.

This use of *put* is normally not available to ordinary folks. Suppose that a friend needs a ride to the airport before 12:30 p.m. the next day, that you cannot provide this ride, but that you tell her that you will find her a ride. I believe you would be more likely to report success in this effort by saying (10a), than by saying (10b).

(10)    a. I can get you to the airport at noon.
        b. I can put you at the airport at noon.

An utterance like (10b) is available to persons who have the socially defined status of Agent, but not to persons who are merely functioning informally as agents. Since (10a) and (10b) differ in both form and literal meaning, it must be that what is held constant in this instance of variation is *S*-Meaning.

Register variation, like politeness variation, involves variation in form and *L*-Meaning, with *S*-Meaning held constant, but unlike politeness variation, which reflects interpersonal relations, register

---

13    On the other hand, if one goes over to a neighbor's home and says, *Do you have any light bulbs?,* your neighbor will surely hear this not as "Do you have any light bulbs for sale?," but as "Do you have any light bulbs for use (i.e., for me to borrow)?" The "select" reading will be discussed in chapter 6 in some detail.

variation involves variations of form and *L*-Meaning which are associated with what people are doing and the socially prescribed statuses and roles of speakers.

## *The sentence–utterance distinction*

Virtually all linguists take the view that the forms of sentences in a language are wholly determined by linguistic rules, that is, by phonological, morphological and syntactic rules, etc. However, in the case of utterances which have illocutionary significance (more specifically, transactional and interactional significance), the principal determinants of utterance form are interaction structure meaning features (which derive from what conditions and domain predicates an utterance specifies) and style, politeness, and register features. The question arises, then, as to how we can reconcile the fact that the factors that seem to determine the forms of utterances seem to be quite different from those that determine the forms of sentences. The answer to this question will depend on what we take the relationship between sentences and utterances to be.

According to what we might call the "standard theory," an **utterance** is a pairing of a sentence with a context, or, put in psycholinguistic terms, an utterance results from producing a sentence in a context (as is implicit in the familiar phrase "utter a sentence").[14] On this view, sentences have *L*-Meanings that they bring with them to contexts and pick up implicatures in context (Grice 1975). On this view, the "full" meaning of an utterance must be said to consist of the *L*-Meaning of the sentence uttered augmented by certain implicated meanings (*S*-Meanings).

A second, "pragmatic" theory of the utterance makes a much sharper distinction between sentences and utterances than does the standard theory. It takes off from the assumption that whereas the form of any **sentence** is determined by linguistic rules (e.g., phonological, morphological, and syntactic rules), the form of any **utterance** is determined by semantic (*L*-Meaning) and pragmatic meaning (*S*-Meaning) features, and certain sociopragmatic features, including discourse, style, politeness, and register features. On this view, there must be some mapping from *L*-Meaning and *S*-Meaning features and

[14] This view of the utterance seems to go back to Bar-Hillel. See Levinson (1983) for a useful discussion of this approach.

sets of sociopragmatic features into the purely linguistic rules of the sentence grammar for the language.

The standard view of the sentence–utterance distinction is very much what one would expect of persons who are engaged in trying to understand language understanding, i.e., to understand what hearers do. The "given" in such a case is a linguistic form that has a particular *L*-Meaning which occurs in a particular context, and the problem is to determine the significance or *S*-Meaning the utterance has in that context.

This approach to the sentence–utterance distinction is not as useful, however, if one is trying to understand utterance production. The problem for speakers is to produce not just an utterance with an appropriate *L*-Meaning that will have an appropriate *S*-Meaning in the context in which it occurs, but an utterance that is **contextually appropriate,** that is, an utterance that is consistent with the discourse context (in that, say, "old" information is presented early on in sentences and "new" information post-verbally), that contains markers of social distance and power appropriate to the relationship between the speaker and addressee (a style consideration), that contains markers displaying an appropriate level of politeness, and markers appropriate to what the speaker and addressee are doing (a register consideration). In short, whereas it may seem reasonable to ignore the issue of interactional significance in doing parsing or language understanding, one cannot ignore this issue in the study of utterance generation if one is ever to understand the basis upon which speakers choose to utter any one sentence over any of its *S*-Meaning equivalents on a given occasion.

Let us suppose that any given utterance (i.e., sentence produced in a particular context) can be represented as a 4-tuple consisting of a linguistic form (LF), an *L*-Meaning (LM), a transactional significance (TS), and an interactional significance (IS). Now, in any given context, as we saw in connection with the examples of (7), there can be a relatively large set of different linguistic forms (LF) which have different LM, the same TS, and different IS, and the problem facing the speaker is to select the LF that has the optimal IS in that context. Given the standard theory of the utterance, the only way one can account for utterance generation is to assume that speakers employ context as a filter. The model that is suggested can be represented as in Figure 1.

$$\langle LF_1, LM_1, TS, IS_1 \rangle$$
$$\langle LF_2, LM_2, TS, IS_1 \rangle$$
$$\langle LF_3, LM_3, TS, IS_1 \rangle$$
$$\cdot$$
$$\cdot$$
$$\cdot$$
$$\langle LF_n, LM_n, TS, IS_n \rangle$$

CONTEXT

$$\langle LF_i, LM_i, TS, IS_i \rangle$$

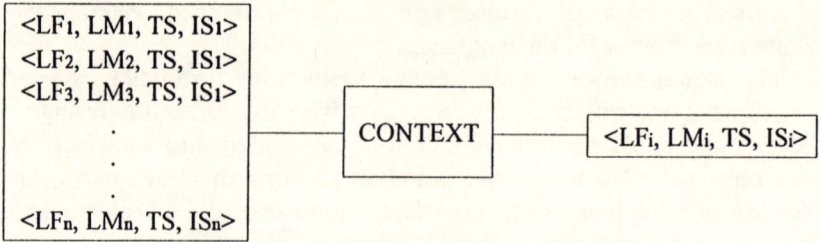

Figure 1. The standard theory of the utterance

In Figure 1 it is assumed that all of the 4-tuples in the left-hand box are *L*-Meaning appropriate and will have the correct transactional significance in that context. That would be true, for instance, of each of the variants of (7). The role of context here is to filter out all but the utterance that has the desired interactional significance. Viewed computationally, this would be a hopelessly inefficient way to do utterance production.

The pragmatic model of the utterance has it that the form of any utterance is determined by a set of transactional *S*-Meaning (SMF) and *L*-Meaning features (LMF), where the *S*-Meaning features are drawn from elements of interaction structures, and a set of socio-pragmatic features (SPF) – discourse, style, politeness, and register features – appropriate to the discourse context, the social distance and power relationships between speaker and addressee, any face-work the speaker wishes to do, the social context and the register. This second model of the relationship between sentences and utterances might be represented as in Figure 2, where "$LF_i$" represent linguistic features of some feature-driven grammar such as Systemic Grammar (Halliday 1985) or Head-Driven Phrase Structure Grammar (Pollard and Sag 1992, 1994).

On this view, the speaker preselects a set of *L*-Meaning, transac-tional *S*-Meaning, and sociopragmatic features which are mapped by the pragmatic stratum into a set of linguistic features (phonological, morphological, and syntactic features) that determine the linguistic form of the utterance. The context in which the speaker finds himself will, of course, play a role in determining which feature preselections he makes.

These two approaches to the sentence–utterance distinction illus-trate the two ways context can interact with utterances in utterance interpretation: a **filtering** role and a **constitutive** role. That context

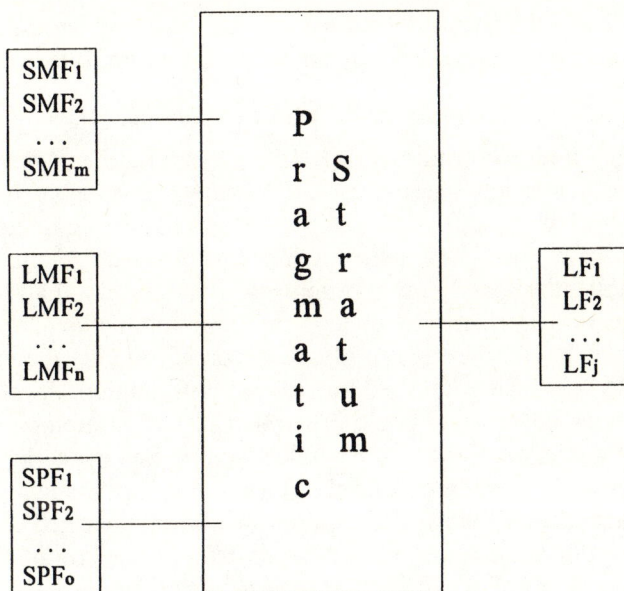

Figure 2. The pragmatic theory of the utterance

plays a filtering role in certain cases might seem to be justified by examples like *The chickens are ready to eat*, which has two possible *L*-meanings. One is equivalent to *The chickens are ready for someone to eat* and the other to *The chickens are ready to eat something*. Suppose that Terry is cooking dinner in a Manhattan apartment for Sandy. He might choose to announce that dinner is ready by saying, *The chickens are ready to eat*, and, in this context, the resulting utterance will be taken to *L*-mean "The chickens are ready for us to eat." The normal assumption is that both readings of this sentence are available in principle to the addressee, for they are properties of the sentence uttered. In this sort of case, it seems therefore that we must say that the role of context is to make one *L*-reading more salient than the other by playing a filtering role.

On the other hand, context determines the referents of indexical expressions on any occasion of use of a sentence. If Terry utters, *I would like to kiss you now*, to Sandy at 9:00 p.m. on Friday, November 24, 1992, then *I* refers to Terry, *you* refers to Sandy and *now* refers to 9:00 p.m. on Friday, November 24, 1992. In this sort of case, context determines not what *I, you,* or *now L*-mean, but what they refer to, and plays a constitutive, not a filtering, role in utterance interpretation.

As these examples illustrate, context arguably can play both a selectional and a constitutive role in determining the *L*-meaning an utterance has in any specific case. The question arises as to whether context can play both of these roles in pragmatics. Though Searle takes pains to say that a sentence like *Can you reach the salt?* is not *L*-meaning ambiguous (my terminology), he does say that when this sentence is being used to make a request it has two illocutionary forces – a literal force (question) and a primary force. Of course, this sentence could also be used to request information. In this case, Searle must say that it has the literal force of a question and the primary force of a request for information. Since Searle saw the request force of conventionalized request forms[15] as being a property of the sentence, it follows that Searle must have conceived context as playing a filtering role in an addressee's effort to determine the force of an utterance of the form, *"Can you* [action predicate]," on any occasion of use.

I shall take the position, however, that in pragmatics, as I conceive pragmatics, context **never** plays a selectional role, but rather, always plays a constitutive role in the determination of *S*-meaning. This follows from the assumption that there are no pragmatic properties of utterances that are properties *simpliciter* of the sentences uttered.[16] As I see it, in utterance understanding, the context in which a sentence is uttered pairs up with the *L*-meaning of the sentence to determine the *S*-meaning of the utterance, with context playing a no less critical and substantive role in determining *S*-Meaning than does *L*-Meaning. On this view, as we shall see in the chapters to follow, the speaker of *Can you reach the salt?* will be heard as making a request in contexts in which (a) people are dining, which makes salient the possibility that someone may need assistance in obtaining items of food or condiments, (b) it is clear

15  Recall the discussion of Searle's views on indirect speech acts on page 8 of chapter 1.
16  Grammaticalization of pragmatic function is widespread, of course, but there are ways of treating it which do not take the simplistic position that the pragmatic functions involved are properties of sentences. Rather, as I shall show in my discussion of the pragmatic stratum, which is the device I employ to account for instances of the grammaticalization of pragmatic function, the appropriate mappings are invariably from *S*-Meanings, *L*-Meanings, and sociopragmatic features to linguistic features, not to sentences as a whole.

50

that the addressee is willing to assist the speaker in obtaining items of food or condiments (a normal presumption of those who agree to dine together), and (c) it is clear that the addressee can reach the salt (a fact about physical context), and (d) it is clear that the addressee is physically able to pass the salt. In such a case, it hardly matters what one says so long as it is consistent with a desire for the salt. One might say, *Can you reach the salt?*, or, *Could you pass the salt?*, or, *Mind giving me the salt?*, or, *The salt, please?*, among many other things. Or one might just point to the salt. The point that has been missed is that what is interesting about *Can you reach the salt?* or *Could you pass the salt?* when being used to request salt, is not the utterance itself, or the sentence uttered, as Searle and most others have believed, but the contexts in which a single utterance like this can be used to do so complex a thing as request someone to do something. The linguistic form of what is actually said is of importance only to the degree to which it provides cues to the L-Meaning of the utterance and highlights those features of context that are relevant to its transactional and interactional significance. The fact that so many forms can be used in any given context to do the same thing demonstrates that the particular utterance employed is less important than the contextual elements (a)–(d) just cited.

### *Psycholinguistic support for a level of S-Meaning*

The thesis that the goal of utterance understanding is to recover the *S*-Meaning of any utterance is strongly supported by a good deal of psycholinguistic research showing that people have better memories for the pragmatic implications of an utterance or for what we might call the utterance's "gist" than for the utterance itself, that is, for the utterance's form and *L*-Meaning. A number of scholars, including Harris (1974), Brewer and Lichtenstein (1975), Brewer (1975, 1977), Harris and Monaco (1978), and Loosen (1981) have established this result in a variety of cued recall experiments.

Brewer (1975) exposed subjects to 30 experimental utterances in each of which there was one word that had a close synonym, and 30 control sentences, and then subjects were given a sentence-completion task. What he found was that subjects more often completed experimental sentences with a predicted or some other synonym, than with the word that actually occurred.[17] For instance, *The girl chose a platinum ring* was more frequently "remembered" as having been heard than the actually occurring sentence, *The girl selected a platinum ring*. It is clear from this that subjects retained what *select* and *choose* have in common (their "gists"), not the specific verb or its actual *L*-Meaning.[18]

In most of the other studies cited above, what was shown is that subjects remember "pragmatic" implicatures as well as or better than the experimental data they were exposed to. Brewer (1977) found that subjects more frequently "recalled" pragmatic implicatures of sentences (e.g. (11a) and (11b)) than the sentences (e.g. (12a) and (12b)) they were exposed to.

(11)   a. The angry rioter threw a rock through the window.
       b. The hungry python ate the mouse.

(12)   a. The angry rioter threw a rock at the window.
       b. The hungry python caught the mouse.

This experiment, like the others cited above, did not embed data in contexts but we can reasonably assume that, if anything, their results would have been all the more robust if they had.

My level of *S*-Meaning does not correspond directly to the "pragmatic implicatures" of these experiments, for they, by and large, are less "pragmatic," than simply "practical" inferences. I say this because the experimental sentences are not presented in contexts that specifically support the inferences, an essential feature of *S*-Meaning. Nevertheless, I think these experiments lend credence to the thesis that recognition of *L*-Meaning is not the goal of language understanding so much as it is a vehicle that is used to reach some deeper, more useful level of understanding of utterances, namely, recovery of their *S*-Meanings.

[17]   In an earlier study, Brewer had found that synonym substitution seems to be directional in that it was often more likely that errors would occur in one direction (e.g., from *select* to *choose* or from *little* to *small*) than in the other. There was movement, then, from the "weak" synonym to the "strong" one, to use my terms. In the experiment being described in the text, experimental sentences contained only weak synonyms.
[18]   Evidence like this supports the view that one of the ways we organize our lexicons is rather like that of a thesaurus, where forms like *select* and *choose* would branch off the same "semantic" feature. I presume a thesaurus-like representation in my formalization of the pragmatic stratum in chapter 6.

Similar experiments have not been done for conversational data, but as I think we can all confirm, we are rather better at remembering the gist of a conversation as a whole and of some of the information obtained from it than what was actually said.

## Conclusion

I have tried to show that there are three senses of the term "meaning" which are of relevance to speech act theory. The speaker who has certain transactional and interactional goals (*I*-Meanings) that she can achieve only through interaction with someone else will normally initiate an interaction that has as its transactional and interactional effects achievement of these goals. Any utterance that appears in the resulting sequence will have an *S*-Meaning that reflects what the utterance contributes to the transactional work of the sequence and will communicate the speaker's perception of the nature of the social relationship between the speaker and the addressee and the speaker's personal feelings about the addressee through the face-work the utterance does. Though the term "*S*-Meaning" is new, the idea that utterances have "pragmatic meaning" is not. What is different about the position I am advocating here is that *S*-Meaning is treated as an actual level of meaning in conversation. I turn in the next chapter to provide a more explicit characterization of what the transactional *S*-Meanings consist of and, in chapters 6 and 7, to providing a formal mapping of utterances into their transactional and interactional *S*-Meanings.

# 3

### The structure of communicative interactions

### Introduction

In this chapter, I turn to consider how speech act theory can be
modified so that it can do for the analysis of conversation what
traditional speech act theory did for the analysis of individual
utterances. The goal of traditional speech act theory was to account
for our ability to recognize the illocutionary point of a speaker in
uttering any sentence. It was assumed that we recognize the point of
an utterance by recognizing the action that the speaker means to be
performing. Thus, according to speech act theorists, if you and I are
dining together and you say, *Can you pass the salt?*, I will recognize
that you mean for me to pass you the salt in virtue of recognizing that
you are requesting me to pass the salt. How, then, do we recognize
what speech act a speaker means to be performing?

According to Searle, a given utterance act is an action of a particular
type if it meets the conditions on that type of act. Thus, for instance, if
an utterance is produced by a speaker that (a) predicates a future
action of the speaker (Searle's propositional content condition) when
(b) it is evident that the speaker is able to perform this action (a
Searlean preparatory condition) and (c) the addressee has made
evident a desire that the speaker perform this action (a Searlean
preparatory condition), then the addressee is entitled to assume that
the speaker means to be making a commitment to the addressee to
perform this action (Searle's essential condition and the illocutionary
point of the act) and that the speaker will in fact perform the action

(Searle's sincerity condition). Viewed from the perspective of the speaker, if a speaker intends to make a commitment to an addressee to perform some action that she believes the addressee wishes her to perform, then she will utter a sentence that predicates a future action of her.

As we have seen, whatever the successes of speech act theory might have been in the analysis of the actions we perform in uttering individual sentences, it provides a very poor platform for the analysis of conversation. The two main failures of traditional speech act theory are the fact that there exists no effective procedure for mapping the utterances of complex multiturn interactions into traditional speech acts and that associating speech acts with individual utterances, even assuming counterfactually that there were an effective procedure for doing so, would shed little or no light on the nature of the interactions in which they occur.

In what follows in this chapter, I turn to consider how speech act theory can be revised so as to facilitate an account of our ability to use and understand language in ordinary conversation. Before doing this, we must consider what the goals of our theory should be.

## Conversational competence

I shall assume that the goal of the study of conversation is to develop a theory of the competence that underlies our ability to converse with others. Such a theory must be able to account for our ability to achieve goals through conversing with others and to recognize and further (or thwart) the efforts of others to achieve their goals. Second, such a theory must be able to account for our ability to produce and understand utterances that are contextually appropriate in that they are consistent in content with Grice's (1975) Cooperative Principle ("make your conversational contribution such that it is consistent with the purposes of the talk exchange"), that are consistent with the discourse context (e.g., obey constraints on the display of new and old information, contain pronouns at appropriate places, etc.), that are consistent in register with the statuses and roles of the participants and with what they are doing and the circumstances in which they are doing it, that are appropriate in style with social distance and power relationships between participants and with the social context, and that display levels of politeness appropriate to the social and inter-personal relationships between the participants.

If a theory of conversational competence is to be of any empirical interest, it must be testable, that is, it must yield testable predictions. There are three ways in which we might imagine testing such a theory. First, we might test its predictions against actually occurring conversational data (the main practice here). Second, we might test its predictions experimentally.[1] And, third, we might implement it computationally in an utterance generation and understanding system (cf. Patten, Geis, and Becker 1992). In the latter case, if the system can produce and understand utterances in interaction with other machines or humans that seem natural (i.e., are fully contextually appropriate) and that further the purposes of the interaction, we would be justified in feeling some confidence in the worth of our theory (but, alas, not justified in believing that it is correct as an account of actual human conversational competence).

At the heart of the theory of conversational competence is the interaction structure, a structure that specifies the goals of the interaction,[2] the conditions that must be met before the goal of the interaction can be achieved, and relevant domain information (i.e., what the interaction is about), among other things. We might approach the question of the nature of interaction structures by considering example (1).

(1)  M and H ride-request. (This conversation took place between a student (H) and a member of the faculty (M) of the student's department following the conclusion of a Linguistic Institute reception in 1993.)
H: Can I ask you something?
M: Sure.
H: Do you have a car?
M: Yes.

---

[1]  Geis and Harlow (forthcoming) describes experiments done on English and French speakers (and French learners) to determine how they do requesting and offering in puzzle-solving. One of the predictions made was that since subjects were instructed to assist each other, there should be no utterances inquiring as to the willingness of the addressee to provide assistance (for that condition on requesting was satisfied in the context). Out of 245 request initiations, there were only two such instances and they were by the same speaker in consecutive, latched utterances. I take this to demonstrate (the obvious point) that context can contribute to the satisfaction of conditions of interaction structures.

[2]  This is the goal of the interaction, but not, presumably, the ultimate goal of the person initiating the interaction, which is, of course, to come to be at her home as a result of this other person's giving her the ride he has committed himself to giving.

H: Could you give me a ride home?
M: Where do you live?
H: University City.
M: Sure.

Prior to initiating this conversation, H had a problem that she needed a solution for, namely, she needed to find a way to get from the reception she had been attending to her apartment. In such a circumstance, if a person had a functional automobile, she might simply drive herself home, or, if she did not, she might take some public mode of transportation (bus, train, or taxi). Or she might attempt to secure a ride home from someone who does have a car. In any case, she must develop some plan of action, the outcome of which is that she ultimately come to be in her apartment.

In this case, H's plan was to attempt to secure a ride from M, a subplan of which was to secure a commitment from M to provide this ride. The "logic" of this plan is clear: if H can cause M to commit himself to provide her a ride home and if M actually undertakes to provide her with this ride home and if M is not hindered from carrying out his commitment (by car trouble or an accident, etc.), then the result will be that H will come to be at her apartment. In this case, as is so often true of conversation, the interaction between H and M is part of some nonconversational ("real world") plan. I shall refer to nonconversational plans as "domain plans,"[3] in contrast with conversational plans.

It is a characteristic, then, of conversational plans that they tend to be goal furthering (elements of larger domain plans), rather than ends in themselves.[4] In this case, since H's goal is to obtain a commitment from M to provide H with a ride, we would expect the interaction to contain language that reflects the fact that before M makes this commitment, he must be **able** to provide this ride and must be **willing** to provide this ride.[5] In this case, we find an inquiry by H as to whether M has a car (with him), which addressed a precondition on his being able to provide this ride, a direct inquiry as to whether M was able to provide this ride, and an inquiry by M as to the destination

[3] I borrow this term from Welker (1994).
[4] Some cases of "idle" conversation may seem to consist of conversation for the sake of conversation. However, these conversations could be argued to further interactional goals. See Cheepen (1988).
[5] Someone's being willing to do something for someone does not entail that they want to do it, of course.

of this ride which addressed a precondition on his being willing to provide the ride, namely that he not find this destination to be inconvenient (i.e., "out of his way"). This illustrates the important point that the utterances that occur in a given interaction address critical transactional (and interactional) matters, including both domain information (which concerns the properties of the desired action – we are dealing with a ride from somewhere to somewhere) and conditions on the initiator's achieving her goal.

What is important about any utterance occurring within an interaction is, then, its transactional and interactional significance – what it contributes to the specification of domain information and to the satisfaction of conditions on goal achievement (including preconditions on same) and to the face-work the utterance does (i.e., the speaker does in uttering the sentence). But, if an account of the transactional and interactional significance of utterances is to be of any empirical interest, it must facilitate an account of the "details of talk" (to borrow Schegloff's (1991) phrase) in conversation, that is, there must be a mapping of some sort from elements of interaction structures to utterances. This thesis gives rise to an important methodological constraint: before an element may be posited in a interaction structure of a particular sort, there must be a demonstration that there are utterance elements that routinely occur in relevant interactions that directly realize (i.e., can be mapped into) that interaction structure element. In this chapter, I will discuss such mappings in somewhat informal terms. A more explicit treatment of colloquial utterances of the sort found in typical service encounters can be found in chapter 6.

## A critique of Searle's speech act structures

Searle's (1969) speech act structures contain four types of conditions, as we saw in chapter 1: a propositional content condition, a set of preparatory conditions, a sincerity condition, and an essential condition. Consider, again, his structure for requests.

(2)  Searle's Conditions on Requests (H is the hearer and S is the speaker)
Propositional content: Future act A of H.
Preparatory:
    H is able to do A. S believes H is able to do A.

58

It is not obvious to both S and H that H will do A in the normal course of events of his own accord.
Sincerity: S wants H to do A.
Essential: Counts as an attempt to get H to do A.

In what follows, I shall argue that Searle's propositional content condition needs to be replaced by a specification of the domain of the interaction (which, in a service encounter, would consist of a representation of the properties of the action or thing desired by the initiator), that Searle's preparatory conditions must be amplified and construed as satisfaction conditions, a subclass of felicity conditions, that Searle's sincerity condition needs to be recast, and that his essential condition needs to be amplified to include other effects of interactions.

Before beginning this examination, we should take note of the fact that Searle gave two formulations of the ability condition on requests, namely

(3)  a. H is able to do A.
     b. S believes H is able to do A.

Searle was concerned here with two quite distinct types of conditions, conditions on **successful** performances of requests (cf. (3a)) and conditions on **felicitous** performances of requests (cf. (3b)). I shall take the position here that what a speaker chooses to say and how she chooses to say it at a particular moment in an exchange will reflect her **beliefs** about what conditions have and have not been satisfied, and that this is an utterance-planning issue. However, since the success of any negotiation ultimately depends on initiator and responder agreement that conditions are satisfied, I shall formulate interaction structure conditions after the manner of (3a), with the understanding that any interaction structure condition is satisfied if and only if it is mutually believed to be satisfied.

### Propositional content condition

Searle's propositional content condition might be said to facilitate an account of the fact that a person in a superior social position might order an inferior to do something in saying something like *You need to go to Boston tomorrow*, for this utterance contains a predication of a future act of the addressee (as is true of orders), or of the fact that

59

one person might make a promise to another in saying *I'll be in my office at noon,* for this utterance contains a predication of a future act of the speaker (as is true of promises). However, a model of utterance generation and utterance understanding in conversation does not want a propositional content condition *per se* for whereas an individual sentence or utterance (the focus of Searle's research, of course) might be said to have a propositional content, multiturn interactions cannot.

In the case of a service encounter, in place of the propositional content condition, there will be a domain that specifies the properties of the action or thing the initiator desires. In this chapter, I shall provide "slot and filler" representations for the domains of interaction structures not unlike those employed in the computational implementation of DSAT in Patten, Geis, and Becker (1992). In chapter 7, I provide representations within the framework of Discourse Representation Theory.

Recall conversation (4).

(4)  Jacobs and Jackson (1983b: 299)
     Carl is standing in the hallway of the speech department, holding the hand of his 15-month-old son, Curtis.

| CARL: | [a] Hey Debbie. [b] Are you going to be free from 1:30 to 2:30? | $T_1$ |
| DEBBIE: | [a] Yeah, I think so. [b] You want me to watch him? | $T_2$ |
| CARL: | Yeah | $T_3$ |
| DEBBIE: | [a] I'd love to. [b] It'd be a pleasure. | $T_4$ |
| CARL: | [a] Okay. [b] Thanks. [c] I'll bring him around then. | $T_5$ |

We might represent the domain of this interaction as in (5), where "A" refers to the action and "i" and "r" are designated discourse referents referring to the initiator and responder in the interaction. I also identify the utterances in which the domain information is established though this is an entirely unofficial part of a DSAT representation.

(5)  Domain(A):[6]
     action(watch child)          $<T_2b, T_3>$

[6]  The provider is the provider of the service, the receiver is the receiver of the service, and the beneficiary (about which more later) is normally the initiator. These predicates identify pragmatic roles. The utterance labels associated with the domain predicates are given in the form of pairs of labels when the information is established via an inquiry and a response and with a single label when just a single utterance provides the information.

| | |
|---|---|
| provider(r) | $<T_2b, T_3>$ |
| receiver(i's child) | $<T_2b, T_3>$ |
| beneficiary(i) | $<T_2b, T_3>$ |
| begin-time(1:30 p.m.) | $<T_1b, T_2a>$ |
| end-time(2:30 p.m.) | $<T_1b, T_2a>$ |
| later(1:30 p.m., now) | $<T_1b, T_2a>$ |
| location(here) | $<T_5c>$ |

Note that the essential information captured in Searle's propositional content condition is preserved. We have a future action (cf. "action (watch child)" and "later(1:30 p.m., now)") which is predicated of the addressee (cf. "provider(r)"). However, as the utterance references to the right indicate, the domain for this interaction structure does not constitute the propositional content of a single utterance. The future time of the action is derived from turns $<T_1b, T_2a>$ and the nature of the action is derived from $<T_2b, T_3>$. The location of the action is derived from $<T_5c>$.

The propositional content condition is of even more problematic usefulness in the case of a conversation like (6) in which we find no utterance predicating an action by the addressee.

(6)  Levinson (1983: 357), drawn from Merritt (1976: 334)
    Position 1: A:  Hi, Do you have uh size C flashlight batteries?
    Position 2: B:  Yes sir
    Position 3: A:  I'll have four please
    Position 4: B:  ((TURNS TO GET))

Within DSAT, this conversation would be assigned domain representation (7), again with an indication of the pair of utterances that establish the information.

(7)  Domain(A)[7]

| | |
|---|---|
| action(sell) | \<context\> |
| provider(r) | $<T_1, T_2>$ |
| receiver(i) | $<T_3, T_4>$ |
| goods(batteries)[8] | $<T_1, T_2>$ |
| size(C) | $<T_1, T_2>$ |

---

[7]  When the beneficiary of the action is also the receiver of the action, I omit it. This is, of course, the default case.
[8]  The predicate "goods" refers to a pragmatic role.

number(4)        $\langle T_3, T_4 \rangle$
at(now)          $\langle T_3, T_4 \rangle$

Clearly, we need to imagine more complex mappings of utterances into the information content of a conversation than is suggested by Searle's thesis that requests are subject to a propositional content condition.

### Sincerity condition

In utterance generation, we choose to engage another in a specific type of interaction because we are in a particular psychological state which leads us to have the goal(s) associated with this type of interaction. Accordingly, I shall argue that each interaction structure contains an "initial-state condition" that stipulates what psychological state the initiator of the interaction (which, again, may not be the initiator of the conversation) must be in. Often, Searle's sincerity condition corresponds to the DSAT initial-state condition. This is certainly true of requests and invitations. There is one major exception worth noting here, and this concerns Searle's sincerity condition on asserting something (cf. (8)).[9]

(8)   S believes P to be true. (Where "P" is the proposition conveyed)

There is no question that someone conveying information to another person cannot do so felicitously unless he believes this information to be true. However, this is certainly not the psychological state that leads us to convey information. That is normally a desire to satisfy the addressee's explicit or implicit desire or need for the information. The relevant interaction type is the information exchange in which one party (the responder) provides information to the other (the initiator) either because the initiator has specifically requested it or because the responder believes that the initiator either wants or needs the information. On this view, the following two conversations equally involve information exchanges.

(9)   I:   Who did Sandy marry?
      R:   Terry.

---

[9]   In DSAT, assertions do not exist except as literal acts. The closest communicative action would be something like conveying information.

(10)  R:  Sandy married Terry yesterday.
      I:  I didn't know that.

These two subtypes of information exchange exactly parallel instances in which someone offers to do something after an explicit request for help (cf. (11)) or because of an evident need for help (cf. (12)).

(11)  I:  I need someone to help me carry these books.
      R:  I'll do it.

(12)  R:  Here, let me help you with those books.
      I:  Oh, thanks.

In my view, the DSAT interaction structures for conversations like (9) and (10) are the same (information-exchange interaction structure) and those for conversations like (11) and (12) are the same (service-encounter interaction structure). The same would be true of more complex, multiturn instances of the two types.

Utterances may specify the initial-state condition directly, of course. Debbie's utterance *You want me to watch him?* at turn $T_2b$ of conversation (4) specifies the initial-state condition of service encounters directly (for it speaks directly to Carl's desire that Debbie watch Carl's child). The utterance clearly advances the conversation forward transactionally in that it facilitates an earlier satisfaction of the initial-state condition, but, as I argued in the preceding chapter, it is present in part for interactional reasons.

Initiators who say things like *I'd like for you to do X* or *I want you to do X* or *I need for you to do X* and responders who say things like *Would you like for me to do x?* or *Do you want me to do x?* or *Do you need for me to do x?* are employing utterances that specify the initial-state condition of service encounters. When the service encounter involves performance of an action, we may represent the initial-state condition as in (13), where A consists of providing the desired thing to the initiator.

(13)  i desires r to do A.

In this representation, as before, "i" and "r" refer to the initiator and responder, respectively. In chapter 6, I provide a formal mapping of utterances like these into condition (13).

63

## The essential condition

Searle's essential condition corresponds to the DSAT transactional effect. My criticism of Searle's speech act structures, in this connection, is not that his essential conditions for acts are incorrect but that we need to recognize other types of effects of interactions.

In the slot occupied by *You want me to watch him?* at turn $T_{2b}$ of conversation (4), we very often find the more general question, *Why do you ask?*, an utterance that seems to specify the transactional effect of the act in that it inquires as to what the prior speaker's goal is. Such an utterance does not advance conversations forward to the same extent as does *Do you want me to watch him?* of course. Notice that (14) gets the same transactional work done that (15) does and in the same number of turns even though it does not contain *Why do you ask?*

(14)   A: Hey Debbie. Are you free from 1:30 to 2:30?
       C: Yeah, I think so.
       A: I need someone to watch my kid. Could you do it for me?

(15)   A: Hey Debbie. Are you free from 1:30 to 2:30?
       C: Yeah, I think so. Why do you ask?
       A: I need someone to watch my kid. Could you do it for me?

The utterance, *Why do you ask?*, seems to play a primarily interactional role for it constitutes an encouraging "go ahead" move, but it also serves to satisfy the curiosity of the responder concerning the initiator's goal.

In the case of many service encounters the responder immediately performs the desired action on recognizing what the intent of the initiator is. However, there are also instances in which the action is performed much later than the giving of the commitment. Accordingly, I shall take the position that the goal of a service encounter is to secure a commitment from the responder to perform an action, rather than to cause the person to perform the action:

(16)   r commits to do A

Though Searle was aware that acts have interactional effects, as well as transactional effects, his speech act structures do not specifically address them. Doing so is essential, however, if we are to provide a full account of conversation. What I shall suggest, then, is that we replace Searle's essential condition with two types of effects of interactions: transactional effects that concern the ostensible goal of the interaction and interactional effects that concern the interpersonal side of the interaction. One other difference between Searle's account and the one being advanced here is that the transactional and interactional effects are not conditions on felicitous or successful performance of some action but are the effects or goal states of the interaction. I shall defer my discussion of interactional effects until the next chapter because very different issues are involved in discussions of transactional and interactional effects.

## Preparatory conditions

Searle's preparatory conditions include two quite different sorts of conditions: nonnegotiable conditions that must be satisfied before an interaction can be felicitously launched and negotiable conditions that must be satisfied before the transactional effect of an interaction can be achieved. Observe that condition (17a) is subject to negotiation and certainly need not be satisfied prior to initiation of a request routine.

(17)  a.  H is able to do A.
  b.  It is not obvious to both S and H that H will do A in the normal course of events of his own accord.

On the other hand, whether or not H will perform an action in the normal course of events, given how Searle meant this condition, is not subject to negotiation.

That there is an ability condition on service encounters and other similar actions, such as invitations, is clear. Observe that turn $T_2$, of conversation (18), contains an occurrence of *can* in an utterance that seems to specify the ability condition on invitations.

(18)  Atkinson and Drew (1979: 58)
  TERRY:  Uh if you'd care to come and visit a little while this morning I'll give you a cup of coffee.  $T_1$
  SANDY:  hehh Well that's awfully sweet of you, I don't think I can make it this morning. .hh uhm I'm running an ad in the paper and-and uh I have to stay near the phone.  $T_2$

65

The presence of *can* in *I don't think I can make it this morning* is, then, a "detail of talk" that motivates postulation of an ability condition, as are utterances in which an ability or inability to perform a desired action is implicated, as would have been the case had B's response been, *hehh Well that's awfully sweet of you, but . .hh uhm I'm running an ad in the paper and-and uh I have to stay near the phone,* where one gives the reason one is unable to perform the action, rather than overtly stating that one is unable to do so. This is an extremely common way of rejecting requests and invitations. In conversation (25) on page 14 below, as we shall see, Marcia provides an ability-based declination of Donny's ride-request, *Yeah:- en I know you want-(.) en I whoa-(.) en I would, but- except I've gotta leave in about five min(h)utes,* where *I've gotta leave in about five min(h)utes,* implicates an inability to accept the request.

I do not mean to overstress the obvious in noting that there are utterances that specify the ability conditions of interactions. My point is both to stress the point that there must be evidence from the details of talk in support of postulation of elements of interaction structures and to give an indication of the specific elements of utterances that are mapped into specific elements of interaction structures. Thus, I would argue that utterances containing *can* and *could* are mapped into the ability condition.[10]

Condition (17b) differs significantly from (17a), for at the point a request is initiated, the responder either had or had not already planned to carry out the action in question. It is not something that can be made true through talk. Similarly, I cannot felicitously request you to do what has already been done (unless it is a repeatable act) and the fact that an act has or has not been done at the time the initiator of a request initiates a request for the act to be performed is nonnegotiable.

In a course paper in which she studied the verbal behavior of persons playing a game of Monopoly, Nicole Schrickel observed that there is a class of utterances occurring in rent requests that tend to void the requests, rather than serve as rejections of them. Thus, if one player lands on another player's property and the latter player demands a rent payment from the other when he does not

---

[10] There are circumstances in which people say that they cannot do things when it is clear that the problem is that they do not want to (as when a speaker declines an invitation saying, *I can't come over. I need some private time*). In such a circumstance we must map *I can't come over* into the ability condition, for the speaker is representing her nonacceptance as ability based.

own the property or has mortgaged it, the former player can void the request by noting that it is out of order. The same would, of course, be true if the real-world owner of an apartment building demanded a rent payment of someone who was not actually renting an apartment (a visitor, say) or demanded payment of someone who had already paid his rent. Schrickel argued that this class of conditions, which she termed "alpha-conditions," is distinct from conditions like the ability condition, on the grounds that the latter provides a basis for rejecting the request, rather than voiding it. Though I accept her distinction, my focus here will be on the negotiable conditions on interactions.

Searle did not include a willingness condition in (2) corresponding to the ability condition. However, it is clear that such a condition is required and most speech act theorists recognize one. It is motivated by utterances in service encounters and other similar interactions that concern the willingness of the responder to go along with the request. Such utterances abound. Marcia's ability-based declination of Donny's ride-request (cf. conversation (25) on page 74), *Yeah:- en I know you want-(.) en I whoa-(.) en I would, but- except I've gotta leave in about five min(h)utes* contains the elliptical expression, *I would* (give you the ride you want), which clearly, even if disingenuously, asserts her willingness to give this ride. The appearance of *would* is a "detail of talk" supporting postulation of a willingness condition.

There are then two ways one can view Searle's "preparatory conditions," as conditions that must be satisfied before the transactional effect can be achieved or as conditions on felicitous launching of the act. In what follows, I shall concern myself only with the former type of preparatory condition, and in order to make this clear shall use the term "satisfaction conditions" to refer to the ability and willingness conditions.

## A DSAT alternative structure

There are basically two types of service encounter: those in which the initiator requests that the responder perform some action on behalf of the initiator and those in which the initiator requests that the responder provide the initiator with some thing, a special case of the action request. Given this distinction, we might provide interaction structure representation (19) for instances of service encounters involving actions.

(19)   Service encounter interaction structure (for actions)
          Effects:[11]
               Transactional: r commits to do A
               Interactional:[12]
          Initial-state condition: i desires r do A
                    Because: P[13]
          Satisfaction conditions:
               r is able to do A
                    If: $\neg$ must(r do A')[14]
               r is willing to do A
                    If: R
          Domain(A):
               action(e)
               provider(r)
               receiver(x)
               begin-time(t)
               end-time(t')
               later(t, now)
               location(p)
               beneficiary(y)[15]
          Domain(A'):
               action'(e')
               e' e
               at(t'')
               $t''$ ε <t ... t'>

---

[11]  In DSAT, the transactional effect of an act is not itself a condition, as in Searle's speech act structures. Instead, it is the effect that is achieved when all other conditions are satisfied.

[12]  I shall defer discussion of the interactional effects of interactions until the next chapter.

[13]  The "Because" condition here and the "If" conditions found in connection with the ability and willingness conditions immediately below represent preconditions on these conditions and play a very important role in conversation, and in the DSAT distinction between direct and indirect communication to be discussed in chapter 8.

[14]  The ability condition precondition, "$\neg$ must(r do A')," which in concert with relevant domain predicates has it that the responder is not engaged in some action other than the desired one at the time of the desired action, holds of all interactions involving the responder's doing something. It is the origin of initiations like, *You doing anything right now?*, *Whatcha doin'?*, and the like.

[15]  One of the important features of service encounters is that the initiator is attempting to cause the responder to do something **for** someone (usually the initiator). Note, for instance, that the predicate *watch him* in Debbie's utterance *You want me to watch him?* could have contained an explicit benefactive phrase, *for you*, as in *You want me to watch him for you?*. In this utterance, the child is the receiver of the action and Carl is the beneficiary.

My thesis is that any utterance that occurs in an action request should be mappable into one or more elements of interaction structures such as this one via the pragmatic stratum of chapter 6 and an appropriately integrated semantic component.

### Personal request service encounters

I would like now to illustrate in detail how an interaction structure like (19) can be employed in the analysis of conversation by reconsidering conversation (4) above.

Carl's utterance *Are you free from 1:30 to 2:30?* at turn $T_{1b}$ has a conventional understanding as an inquiry as to whether or not the responder is engaged in some activity during the time period in question. However, addressees recognize an initiation such as this as an attempt to determine whether they are **available** to engage in some activity during the indicated time. We can account for this by mapping the utterance into the precondition, "$\neg$ must(r do A')," of the ability condition.

In general, the responder cannot know whether the initiator of an inquiry like this means to request the responder to do something for the initiator or with the initiator or suggest that the responder do something the initiator thinks she might find interesting (go to a talk, say). All that can solidly be inferred is that the initiator means to cause the responder to be engaged in some action at the time in question. I shall assume then that utterance $T_2b$ is mapped via the pragmatic stratum into **all** interaction structures consistent with the information content of (20), where "?" indicates that the utterance is explicitly value-requesting in nature.

(20)   D and C interaction structure representation after *Are you free from 1:30 to 2:30?*
Transactional effect: r commits to do A
Initial-state condition: i desires r do A
Satisfaction condition: r is able to do A
    If: $\neg$ must(r do A') [?]
Domain(A):
    action(e)
    begin-time(1:30 p.m.)
    later(1:30, now)
    end-time(2:30 p.m.)

Domain(A')
    action(e')
    e' ≠ e
    at(t)
    t ε <1:30 ... 2:30>

An important benefit of this approach is that the implicature of *Are you free from 1:30 to 2:30?* that Carl is inquiring as to the **ability** of Debbie to engage in some activity from 1:30 till 2:30 is accounted for completely automatically, for an inquiry as to whether a precondition of some interaction structure condition holds automatically implicates an inquiry whether the condition holds. This utterance also quite automatically implicates that Carl's intended transactional effect is that r commit to engage in some sort of action, for only interactions with this sort of transactional effect have ability conditions of this type. Debbie need therefore do no Gricean calculation in order to recognize that Carl is "really" asking whether she is available to engage in some activity from 1:30 p.m. till 2:30 p.m. or to recognize that Carl's goal is to cause her to commit to engaging in the activity. It is a signal virtue of the DSAT approach to interaction that most routine speech-act-theoretic implicatures are automatically computed, rather than calculated in a traditional Gricean manner.

When Debbie replies with *Yeah,* she provides the value "true" ("T") for this precondition. Since the precondition on the ability condition is satisfied, unless Debbie introduces some other precondition on this condition, it will be understood that the ability condition is satisfied. The resulting interaction structure representation is presented in (21).

(21)    D and C interaction structure after Debbie's, *Yeah, I think so.*
    Transactional effect: r commits to do A
    Initial-state condition: i desires r do A
    Satisfaction condition: r is able to do A [T]
        If: ¬ must(r do A') [T]
    Domain(A):
        action(e)
        begin-time(1:30 p.m.)
        later(1:30, now)
        end-time(2:30 p.m.)
    Domain(A'):

action(e')
e' ≠ e
at(t)
t ε <1:30 ... 2:30>

Debbie goes on to say, *You want me to watch him?*, at turn $T_{2b}$,[16] which constitutes a request for the value for the initial-state condition. The resulting interaction structure is given in (22).

(22)   D and C interaction structure after Debbie's, *You want me to watch him?*
Transactional effect: r commits to do A
Initial-state condition: i desires r to do A [?]
Satisfaction condition: r is able to do A [T]
    If: ¬ must(r do A') [T]
Domain(A):
    action(watch child)
    provider(r)
    receiver(i's child)
    beneficiary(i)
    begin-time(1:30 p.m.)
    later(1:30, now)
    end-time(2:30 p.m.)
Domain(A'):
    action(e')
    e' ≠ e
    at(t)
    t ε <1:30 ... 2:30>

When Carl says *Yeah,* he indicates that the value for the initial-state condition in (22) is true. The effect of this utterance on the baby-sitting interaction structure is as in (23).

(23)   Baby-sitting interaction structure representation, after Carl's *Yeah.*
Transactional effect: r commits to do A

---

[16] We cannot know why she is able to opine that this is what Carl wants. It could be that she has watched the child before or has inferred that this is what he wants on the grounds that she knows he has a class at the time in question and knows that the child will not be welcome at the class.

Initial-state condition: i desires r to do A [T]
Satisfaction condition: r is able to do A [T]
    If: ¬ must(r do A') [T]
Domain(A):
    action(watch child)
    provider(r)
    receiver(i's child)
    beneficiary(i)
    begin-time(1:30 p.m.)
    later(1:30, now)
    end-time(2:30 p.m.)
Domain(A'):
    action(e')
    $e' \neq e$
    at(t)
    $t \, \varepsilon <1:30 \ldots 2:30>$

At this point in the conversation, Debbie is, for all practical purposes, committed to watching Carl's child. Note, for instance, how unexpected – even rude – it would be were Debbie to have said, *I'm sorry, I can't*, after Carl's, *Yeah*. One might argue that her utterances, *I'd love to* and *It'd be a pleasure*, instantiate the willingness condition, but I would argue that although they seem to confirm her willingness to watch Carl's child, they are present for interactional, not transactional reasons. Note, for instance, that had Carl opened the exchange saying, *Say, Debbie, would you watch my child from 1:30 to 2:30?*, and had Debbie replied, *Yes, I'd love to*, we would see her *Yes* as having transactional, and her *I'd love to* interactional significance. The situation in conversation (4) is no different.

Note that once conversation (4) is over, Debbie is committed to watching Carl's child from 1:30 to 2:30 on the afternoon in question, but she has made no overt promise to do this. In fact, Carl has not made an overt request that she do so. The question therefore arises as to how exactly this commitment gets made. The answer is, I submit, that among many, if not most or all, speakers of American English, it is understood that if one person has some evident need or desire[17] and some other person makes evident **either** a willingness **or** an ability to satisfy that need or desire, this latter person is understood to be

---

[17] This need for assistance might be evident simply from the context itself. Thus, someone carrying more books than he can comfortably carry has an evident need for help.

committed in principle to satisfying this need or desire. I shall refer to this axiom as the "axiom of commitment."

The axiom of commitment is critical to understanding the dynamics of commitment-making in conversation. It is because of this axiom that we are able to make requests using single sentences like *Could you watch my child from 1:30 to 2:30?* or *Would you watch my child from 1:30 to 2:30?* In each case the initiator implicates a desire that the responder watch his child and should the responder reply in the affirmative, she will be taken as being committed to watching the child even though technically all she has conceded is an ability to watch the child (the first example) or a willingness to do so (the second example). Once Carl confirms that he desires that she watch his child, the axiom of commitment kicks in to assign the value "true" to the willingness condition, for Debbie has conceded an ability to watch Carl's child. The only other utterance that has specific transactional consequences is Carl's *I'll bring him around then,* which serves to specify the location predicate of the interaction structure. (Carl's *Okay* signals that he is satisfied that the transactional work of the exchange is completed.)

The final interaction structure would be instantiated as in (24), where I have indicated the utterance or utterance pairs that do the work of instantiating the various conditions and domain predicates.

(24) Final D and C interaction structure
Effects:
　　　　　Transactional: r commits to do A [Achieved, $T_3$]
　　Initial-state condition: i desires r to do A [T, $<T_2b, T_3>$]
　　Satisfaction conditions:
　　　　　r is able to do A [T, $<T_1b, T_2a>$]
　　　　　　　If: $\neg$ must(r do A') [T, $<T_1b, T_2a>$]
　　　　　r is willing to do A [T, $<T_2b>$, axiom of commitment]
　　Domain(A):
　　　　　action(baby-sit)　　　　　$<T_2b, T_3>$
　　　　　provider(r)　　　　　　　$<T_2b, T_3>$
　　　　　receiver(i's child)　　　　$<T_2b, T_3>$
　　　　　beneficiary(i)　　　　　　$<T_2b, T_3>$
　　　　　begin-time(1:30 p.m.) $<T_1b, T_2a>$
　　　　　end-time(2:30 p.m.)　$<T_1b, T_2a>$
　　　　　later(1:30, now)　　　　$<T_1b, T_2a>$
　　　　　location(here)　　　　　$<T_5c>$
　　Domain(A'):

$$action(e')$$
$$e' \neq e$$

| | |
|---|---|
| at(t) | $<T_1b, T_2a>$ |
| $t \, \varepsilon <1{:}30 \ldots 2{:}30>$ | $<T_1b, T_2a>$ |

This representation provides information as to what utterances specify which conditions and domain predicates. Though it is not an official part of a DSAT representation of a conversation, this mode of representation can be utilized to exhibit structural information deemed critical by conversation analysts, including, in particular, what pairs of utterances constitute adjacency pairs (e.g., $<T_1b, T_2a>$ and $<T_2b, T_3>$).

Before continuing, let me note that though we may not wholly unreasonably say that Carl was doing requesting (a communicative action) in this conversation and that Debbie was making an offer (a communicative action) when she said, *You want me to watch him?*, and that she ultimately made a promise to watch Carl's child (a communicative action), these action descriptions have no official status in DSAT. They are clearly unneeded in order to understand the progress of this conversation. What we need, instead, and all we need, is a mapping of utterances into the interaction structure conditions and domain predicates along the lines suggested in the discussion, for this suffices to account for the fact that by the time Carl says, *Yeah*, Debbie is committed to watching Carl's child, i.e., Carl's goal is attained. There is no harm, when discussing interactions, to make informal reference to the communicative actions of participants. However, it must be recognized that calling an action a "request" or "offer" can contribute nothing to the actual account of the interaction in which it occurs until some effective way of mapping utterances into communicative actions like these is provided and shown to be of some systematic theoretical interest.

Let us turn now to an example of a rejected request of a ride. In this case, I shall also focus exclusively on the transactional work of the exchange.

(25)  Schegloff (handout)[18] – 18-second conversation
      (1+ rings)

---

[18]  A slightly different transcript of this conversation can be found in Mandelbaum and Pomerantz (1991: 153f). The present transcript, as well as an airing of the taped conversation, was provided by Manny Schegloff at a talk in April, 1993 at NATO advanced workshop on discourse in Maratea, Italy.

| | |
|---|---|
| MARCIA: | Hello? |
| DONNY: | 'lo <u>Marcia</u>,=[19] |
| MARCIA: | Yea[:h][20] |
| DONNY: | =[('t's) D]onny. |
| MARCIA: | Hi, Donny. |
| DONNY: | Guess what.hh[21] |
| MARCIA: | What. |
| DONNY: | .hh My <u>ca</u>:r is sta::lled. |
| | (0.2) |
| DONNY: | ('n) I'm up here in the Glen? |
| MARCIA: | O<u>h</u>::. |
| | (0.4) |
| DONNY: | (.hhh) |
| DONNY: | A:nd.hh |
| | (0.2) |
| DONNY: | I don' know if it's po:ssible, but {.hhh/(0.2)}[22] see I haveta open up the <u>ba</u>:nk.hh |
| | (0.3) |
| DONNY: | a:t uh: (.) in Brentwood?hh= |
| | (0.4) |
| MARCIA: | =Yea<u>h</u>:- en I know you want-(.) en I whoa-(.) en I <u>wo</u>uld, but- except I've gotta leave in about five min(h)utes.[(hheh)[23] |
| DONNY: | [=Okay then I gotta call somebody else.right away. |
| | (.) |
| DONNY: | Okay?= |
| MARCIA: | =Okay [Don] |
| DONNY: | [Thanks] a lot.=Bye-. |
| MARCIA: | =Bye:. |

Aligned markers in right margin: T₁ (Guess what.hh), T₂ (What.), T₃ (.hh My ca:r is sta::lled.), T₄ ((0.2)), T₅ (('n) I'm up here in the Glen?), T₆ (Oh::.), T₇ (haveta open up the ba:nk.hh), T₈ ((0.3)), T₉ (a:t uh: (.) in Brentwood?hh=), T₁₀ ((0.4)), T₁₁ (min(h)utes.[(hheh)), T₁₂ ([=Okay then I gotta call somebody else.right away.)

In this conversation, following the initial greetings sequences, Donny initiates his ride-request service encounter with what conversa-

---

[19]  The "=" sign indicates latched utterances of different speakers or utterance parts of the same speaker. Underlining indicates a hard attack – emphasis of some sort.

[20]  Material enclosed in brackets "[ ]" in successive turns indicates that the talk so bracketed was simultaneous.

[21]  A period before "h" indicates inhalation.

[22]  This represents that the tape was unclear as to whether there was an inhalation or silence at this point.

[23]  The "h's" not preceded by a period indicate exhalations.

tion analysts (Schegloff 1988) call a pre-announcement, an utterance that prefigures an announcement of "news," often "hot news." Normally, offering news to others is socially configured as providing them with information the speaker believes they may want to know.[24] However, Donny's news in no way satisfies any need or desire for information on Marcia's part, and, thus, Donny's pre-announcement must be said to be disingenuous.

In order to give a formal treatment to this conversation, we must decide whether we have two interactions here, an aborted announcement sequence followed by the ride-request service encounter, or just a single interaction, with the "pre-announcement" being part of the service encounter. Given the methodological principle that for a set of utterances to comprise an interaction, each of them must contribute to the work of that interaction, we must say that turns $T_1$ and $T_2$ do not belong to the service encounter, for they do not address conditions on or domain predicates of this type of interaction.

What Marcia gets instead of "news" is the opening move of a ride-request interaction, as I shall term this service encounter. Now, the question arises as to how Marcia comes to recognize that Donny is not presenting news for her benefit, but means to request a ride from her, which is, of course, the question of how she comes to recognize what Donny's goal is. There are basically two kinds of answers one can give to this question. The first is that Marcia must engage in a full-blown Gricean calculation. On the second, the utterance, *My car is stalled*, is mapped into the "Because" precondition of the initial-state condition fairly directly.

Consider, first, the Gricean account. Marcia can be expected to recognize that for the utterance, *My car is stalled*, to be true, it must be true that Donny was trying to get from point $P_o$ to $P_d$, but that the car ceased moving of its own accord at point $P_s$, where $P_s$ is either identical to $P_o$ or lies between points $P_o$ to $P_d$. Marcia may reasonably infer from the fact that Donny is a rational agent and has given no indication of any change of plans that he still wants to get to $P_d$ and, further, that Donny must therefore get someone to fix his car so that he can drive himself to $P_d$ or must get someone to take him to $P_d$, among other possibilities.

[24] One's car being stalled constitutes a kind of trouble and we often tell our troubles to others because (often mistakenly, I think) we believe our conversational partners care enough about us to want to hear them or we know they have suffered similar troubles and may want to hear about our trouble for that reason.

In saying that one's car is stalled, one clearly implicates that one has a problem and needs help, and the fact that Donny has called Marcia to tell her that his car is stalled implicates (Grice's Maxim of Relevance) that he wants her to play a role in solving his problem (which might be to come fix the car, give him a ride somewhere, come pick something up from him he was carrying to some destination and carry it there herself, go open the bank, etc.). On this approach, Marcia's drawing the inference that Donny's car's stalling constitutes a problem for him that he hopes she can help him solve requires creative thinking – employment of one's imagination and one's reasoning powers.

On the second approach, it is held that most inference drawing in conversations involving familiar interactions in familiar circumstances is accomplished in a highly automatic manner, or, put in computational terms, the inferences are compiled (cf. Patten, Geis, and Becker (1992) for a discussion of the relevant sense of "compilation"). This view treats interaction structures as determining the possible "relevance" of utterances (in the sense of Sperber and Wilson (1986)) and requires that interaction structures be relatively highly articulated.

Utterances that initiate interactions in which no conditions can be assumed to be satisfied at the outset and no domain predicates are understood to be instantiated (i.e., this is an unprecedented interaction between the parties to the conversation) normally specify either the ability condition or the initial-state condition of some interaction (normally also specifying one or more domain predicates).[25] Such utterances may specify the condition directly (as with *Could you give me a ride home after work?*, for the ability condition, or *I need a ride home after work*, for the initial-state condition) or indirectly (the utterance instantiates a precondition on the condition, as with *Do you have your car?*, for the ability condition, or *My car is in the shop*, for the initial-state condition).[26] I will argue here, as in the case of the baby-sitting example just discussed, that the preconditions typically associated with the conditions of specific types of interactions are stored as parts of the interaction structures and that these preconditions play critical roles in goal recognition.

[25] I shall discuss how speakers negotiate paths through interaction structures in chapter 8. Such paths are determined by both transactional and interactional considerations, that is, by what conditions and domain predicates need to be instantiated and by efforts to redress face threats, which can lead to attacks on satisfaction conditions (*Could you pass the salt?*) rather than the initial-state condition (*I need the salt*).

[26] I shall discuss the distinction I am drawing between direct and indirect communication in chapter 8.

There is, for instance, a precondition on the ability condition of ride-requests stating that the responder possess a car and that the responder (and his car) be at the place the ride would be expected to commence at the time it would be expected to commence. Not surprisingly, ride requests are often initiated with utterances like *Do you have your car today?* (as in the case of conversation (1)). I shall argue that this sort of utterance requests a value for precondition (26a) of the ability condition.

(26)  a.  possess(r, car)
      b.  be-at(r, p, t) & depart-place(p)

Ride requests are also frequently initiated with utterances like, *Are you going to go to the faculty meeting today?* or *Are you going to be on campus this afternoon?*, etc., which are normally heard as bearing on the precondition of the ability condition that the responder be at the place at which the ride should originate at the desired time of departure (cf. (26b)). Normally, the significance of inquiries addressing (26b) will not be as easily recognized as implicating a need for a ride as are those that address (26a) and require additional contextual information, as we shall see below.

As I noted, when we hear an utterance indicating that someone is having car trouble or is stranded somewhere, when it is clear that the information is not being offered simply for its news value, I submit that we instantly recognize that the speaker has a problem and wants some sort of help from the addressee, the nature of the help being determined by what sort of help the addressee is able to afford (a ride, help repairing the car, etc.). In the normal case, since few of us can repair automobiles, we recognize that what is wanted is a ride. The view that we instantly recognize the import of claims of others that they are having car trouble or are stranded as implicating a desire for a ride presupposes that we maintain an ontology of "troubles" typical of humans and a mapping of particular types of troubles into particular types of help that responders can provide. We may imagine, for instance, that "i has car trouble" and "i is stranded" are linked to the precondition of the initial-state condition (cf. "P" of (19)) of the ride-request interaction structure in the normal case of persons who cannot repair cars. Someone working for an automobile repair shop would, of course, hear an utterance like *My car is stalled* quite differently.

This approach gives rise to specific subtypes of service encounters. We have (again using an unofficial way of talking) ride requests, requests for gifts and loans, and requests for baby-sitting help, each of which is subject to special conditions. In the case of the baby-sitting conversation above, we saw that it involved the responder's watching or taking care of a child throughout a period of time at some location. In the case of a gift, there is the transference of some object from the responder to the initiator at some time at some place. In the case of a loan, there is the transference of some object from the responder to the initiator followed by the transference of that object (a borrowed lawn mower) or an equivalent object (a different cup of sugar) to the responder.

In (27), I provide the architecture of ride-request interaction structures.

(27)    Ride-request interaction structure
        Effects:
                Transactional: r commits to do A
                Initial-state condition: i desires r to do A
                        Because: P(often a ride-request related "trouble")
        Satisfaction conditions:
                r is able to do A
                        If:
                                possess(r, car)
                                be-at(r, $p_1$, t)
                r is willing to do e
                        If:
                                $\neg$ inconvenient($p_2$, r)
        Domain(A):
                action(ride)
                provider(r)
                receiver(i)
                instrument(car)
                depart-time(t)
                depart-place($p_1$)
                arrive-place($p_2$)

The ability condition in this interaction structure is subject to two preconditions, namely that the responder possesses a car and be at the place at which the ride should begin at the time it should begin. The willingness condition is subject to the precondition that the responder not find the destination to be inconvenient, i.e., far out of the responder's way. The reason for the preconditions on the ability condition are, as noted above, that we routinely find ride-requests being initiated with utterances that specify these preconditions (e.g., *Do you have your car?* and *Are you going to the talk today?*). The reason for postulating the precondition of the willingness condition is that before responders commit to providing rides they normally attempt to determine where the initiator wants to go (e.g., *Where do you live?* in conversation (1)). One of the reasons to ask is to determine whether one is willing to travel the route required to get to that destination. Moreover, initiators may initiate a ride-request with an utterance that specifies this precondition (e.g., *Do you live anywhere near Henderson and High?*).

Propositional variable "P" provides a "slot," then, for sequence-initiating items that are hearable as giving reasons for initiating a ride request. The transactional significance of Donny's utterance, *My car is stalled*, is, then, that it instantiates P. The information content of this utterance (that the responder's car is stalled) is given in (28).

(28)   D and M Ride-request interaction structure
          Initial-state condition: i desires r to do A [T]
                  Because: stalled(i's car) [T]

This utterance automatically implicates a desire for a ride in any case in which the responder associates an initiator's car trouble with a need for a ride, and this in turn constitutes an **implicit** questioning of Marcia's willingness and ability to provide this ride. I shall indicate an implicit request for the value of a condition with "$?_i$" and use "?" for explicit or explicitly implicated requests for values. Being implicit, the inquiry is ignorable.

(29)   D and M Ride-request interaction structure after *My car is stalled.*
          Transactional effect: r commits to do A
          Initial-state condition: i desires r to do A [T]
                  Because: stalled(i's car) [T]
          Satisfaction conditions:
                  r is able to do A [$?_i$]
                      If:
                              possess(r, car) [T, contextual presupposition]

$$be\text{-}at(r, p_1, t)$$

r is willing to do A [?$_i$]

If:

$$\neg\, inconvenient(p_2, r)$$

Domain(A):

action(ride)
provider(r)
receiver(i)
instrument(car)
depart-time(t)
depart-place($p_1$)
arrive-place($p_2$)

Were we not to say that an implicit inquiry concerning Marcia's willingness and ability to perform the implicated action had been made, we could not justify the claim that her failure to respond with something more than silence (at $T_4$) and *Oh* at ($T_6$) constitute dispreferred responses.[27]

In fact, Donny is greeted with silence (for 0.2 seconds) and continues on to provide domain information at turn $T_5$, which I give in (30).

(30)   Domain(A):

action(ride)
car(x)
provider(r)
receiver(i)
instrument(car)
depart-time(now)[28]
depart-place(the Glen)
arrive-place($p_2$)

At this time, the variable "$p_2$" is uninstantiated.

It is clear from Donny's rather long delay after Marcia's *Oh* and his stumbling resumption followed by another delay that he had hoped for more – perhaps an offer of a ride after the manner of Debbie's offer to

---

[27]   Dispreferred responses are responses that are less than fully socially expected. I discuss this notion in the next chapter.

[28]   A broadly construed "now."

watch Carl's child in conversation (4). He then comes up with the very interesting utterance

(31)  I don' know if it's: po:ssible, but .hhh see I haveta open up the ba:nk.hh

Note that an utterance like (32a) would, if contemplated in isolation of any particular context, very probably be heard as equivalent in *L*-Meaning to (32b).

(32)  a.  I don't know if it is possible, but I have to open the bank.
      b.  I don't know if it is possible for me to open the bank, but I have to open it.

Instead, Donny's utterance has an *S*-Meaning along the lines of (33).[29]

(33)  I don't know if it is possible **for you to give me a ride**, but I **need for you to do so because** I have to open the bank.

In short, the first clause specifies the ability condition of the ride request (as a result of the lexical item *possible*) and the second specifies the initial-state condition, because *I have to open the bank* will be heard as a further instantiation of the propositional variable "P" of (27). This utterance further specifies the domain by providing a value for "$p_2$." The resulting interaction structure is:

(34)  D and M Ride-request interaction structure, after $T_9$
      Effects:
              Transactional: r commits to do A
      Initial-state condition: i desires r to do A [T]
              Because: stalled(i's car) & must(open(i, Brentwood bank))

---

[29] It is worth noting that no view of utterance generation predicated on conventional theories of syntax and semantics alone could possibly account for utterance (33). Indeed, it would have to be regarded as ungrammatical on the intended interpretation. I would argue that this datum provides compelling evidence that utterance generation is pragmatically, as opposed to semantically, driven in that the goal is to produce an utterance that has the desired (transactional) *S*-Meaning, as opposed to a specific *L*-Meaning (except, perhaps, in rare cases in which precision is necessary) and which has the desired interactional effect, where, in this case, the input consists of a complex conjunction of the interaction structure ability condition and a precondition of the initial-state condition.

Satisfaction conditions:
  r is able to do A [?]
    If:
      possess(r, car) [T, contextual presupposition]
      be-at(r, Glen, now)
  r is willing to do e
    If:
      ¬ inconvenient(r, bank in Brentwood)
Domain(A):
  action(ride)
  provider(r)
  receiver(i)
  instrument(car)
  depart-time(now)
  depart-place(Glen)
  arrive-place(bank in Brentwood)

Marcia's reply, *Yeah:- en I know you want-(.) en I whoa-(.) en I would, but- except I've gotta leave in about five min(h)utes*, has the transactional significance of (35).

(35)  I know you want **a ride to the bank at Brentwood** and I would **be willing to give you this ride** but **I am not able to do so because** I've got to leave in about five minutes.

This utterance, like Donny's before it, also complexly mixes interaction structure elements, specifically, the initial-state condition (*I know you want* [for me to give you a ride]), the willingness condition (*I would* [give you a ride]), and a precondition on the ability condition ([I am not able to give you a ride because] *I've got to leave in about five minutes*).[30] On this view, Marcia's declination of the request will be heard as ability-based, not willingness-based, for she has asserted her willingness in principle to do so (cf. *I would*). Specifically, it falsifies the precondition "be-at(r, Glen, now)" of the ability condition, as opposed to falsifying the willingness condition (even though it is implicated to be false in the present circumstances). Marcia cannot be

---

[30]  Again, let me note that we cannot hope to account for Marcia's production of this utterance unless we suppose that the input consists of complexly conjoined interaction structure elements, as opposed simply to purely semantic elements. See footnote 29 for further discussion.

where the ride would need to begin at the time it would need to begin because she has to leave soon to go be somewhere else.

The resulting interaction structure for this conversation is (if we ignore the interactional effects of the utterances that comprise it):

(36)   The final D and M Ride-request interaction structure
       Effects:
             Transactional: r commits to do A [Failed]
       Initial-state condition: i desires r to do A [T]
             Because: stalled(i's car) & must(open(i, Brentwood bank))
             [T]
       Satisfaction conditions:
             r is able to do A [F]
                   If:
                         possess(r, car) [T, contextual presupposition]
                         be-at(r, Glen, now) [F]
             r is willing to do e [T]
       Domain(A):
       action(ride)
             provider(r)
             receiver(i)
             instrument(car)
             depart-time(now)
             depart-place(Glen)
             arrive-place(bank in Brentwood)

Interaction structure (36) represents the common ground between Donny and Marcia at the conclusion of this excerpt insofar as the transactional significance of the utterances is concerned. In order to account for the dynamic nature of this interaction, it would be necessary to associate an interaction-structure representation with the conversation after each utterance of each turn as we did in the case of the baby-sitting example. The change in successive representations would reflect the transactional (and interactional) significance of the intervening utterance.

## Commercial service encounters

There is considerable data on commercial request interactions. In this section I shall draw on Merritt's (1976) study of service encounters.

84

Merritt's paper focuses on cases in which an opening question is followed up by another question, either from the customer (cf. (37)) or the clerk (cf. (38)).

(37)  Merritt (1976: 337)

| | | |
|---|---|---|
| CUSTOMER: | Do you have hot chocolate? | $T_1$ |
| CLERK: | mmhmm | $T_2$ |
| CUSTOMER: | Can I have hot chocolate with whipped cream? | $T_3$ |
| CLERK: | Sure ((leaves to get)). | $T_4$ |

(38)  Merritt (1976: 325)

| | | |
|---|---|---|
| CUSTOMER: | Do you have Marlboros? | $T_1$ |
| CLERK: | Yeah. Hard or Soft? | $T_2$ |
| CUSTOMER: | Soft please | $T_3$ |
| CLERK: | Okay | $T_4$ |

Merritt does not provide data on the payment side of these transactions.

There are two reasons to believe that the payment side of commercial transactions should be separated from the service side. The best reason is that the initiator-responder relationship is reversed. It is the server's desire that he be paid that is the occasion for payment. Another reason is that the payment sequence often occurs substantially after the service sequence. This is particularly true in restaurants. I would argue that the willingness condition of commercial requests is subject to the precondition that the initiator commit to paying the required amount of money for the services or things provided, and that the payment side of the interaction involve something akin to a demand for payment, where the initial-state condition is that the initiator desire payment, and the precondition of the initial-state condition is that the customer owes the money. In the normal case, the ability and the willingness of the customer to pay are not at issue for the customer implicitly agrees to pay by accepting the services or things involved.

Commercial requests are intrinsically reciprocal in that there is not only a commitment by the clerk to supply some product, there is a commitment by the customer to pay for the product. There are reciprocal personal requests, as well, of course, though I have neither collected one nor seen one in print. The sort of example I have in mind is illustrated in (39).

(39)   A:   Could you give me a ride to work tomorrow?
       B:   Yeah, if you give me one the day after.

I see such a case as not at all different in character from one like (40).

(40)   A:   Could you give me a ride to work tomorrow?
       B:   Yeah, if my car is back from the shop.

In the case of (40), the *if*-clause functions as a precondition on the **ability** of B to provide this ride. I would see the *if*-clause of (39) as being a condition on the responder's **willingness** to give this ride.

In commercial service encounters, the action at issue is for the responder to provide some product or perform some service in exchange for a certain amount of money. One such class of requests I shall refer to as "thing-requests" – requests for things and for services that we are able to refer to with a simple noun phrase (*a haircut, a shave, a massage, a manicure*, etc.). These are of special interest, for we find somewhat specialized language in connection with them. The verbs *have* and *take*, which normally cannot occur with verbal complements describing actions (except for *have*, when it is interpreted causatively) (cf. (41)), can occur with simple object noun phrases, as in (42) and (43), even when the noun phrase refers to a service (action).

(41)   a.   *I'll have your cutting my hair.
       b.   *I'll take your rubbing my back.

(42)   a.   I'll have a pineapple yoghurt.
       b.   I'll take a pineapple yoghurt.

(43)   a.   I'll have a haircut.
       b.   I'll take a back rub.

As I demonstrate in chapter 6, utterances like (42) and (43) have *S*-Meanings along the lines of (44).

(44)   a.   I (herewith) select a pineapple yoghurt.
       b.   I (herewith) select a haircut.

We also find the verbs *have* and *take* being used in this way in noncommercial thing-requests as well.

Still another verb that recurs in requests for things both in personal requests and in service encounters is *give*. (When *give* occurs in service encounters, it *S*-means "transfer for money," as opposed to "transfer gratis.") Note that the pattern observed in connection with (42)–(41) applies also to *give*.

(45)   a.   *Why don't you give me your cutting my hair today?
       b.   Why don't you give me a pineapple yoghurt?
       c.   Why don't you give me a hair cut today?

The same verb occurs, of course, in personal requests for things, as in *Could you give me a glass of water/back rub?* These linguistic facts support positing the thing-request as a specific subclass of service encounter, whether the interaction is commercial or personal.

Thing-requests not uncommonly begin with possession questions like those that initiate (37) and (38), e.g., *Do you have hot chocolate?* and *Do you have Marlboros?* In both cases, the utterances instantiate domain predicates, specifically an object predicate, and instantiate a ubiquitous precondition on thing-requests that the responder possess the thing desired or offer the service desired in the case of services like haircuts, back rubs, and the like. Accordingly, I propose the interaction structure (46) for commercial thing-requests.

(46)   Retail sales thing-request interaction structure
      Transactional effect: r commits to provide o to i
      Initial-state condition: i desires r to provide o to i
      Satisfaction conditions:
          r is able to provide o to i
             If:
                  r possesses o
          r is willing to provide o to i
             If:
                  i commits to pay m to r
      Domain(o):
          object(o)
          num(n)
      Domain(m):
          $(m)

Now, in cases in which there is an interaction about how much money should be paid for the thing desired or what quality or what size of thing should be given for what amount of money, the resulting talk will be understood as simply negotiating the properties of o and the amount of m. In the informal study of the language of Monopoly games in German and English done by my students Bettina Migge, Nicole Schrickel, Michela Shigley-Giusti, and Tracy Weldon, they observed that selling and trading of properties often involved just such negotiations.

Let us examine conversation (37) from the perspective of interaction structure (46). The customer's utterance, *Do you have hot chocolate?*, at turn $T_1$ instantiates the "object" predicate of the domain, as well as the precondition on the ability condition (from which it gets the verb). It furthermore implicates that the initiator desires the object named. The effect is represented in (47).

(47)   Hot chocolate interaction structure after *Do you have hot chocolate?*
       Transactional effect: r commits to provide o to i
       Initial-state condition: i desires r to provide o [T, $<T_1>$]
       Satisfaction condition
           r is able to provide o to i [?, $<T_1>$]
               If:
                       r possesses o [?, $<T_1>$]
               r is willing to provide o to i [T]
               If:
                       i commits to pay m to r [T, implicitly]
       Domain(o):
           object(hot chocolate) $<T_1>$
           num(1) <Context>

When the clerk replies *mmhmm*, the value of the precondition on the ability condition and that of the ability condition itself is set to "True," as in

(48)   Hot chocolate interaction structure after *Sure*
       Transactional effect: r commits to provide o to i
       Initial-state condition: i desires r to provide o [T, $<T_1>$]
       Satisfaction condition
           r is able to provide o to i [T, $<T_1,T_2>$]

88

If:

        r possesses o [T, $<T_1,T_2>$]

r is willing to provide o to i [T]

    If:

        i commits to pay m to r [T, implicitly]

Domain(o):

    object(hot-chocolate) $<T_1,T_2>$

    num(1) <Context>

The customer's next utterance, *Can I have hot chocolate with whipped cream?*, is more interesting. The question arises whether the interrogative form of this sentence reflects the fact that she is requesting information ("Is whipped cream available?") – a value-requesting utterance – or providing it ("I want hot chocolate **with whipped cream**") – a value-positing utterance. This would turn on whether or not she believed that whipped cream is available. Let us assume that the initiator means to be requesting the value of the "r possesses y" predicate of (49).

(49)  Hot chocolate thing-request interaction structure after *Can I have hot chocolate with whipped cream?*

Transactional effect: r commits to provide o to i

Initial-state condition:

    i desires o [T, $<T_1>$]

Satisfaction condition:

    r is able to transfer o to i [?, $<T_1,T_2>$]

        If

            r possesses o [T, $<T_1,T_2>$]

            r possesses y [?, $<T_3>$]

    r is willing to provide o to i [T]

        If:

            i commits to pay m to r [T, implicitly]

Domain(o):

    object(hot-chocolate) $<T_1,T_2>$

    num(1) <Context>

    with(hot-chocolate, y) $<T_3>$

Domain(y):

    object(whipped-cream) $<T_3>$

Note that this causes the value of the ability condition to go from "T" to "?." The reason is that a novel precondition has been posited by the customer.

When the clerk says, *Sure*, the "ordering" phase of the thing-request is completed. The net result is:

(50)   The final hot chocolate interaction structure
Transactional effect: r commits to provide o to i [achieved, $T_4$]
Initial-state condition: i desires r to provide o [T, $<T_1>$]
Satisfaction condition:
   r is able to transfer o to i [T, $\{<T_1,T_2><T_3,T_4>>\}]$
      If
         r possesses o [T, $<T_1,T_2>$]
         r possesses y [T, $<T_3,T_4>$]
   r is willing to provide o to i [T]
      If:
         i commits to pay m to r [T, implicitly]
Domain(o):
   object(hot-chocolate) $<T_1,T_2>$
   num(1) <Context>
   with(hot-chocolate, y) $<T_3,T_4>$
Domain(y):
   object(whipped-cream) $<T_3,T_4>$

In this case, again, we can easily recover some of the structure of this conversation, for we see in connection with the two preconditions on the ability condition that utterances $T_1$ and $T_2$ are paired and that utterances $T_3$ and $T_4$ are paired. However, in my view, this is an entirely unofficial part of DSAT interaction structure representations.

### Invitations

Invitation interactions enjoy some family resemblances to service encounters. In both cases, the initiator acts out of a desire to cause the responder to perform some action and the responder must be willing and able to perform this action before it will be accepted.

Invitations, like action requests, can begin with some sort of availability question such as those in (51).

(51)   a.   Whatcha doin'?
       b.   Doing anything?

As a consequence, we will need to place the precondition on the ability condition of invitations that the responder not be otherwise engaged, just as in the case of service encounters.

One major difference between service encounters and invitations is that in the case of service encounters, the action is to be done **for** someone, whereas in the case of an invitation the action is to be done **with** someone, normally the initiator. A second major difference is that invitations, unlike service encounters, very commonly contain utterances that make reference to the desires of responders, such as we find in (52).

(52)  a.  Wanna cum down'n av a bighta lu:nch with me:? (Drew 1984: 130)
      b.  Would'ja like to get out? (Drew 1984: 141)

There are two ways in which one might try to deal with these utterances. We could see them as invitation-specific instantiations of the willingness condition. Alternatively, we could argue that the willingness condition in invitations is stated in terms, not of what the responder is **willing** to do, but in terms of what he **desires** to do. The similarity in the forms found in (52) to those that instantiate the initial-state condition in service encounters favors the latter option.[31]

I shall posit the following as the invitation interaction structure:

(53)  Invitation interaction structure
      Transactional effect: r commits to do A
      Initial-state condition: i desires r to do A
      Interactional effects:
      Satisfaction conditions:
          r is able to do A
              If:
                          $\neg$ must(r do A'))
          r desires to do A
      Domain(A):
          action(e)

---

[31]  The forms present+*need*, present+*want*, and *would*+*like* occur as realizations of the initial-state condition. However, in invitations, we get present+*want* and *would*+*like*, but not present+*need*. So, we can say, *Would you like to come over?* or *Do you want to come over?*, but normally not, *Do you need to come over?*, by way of initiating invitation interactions.

host(i)$^{32}$
guest(r)
at(t)
Domain(A′):
action(e$_1$)
e $\neq$ e$_1$
at(t$_1$)
t = t$_1$

In conversation (54), we find both parties using forms that realize the interaction structure predicate "desires," providing support for the thesis that not only the initial-state condition, but also the "responder-willingness" satisfaction condition, is defined in terms of this predicate.

(54)  London–Lund Corpus. (B has determined that A will be visiting A's university.)
  B:  Do you want to have lunch with us in college or will you be being lunched?                                          T$_1$
  A:  I shouldn't think I'm I [sh] I shall be being lunched.     T$_2$
  B:  Will you will you be at your college at lunchtime?     T$_3$
  A:  I will be at my college at lunch-time lunching in the canteen and would be very ((2 to 3 sylls)) if you would join us     T$_4$
  B:  Well I'd like to come along. I would like to do that please
                                                              T$_5$
  A:  [m] do that                                             T$_6$

This conversation is of particular interest because it demonstrates the interactive nature of invitations in that it begins with B playing the host role, but ends with A proposing that A be the host. B's first utterance addresses both the responder-desires satisfaction condition and the precondition on the ability condition that the responder not be otherwise engaged thereby providing a basis for rejection (A's being

---

32  The predicates "host(x)" and "guest(x)" refer to pragmatic roles. The different responsibilities associated with these roles varies from case to case. If i invites r to go to a movie, the default assumption is that i will drive, but this can be negotiated. Whether or not i will pay for r's ticket would depend on the relationship. If i invites r to come to i's home for dinner, i must, of course, provide drinks and food and actively do things that will entertain r. The predicate "host(x)" can be realized linguistically via the phrase *with x*.

taken to lunch by others). The interaction structure representation of the conversation at this point is as in (55).

(55)   The invitation interaction structure after $T_1$
        Transactional effect: r commits to do A
        Initial-state condition: i desires r to do A [T]
        Satisfaction conditions:
            r is able to do A [?]
                If:
                        $\neg$ must(r do A')) [?]
            r desires to do A [?]
        Domain(A):
            action(have lunch)
            host(i)
            guest(r)
            at(i's college)
            at(lunch time)
        Domain(A'):
            action(have lunch)
            host(r's college mates)
            guest(r)
            at(r's former college)
            at(lunch time)

B's asking specifically whether she will be being taken to lunch does not exhaust the ways in which A might be otherwise engaged and when A replies that she thinks she will not be being lunched (i.e., that her college mates will not be hosting her though she will be dining with them), B is left without an answer to her question whether A wants to come to B's college for lunch. B then takes another tack with respect to the precondition that A not be otherwise engaged when she says, *Will you be at your college at lunchtime?* This is an *L*-Meaning inquiry as to where A will be at the time the proposed invitation will take place, but I would argue that it too counts as an *S*-Meaning inquiry as to whether A is otherwise engaged, specifically whether A, though not being taken to lunch, nevertheless had lunch plans. If this is correct, the only respect in which this utterance affects representation (55) is that the value of the predicates "host(x)" and "guest(x)" change to "nil" in "Domain(A')."

At $T_4$, A answers B's *L*-Meaning inquiry affirmatively, and then invites B to join A for lunch. The question arises whether we should characterize what B has done as altering the terms of the original invitation or as initiating a wholly new invitation. I would argue that the former is true, that is, that it is still B's original goal – that A and B have lunch with each other – that is under negotiation. What has changed is who will play the host and guest roles and the location of the lunch. On this view, the resulting interaction structure would be something like that in (56).

(56) The invitation interaction structure after $T_4$
Transactional effect: r commits to do A
Initial-state condition: i desires r to do A [T]
Interactional effects:
Satisfaction conditions:
    r is able to do A [T]
    r desires to do A [T]
Domain(A):
    action(have-lunch)
    host(r)
    guest(i)
    at(r's college)
    at(lunch time)

As I noted, we might have argued that this conversation consists of two sequences – an invitation sequence in which B is the initiator and a subsequent invitation sequence in which A is the initiator. However, I would argue that invitations should be seen more flexibly as proposals for social interaction with the nature of the interaction being up for negotiation. In the case at hand, all that changed was who was joining whom where, not whether they would be dining together, which was, presumably, the primary aim of the initiator. When the initiator says, *Well I'd like to come along. I would like to do that please*, she commits to the terms of the altered domain. The original goal of the initiator – to cause the responder to agree to have lunch with her – has been achieved, though the precise nature of the lunch engagement has changed. In other cases, an alternative activity on another day might ultimately be agreed to. The fact that invitations (proposals for social interaction) contain a responder-specific satisfaction condition that is the reciprocal of the initial-state condition is arguably what allows responders to seize the initiative in proposals for social interaction (i.e., invitations).[33] The responder's desires rank equally with those of the initiator.

## Conclusion

In this chapter, I have argued that Searle's speech act structures need to be revised in five ways. First, the propositional content condition must be replaced with a domain. This change is required because the domain of a typical conversation is not communicated through a single utterance. Nevertheless, the domain is very much like the propositional content condition in regard to the nature of the information it contains. Second, Searle's essential condition must be split into both a transactional effect (Searle's essential condition) and an interactional effect. Third, Searle's sincerity condition must be abandoned in favor of a condition stipulating the psychological state from which the interaction is launched. As was noted, the resulting initial-state condition is sometimes equivalent and sometimes not equivalent to Searle's sincerity condition. Fourth, those of Searle's preparatory conditions that are concerned merely with issues of felicity should be given over to the utterance planner. The idea here is that we initiate interactions when we believe the circumstances are felicitous, but the resulting interaction is focused on determining values for interaction structure satisfaction conditions and domain predicates. Fifth, a willingness condition of some sort needs to be added in the case of interactions in which the responder is being asked to make a commitment to do something.

A second basic difference between Searlean speech act theory and DSAT is that DSAT sees its interaction structures as being highly domain-specific in that the conditions on different subtypes of a given type of interaction will typically contain domain-specific preconditions. Thus, service encounters involving actions contain a precondition on the ability condition that the responder not be otherwise engaged, whereas those involving the transference of things contain the precondition that the responder possess the thing. Similarly, ride-requests, which are a species of service encounter involving actions, are subject to a specific precondition on the willingness condition that the responder find the proposed destination

---

[33] Obviously the terms of some invitations aren't negotiable. If you are invited to the White House for a formal dinner, the President would surely not entertain the proposal that he move the dinner to your home.

not to be inconvenient and preconditions on the ability condition that the responder have a car with him and that he be able to be at the place the ride should take place at the time it should take place. These facts lead me to suggest that we may have a host of subtypes of particular interactions subject to Wittgenstein's "family resemblance" relationship, with cases like someone's requesting a beer from a friend resembling ordering a beer in a bar and requesting a ride from a friend resembling contracting with a taxi driver for a ride, and so on. I submit that growing up in a given culture involves learning these very specific interaction types and that when we engage in a novel interaction, we rely on what we know about similar interactions.

The greatest difference between DSAT and traditional speech act theory lies in the use to which interaction structures are put. The DSAT position is that individual utterances do not have illocutionary force in the sense Austin and Searle used this term. Instead, individual utterances are said to have an illocutionary significance (i.e., more precisely, a transactional and interactional significance) that derives from what they contribute to satisfaction of interaction structure conditions and instantiation of domain predicates and to the facework of an interaction, the concern of the next chapter. The most important single consequence of this is that it allows us to capture the dynamic nature of conversation, the fact that the successive utterances that comprise a conversation alter belief-states. By giving a sequence of interaction structure representations to a conversation representing what each utterance contributes to the work of an exchange, we can make quite explicit what an utterance contributes to an conversation: the significance of any utterance can be represented as the difference between the interaction structure representation prior to the utterance and the interaction structure representation immediately consequent to the utterance. This allows, then, for a fully explicit theory of conversation. This is clearly not possible for a theory of the actions – speech acts or communicative actions – we perform in interactions.

# 4

## Interactional effects

### Introduction

In the preceding chapter, we focused on the transactional side of two types of interactions, service encounters (i.e., exchanges in which one person is trying to cause another to do something for him), and invitations (i.e., exchanges in which one person is trying to cause another to do something with him). In this chapter, we turn to consider interactional effects in interactions such as these.

The concept of an interactional effect is critical to an account of conversation in at least three ways. First, utterances appear in conversation that do transactional work, but the fact that the speaker troubles to utter them itself has interactional implications. Second, there are certain utterances that appear in conversations that seem only or primarily to do face-work. Third, certain features of the forms of transactionally significant utterances reflect the interactional effects of participant actions. In this chapter, I shall focus on the first two phenomena, reserving the third for chapter 6.

There exist two approaches to interactional phenomena of interest to us here, Brown and Levinson's (1987) politeness theory and the conversation-analytic theory of preference. According to Brown and Levinson, people have two face-needs, a negative face-need not to have their freedom of action restricted, and a positive face-need to be valued and to have what they value be valued. The importance of these observations lies in the fact that many of the actions we engage others in threaten face. Requesting a friend to do some favor (as in the case of a service encounter) threatens her freedom of action. Rejecting a request by a friend threatens the requester's positive face. And, criticizing someone threatens that person's positive face. Brown and Levinson refer to such acts as face-threatening acts (FTA).

As Brown and Levinson observe, those who commit FTA commonly attempt to mitigate or redress the face-threat, and much of their study is focused on how speakers go about doing this. They note, for instance, that (p. 136) if one chooses to perform an FTA against one's addressee's negative face-want to be free of imposition, one can redress the face-threat by displaying either negative or positive politeness, with "negative" and "positive" referring here to whether the redressive action is directed at the addressee's negative face or positive face. One might display negative politeness by choosing to make minimal assumptions about this person's wants (cf. (1a)), by choosing not to coerce her by not assuming that she is willing (cf. (1b)) or able (cf. (1c)) to perform some desired action, or by choosing to be pessimistic (cf. (1d)), etc.

(1)  a. Do you want to sign these forms?
     b. Would you mind signing these forms?
     c. Could you sign these forms?
     d. I don't suppose you would sign these forms.

One might display positive politeness by attending to the responder's needs (cf. (2a), down-playing disagreement (cf. the token *yes* in (2b)), showing affiliation with the addressee (cf. (2c)), etc.

(2)  a. You must be hungry. Wanna go get lunch?
     b. Yes, but don't you think he's smarter than he looks?
     c. Say, buddy, could you spare a dime?

Each of these latter utterances displays respect for the addressee's positive face.

Though Brown and Levinson do discuss how response forms can threaten face (as when someone rejects a request) and how such FTA can be redressed, most of their focus was on initiator actions. Conversation analysts (see Davidson 1984, Drew 1984, Levinson 1983: 332–45, and Pomerantz 1984), on the other hand, have focused exclusively on responder actions. They have argued that responses to first members of adjacency pairs[1] are socially graded with respect to whether or not and to what degree they are "preferred" or "dispreferred."[2] If one is in a position to supply the preferred response to a question, request, invitation, or the like, then normally one supplies this response simply and with no delay (Heritage 1984: 266). However, in cases in which we are unwilling or unable to satisfy someone else's expressed needs or desires, we (Levinson 1983: 307) sometimes hesitate before replying, or utter some sort of "pause filler" (such as *uh*), initiate our response with certain discourse markers that are associated with dispreferred responses such as *well* or *Oh gosh* or the like, provide explanations for our inability to supply the expected/desired response, or provide mitigation (*Oh, I'd like to, but...*). Such "structural" details (cf. Levinson 1983: 307) as these serve conversation analysts as the criteria for identifying dispreferred responses and distinguishing them from preferred responses.

The presence of dispreference markers such as these in utterances clearly plays a role in how they are interpreted. Consider, for instance, how the two-second pause in the following example from Levinson is interpreted:[3]

(3)   Levinson (1983: 320)
      C: So I was wondering would you be in your office on Monday
         (.) by any chance?
      R: (2 second pause)
      C: Probably not
      R: Hmm yes =
      C: =You would?
      R: Ya
      C: So if we came could you give us ten minutes of your time?

In this conversation C construes R's failure to respond immediately to C's question as prefiguring a rejection of the request. And in

---

[1]   Adjacency pairs are pairs of utterances that are related in that when the first occurs the second becomes immediately expectable, as with questions and answers, requests and acceptances and rejections. I discuss this notion at some length in chapter 7.

[2]   Bilmes (1988) has provided a survey of different uses of the term "preference" in the conversation-analytic literature. As he notes, there is no uniform theory of preference.

[3]   The notation "(.)" indicates a very brief pause and "=" indicates that the two utterances are latched, i.e., there is no period of silence between them.

the lunch invitation fragment (14) below, when the responder says, *Wul yer ril sweet hon:, uh::m,* the initiator replies with, *or d'yuh'av sump'n else,* which clearly indicates that she heard this response (which contains the discourse marker *well* as well as a mitigator) as implicating a rejection of the invitation.

How we interpret preference markers reflects the fact that an addressee's choices of action in response to what someone else has said are institutionally ranked (Atkinson and Heritage 1984: 53), and as such, communicate important social information. The notion "preferred response" does not necessarily correspond to what the speaker prefers, though in many cases it does, but rather to what is institutionally configured as preferred. Perhaps the clearest case of a mismatch between what a speaker might prefer and what is socially preferred occurs in accusations, where the preferred response is a denial of guilt, rather than a confession of guilt (Levinson 1983).[4] The reigning principle is that preferred responses are those that are best calculated (Pomerantz 1984: 77) to maintain "sociability, support, and solidarity." That the organization of preference is designed to maintain sociability, support, and solidarity is nicely demonstrated by the fact that while the preferred response to a negative assessment of someone else (*He sure is stupid!*) is agreement (*He sure is!*); the preferred response to a negative self-assessment (*I sure am stupid*) is disagreement (*No you're not. You're very smart*), as Pomerantz (1984) has noted. In each case, the preferred response is the one that best preserves sociability, support, and solidarity.

One difficulty with the theory of preference of conversation analysts is that the utterances that initiators of interactions employ sometimes contain precisely the same markers found in dispreferred responses. In the Donny and Marcia ride-request discussed on page 74 of the preceding chapter, Donny, on failing to get Marcia to volunteer to help him out, is finally forced to be more explicit about what he wants from her. The result is (4).

---

[4]   One might think that a person who accuses another of some offense would prefer a confession, for that would confirm his suspicions. Moreover, *qua* assertion, the preferred response to an accusation would be agreement. However, conversation analysts have argued that the reverse is true (Levinson 1983). Note that if one person accuses a lover of infidelity, and the latter denies it, they will be in a better position to get on with their relationship than if this person were to confess guilt, which might call for a substantive loss of trust in this other person or even breaking the relationship off.

(4)   (0.4) (.hhh) A:nd.hh (0.2) I don' know if it's: po:ssible, but
      {.hhh/(0.2)} see I haveta open up the ba:nk.hh (0.3) a:t uh: (.) in
      Brentwood?hh

This utterance begins with a longish four-tenths of a second pause,
contains a significant internal pause of two-tenths of a second, a
second short pause or inhalation (marked by a period followed by an
"h"), contains three (or four) instances of inhalations, and an
explanation for his actions (*but .hhh see I haveta open up the ba:nk.hh*).
  Some of these disfluent[5] elements – specifically, some of the pauses
– reflect time spent waiting for uptake by Marcia. Other elements,
including some pauses – the one after *but*, for instance – clearly have
some other cause. I see no reason to see these disfluencies any
differently from those found in Marcia's dispreferred reply (5).

(5)   Yeah:- en I know you want-(.) en I whoa-(.) en I would, but-
      except I've gotta leave in about five min(h)utes.

In this reply, we have pause-fillers (e.g., *and* = 'en'), false starts (*but-
except, I whoa-(.) en I would*), brief pauses, a mitigator (*en I would, but*),
and an explanation for her action (*I've gotta leave in about five
min(h)utes*).
  In order to account for the fact that utterances like (4) and (5)
exhibit essentially the same indicators of dispreference, we could coin
a new concept "dispreferred initiation." But a better approach would
be to treat these very similar initiator and responder behaviors as
instances of the same phenomenon. We can do just this if we see
preference organization as being a consequence of face-work, as
Brown and Levinson (1987: 38) have suggested. Note that in asking
Marcia to give him a ride, Donny is threatening Marcia's negative face
in that he is proposing to restrict her freedom of action and that in
rejecting this request, Marcia is threatening Donny's positive face in
that she is communicating that she does not, at least in this instance,
sufficiently value Donny's needs to provide him with help. We may
imagine that the dispreference markers that occur result from the
difficulty speakers have in formulating FTA in a way that does not
threaten "sociability, support, and solidarity."
  In what follows in this chapter, I propose to discuss the interactional

[5]   I don't mean to be using this term pejoratively.

sides of service encounters and invitations. Before doing so, let me draw attention to a problem with Brown and Levinson's account. Brown and Levinson argue that we can mitigate or redress an FTA by displaying negative or positive politeness. One may display positive politeness by paying respect to one's addressee's positive face. However, I have argued that we must make a distinction between a speaker's employing positive politeness by way of redressing some FTA that he is himself committing (the exclusive concern of Brown and Levinson in regard to positive politeness) and *sui generis* displays of positive politeness, as when one compliments someone else.

## Some general remarks on politeness

In chapter 2, I distinguished style, which I associated with power and social distance relationships between participants, and politeness, which I associated with face-work. Though I would argue that style and politeness, so defined, are distinct phenomena (in part because style variation involves variation in form with *L*-Meaning being held constant and politeness variation involves variation in both form and *L*-Meaning with *S*-Meaning being held constant), both power and social distance relationships influence the politeness choices we make.

In the United States, when there is an asymmetric power relationship between an initiator who has higher status (H) than the responder (L) in a particular context (employer vs: employee or customer vs: clerk), contextually legitimate acts performed by H – legitimate work-related requests by an employer, for instance – may not be socially configured as FTA. An employer might reasonably request an employee to perform some work-related task saying something like *I want you to finish the Brower report this afternoon,* which is egocentric and does not give the employee an option as to whether or not he will comply with the request. Moreover, the employer might not even express appreciation when the employee agrees to do what is wanted. Though we must expect some individual variation on this point, many employees would not, I think, feel insulted by such behavior. If my intuitions are correct, we are presented with the choice of saying either that contextually legitimate requests by H of L are not socially configured as FTA or we could say that there is simply no expectation or requirement that such requests be redressed. I am inclined to prefer the former analysis, but have no compelling evidence supporting it.

Even when routine work-related requests are nononerous and

arguably not FTA, H nevertheless sometimes employ polite forms in addressing L, as when H makes the request discussed in the preceding paragraph by saying, *Could you finish the Brower report this afternoon?*, which is exocentric and (counterfactually) treats the employee as having an option as to whether he will comply. Because of this, we must distinguish displays of politeness in the redress of genuine FTA from cases in which the initiator displays politeness simply to **be** polite when she is not obligated or even expected to be. I believe that H engage in these spontaneous displays of politeness for many reasons, ranging from the desire to contribute to a more solidary relationship with L or because one feels sympathy for the responder. I am told by persons who have themselves clerked that they employ spontaneous displays of politeness with clerks they interact with because they know such persons are often treated quite badly by some customers.

When we look at the language employed by the initiator of an act, if the initiator is H and the responder is L, the fact that H might employ language characteristic of the redressing of a face-threat is not conclusive evidence then that there was a face-threat associated with the act, for H may simply be displaying spontaneous politeness. We must therefore look to other cues to what sort of face-threat is involved, if any. One important source of evidence lies in how responders respond.

If I request a friend to give me a ride home, he will almost certainly not thank me for requesting him to do this, nor will he thank me when he delivers me to my destination. In the normal course of events, I would thank him for accepting the request and he would say, *You're welcome*, or, *no problem*, or something of the like and I would thank him for giving me the ride and he would likely respond by saying something like *You're welcome*, or, *no problem*. On the other hand, if I invite him over for dinner, he will likely thank me for doing so and I might say, *You're welcome*, or, *no problem*, or something of the like, and on departing my home, he will likely thank me for having him over and I would surely thank him for coming. These fundamental differences in responder behavior in the two cases provides compelling evidence that service encounters and invitations are configured quite differently socially, with the former threatening the negative face of responders (which is why responders do not express thanks) and latter paying respect to the positive face of responders (which is why responders express thanks). The fact that responders tend to thank initiators for proffering invitations provides compelling evidence that the initiator is not only not threatening the responder's negative face (we do not get this behavior in the case of requests, recall), but is, in fact, paying respect *sui generis* to the responder's positive face. The initiator cannot in such a circumstance be said to be redressing some FTA, for there is no FTA to be redressed. This provides evidence for *sui generis* face-respecting acts (FRA) as distinct from redressive displays of positive politeness.

## Interactional effects in DSAT

I have argued that interactions have both transactional and interactional effects and that a person who chooses to initiate an interaction with others will choose to initiate a particular type of interaction because it will have the desired transactional and interactional consequences. Thus, if I want fifty dollars from you, I could beg you for the money (which threatens your negative face and poses a significant risk to my positive face), request that you loan the money to me (which threatens your negative face and potentially threatens my positive face, but not in the way or to the degree that begging for the money would), or threaten you with bodily harm (which would very severely threaten your negative face and – a social, as opposed to an interactional effect – might land me in jail). Each of these choices might have the desired transactional effect of causing you to hand over the fifty dollars. My choice of interaction would presumably depend on some sort of cost-benefit analysis of the various interactional (and social) effects.

I shall argue that different types of interactions have intrinsically different interactional effects. Moreover, the utterances that occur within a given interaction will have an interactional significance (interactional *S*-meaning) that reflects the face-work that they do (or, more precisely, the face-work the participant does in uttering the sentence) with regard to the interactional effects associated with that type of interaction.

I would suggest that in typical service encounters the initiator threatens the responder's negative face in that the goal is to cause the responder to commit to doing something for the initiator, and there is no positive face-threat to the initiator. On the other hand, the responder has two basic choices – to agree to or decline to undertake this commitment. The former choice constitutes a positive face-respecting response and is therefore an FRA; the latter constitutes a positive face-threatening act and is therefore an FTA. Simply to agree to undertake a commitment is to pay respect to the initiator's positive face. In what follows in this chapter, I shall therefore take the position that initiator actions may either threaten the responder's negative face (FTA) or pay respect to the responder's positive face (FRA) and that when responders give what conversation analysts call dispreferred responses they are engaging in FTA, but when they give preferred responses they are engaging in FRA, not to redress a threat to the initiator's positive face for none has been made, but because they are simply being agreeable for one reason or another.

One last point. As in our discussion of the transactional side of interactions in the preceding chapter, it is necessary to show in the details of talk evidence of the face-work we say is going on. We might point to the disfluent elements of (5), as conversation analysts do, as evidence of the threat to the initiator's positive face associated with refusing to undertake commitments desired by the initiator. The disfluent elements of (4) provide similar evidence of the negative face-threat associated with asking others to undertake to commit to do things for us.

## Interactional effects in service encounters

In the preceding chapter, we considered how the utterances that comprise conversations can be mapped into interaction structure conditions and domain predicates by way of tracking the progress of a conversation. In this section, we shall turn to consider how utterances can be mapped into the interactional effects of interactions. We shall examine the successful baby-sitting example (between Carl and Debbie) and the failed ride-request example (between Donny and Marcia) of the previous chapter and a novel failed invitation.

### THE BABY-SITTING EXAMPLE

Recall that in the baby-sitting example (6) discussed in the preceding chapter, I argued that the transactional work of the exchange was accomplished primarily through utterances $T_{1b}$, $T_{2a}$, $T_{2b}$, $T_3$, and $T_{5c}$.[6]

---

[6] Utterance $T_{5a}$ seems to communicate that insofar as Carl is concerned the goal of the interaction has been achieved, and thus also does transactional work.

(6)  Jacobs and Jackson (1983b: 299)
     Carl is standing in the hallway of the speech department, holding
     the hand of his 15-month old son, Curtis.

     CARL   [a] Hey Debbie. [b] Are you going to be free from 1:30
            to 2:30?                                            $T_1$
     DEBBIE: [a] Yeah, I think so. [b] You want me to watch him?
                                                                $T_2$
     CARL:  Yeah                                                $T_3$
     DEBBIE: [a] I'd love to. [b] It'd be a pleasure.           $T_4$
     CARL:  [c] Okay. [b] Thanks. [c] I'll bring him around then.
                                                                $T_5$

There are four things that cannot be accounted for solely in terms of
the transactional effect of requests: the fact that Carl initiates the
service encounter with an utterance that addresses a precondition on
the ability condition, the fact that Debbie troubled herself to say, *You
want me to watch him?*, at turn $T_{2b}$, her utterances at turn $T_4$, and
Carl's saying *Thanks* at turn $T_5$.

   Carl could have initiated this service encounter with any of the
utterances of (7), among many others.

(7)  a.  Would you watch my kid this afternoon from 1:30 till 2:30?
     b.  I need someone to watch my kid this afternoon from 1:30 till
         2:30. Could you do it?
     c.  If you're not doing anything between 1:30 and 2:30, I'd like
         to ask you to watch my kid.

Like the utterance he chose, none of these utterances presumes
Debbie's availability to do what he wants. Why, then, did he choose to
initiate the interaction in the way he did? Levinson (1983) argues that
we initiate interactions in this way to minimize the chances of a
dispreferred response, i.e., to minimize the possibility of a response
that threatens our positive face. Alternatively, we could say that we do
this by way of mitigating or redressing the threat against the
responder's negative face by affording the responder an early opportunity to opt out of the interaction. Should Debbie see what was coming
(as she clearly did) and not want to do this baby-sitting, she could opt
out simply by manufacturing some prior obligation at the time in
question (yes, this is something we sometimes do). In fact, these two
accounts are not inconsistent with each other, for it is because the

indirect approach offers the responder a chance to opt out before the request-intent is made explicit that the indirect approach reduces the possibility of a threat to the initiator's positive face.

Debbie's utterance, *You want me to watch him?*, at turn $T_2$ specifies the initial-state condition of personal requests and thus clearly does transactional work. However, Debbie had the option of remaining silent after saying, *Yeah, I think so*, thereby forcing Carl to say something like *Would you watch my kid?* Such a move would not even have been uncooperative, for failing to confirm a discourse presupposition one has formed does not *per se* count as an FTA (unless perhaps it is clear to both that the responder knows what the initiator has in mind). Thus the fact that Debbie troubled herself to say, *You want me to watch him?*, needs to be explained.

In the slot occupied by *Do you want me to watch him?*, we sometimes find *Why do you ask?*, as I have previously noted. The transactional difference between them is that in the first case the responder has a specific supposition about why the initiator has initiated the act, but in the second case the responder does not know or is at least acting as if she does not know what the initiator has in mind. When a *Why do you ask?*-Question occurs in contexts like (8), it counts as an inquiry as to what A's goal is.

(8)   A: Hey Debbie. Are you free from 1:30 to 2:30?
      C: Yeah. Why do you ask?

However, such utterances do not advance the conversation forward transactionally, for all they accomplish is to request the initiator to say what he would normally say anyway. Because of this, I think we must say that this utterance is doing purely interactional work, functioning as what conversation analysts call a "go ahead" signal in that it communicates a willingness in principle to entertain what follows. Debbie's utterance, *Do you want me to watch him?*, also constitutes a go ahead move. However, there is a large difference between these two "go ahead" signals. The person who says *Why do you ask?* has not committed herself to doing anything. However, Debbie implicates her willingness to accept the imposition she has inferred is coming in saying *Do you want me to watch him?*

Since Debbie has committed no FTA that need redressing we must regard her saying, *Do you want me to watch him?*, as paying respect to Carl's positive face. Brown and Levinson assume that "people cooperate (and assume each other's cooperation) in maintaining face in interaction, such cooperation being based on the mutual vulner-ability of face" (1987: 61). We may assume then that Debbie said, *Do you want me to watch him?* in an effort to carry out her responsibility to cooperate with Carl in their joint effort to maintain face. Debbie's utterances, *I'd love to* and *It'd be a pleasure,* constitute additional examples of FRA as we have seen. At the time she says these things, the transactional work of the exchange is completed (with the exception of Carl's saying that he will bring his child to her), for Debbie has conceded her availability to perform the act Carl wants her to perform when she says *Yeah, I think so* and has implicated her willingness to do so when she says *You want me to watch him?* There is therefore nothing left to negotiate transactionally (with the exception noted) at the point these utterances occur, since the axiom of commitment kicks in to effect the making of the commitment.

Semantically, *I'd love to watch your child* expresses an attitude toward watching the child, not a willingness to do so. The same is true of *It'd be a pleasure.* What these forms do is communicate that Debbie values what Carl wants (i.e., values what Carl values), which is the defining feature of positive face-work.[7] Further evidence that Debbie is doing positive face-work in saying these things is the fact the forms are redundant and exaggerated.[8] *It'd be a pleasure* adds virtually nothing to what *I'd love to* communicates.

The last feature of this conversation that needs to be explained is Carl's saying *Thanks. Thanks* is a conventional form for showing appreciation to someone for accepting an imposition or in recipro-cating an FRA. In this conversation, I would argue that Carl is showing appreciation for Debbie's positive-face-respecting acceptance of the imposition, and is thereby reciprocating her display of respect to his positive face. Brown and Levinson take a different view of expressions of gratitude.

Brown and Levinson treat expressing thanks as offending the speaker's positive face in that the speaker implicitly accepts a debt and humbles himself (1987: 72). I find the view of interaction this account presupposes to be rather pessimistic – even paranoid. The fact is that

---

[7] There is some obligation for her to speak again at the point she says these things. However, she could simply have said something much less face-respecting like, *Okay, then. Will you bring him around?*

[8] Brown and Levinson (1987: 104–6) note that exaggeration plays an important role in displays of positive politeness. This would presumably be as true of FRA as in displays of positive politeness in redressing face-threats.

it is in attempting to cause Debbie to agree to help him that Carl acquires a debt to her, not in saying, *Thanks*. In agreeing to watch Carl's child, Debbie pays respect to Carl's positive face for she implicates that she sufficiently values him to restrict her freedom of action during the time she is watching his child. Her utterances, *I'd love to* and *It'd be a pleasure* explicitly pay respect to his positive face in that they communicate that she values what he values (namely, her watching his child). Carl reciprocates these FRA with one of his own, albeit not a very effusive one.

We may summarize what has been said about the interactional effects of this service encounter as follows:

- Carl's initiating an interaction the goal of which is to cause Debbie to undertake an obligation to watch his child threatens Debbie's negative face. Carl mitigates the FTA at $<T_{1b}>$ by initiating the interaction indirectly, specifically by employing an utterance that specifies a precondition on the ability condition.
- Debbie invites (and therefore implicitly accepts) the imposition, an FRA at $<T_{2b}>$ in saying, *You want me to watch him?*
- Debbie employs two FRA at $<T_{4a}>$ and $<T_{4b}>$.
- Carl reciprocates Debbie's FRA by expressing appreciation, itself an FRA.

### THE DONNY AND MARCIA RIDE-REQUEST

The Donny and Marcia ride-request excerpt begins, as we saw, with what conversation analysts call a "pre-announcement sequence" ($T_1$–$T_2$) followed by a piece of information at $T_3$ to which Marcia does not respond.

| | | |
|---|---|---|
| (9) DONNY: | Guess what.hh | $T_1$ |
| MARCIA: | What. | $T_2$ |
| DONNY: | .hh My ca:r is sta::lled. | $T_3$ |
| | (0.2) | $T_4$ |
| MARCIA: | Oh::. | $T_6$ |

The very brief pause at $T_3$ is clearly significant. Donny has told Marcia of some trouble he is having. Now, troubles come in two varieties – troubles that constitute a problem that needs a solution and troubles that do not. If I tell you that my favorite aunt has died, I do not expect you to do anything about this, for this is not a problem that can be fixed. Instead, I might expect you to show sympathy. However, Donny's trouble does constitute a problem that needs a solution, and we may expect that Marcia fully recognizes that and that Donny recognizes that she will recognize this.

Though Donny's initiation of his ride-request is indirect, it is highly egocentric. It focuses on his problem, not her ability or willingness to help. It is more polite than saying, *I want you to come to the Glen, pick me up, and take me to the bank in Brentwood,* for it indicates that his effort to get her to give him a ride has been forced on him rather than being ego driven. However, it does not provide Marcia the opportunity to opt out on ability grounds for his utterance does not speak to that issue (unlike his later, *I don't know if it's possible*).

Marcia's possible responses include offering some sort of solution, expressing sympathy, or saying nothing. Now, Marcia was not in a position to provide a solution to Donny's problem. The next best thing would be a display of sympathy, which would pay respect to Donny's positive face by indicating that she shares his unhappiness at his fate. The problem with this response is that it would constitute a kind of "go ahead" move, encouraging Donny to believe that he might be successful in achieving his goal, something that was not true. Thus, silence must have seemed to be all that was available to her. However, her silence clearly threatened Donny's positive face for in failing to display sympathy with Donny's troubles, she communicates that she does not share his unhappiness at his fate.

At turn $T_5$, Donny employs what seems to be a rising tune in saying, *('n) I'm up here in the Glen?*, which has the discourse significance of forcing a response from Marcia. However, she is in precisely the same situation as before, for he has advanced the conversation forward only minimally. She comes up with a minimal, noncommittal verbal response in saying, *Oh::* (elongated vowel). This has the minimal transactional significance of signaling understanding of what he has said, and is as threatening to Donny's positive face as was her earlier silence for, again, she has not displayed sympathy with his plight. It is at this point that Donny makes somewhat more explicit the nature of his problem.

(10)    DONNY:    (0.4) (.hhh) A:nd.hh (0.2) I don' know if it's po:ssible,
             but {.hhh/(0.2)} see I haveta open up the ba̲:nk.hh
             (0.3) a:t uh: (.) in Brentwood?hh

MARCIA: Yea<u>h</u>:- en I know you want-(.) en I whoa-(.) en I
<u>wo</u>uld, but- except I've gotta leave in about five
min(h)utes.

In the face of two FTAs from Marcia, it is perhaps not surprising that
Donny has difficulty in framing his utterance, the cause, I have
suggested, of disfluent utterances like his. What he says is face-
threatening, and he includes two redressive elements, *I don' know if
it's: po:ssible* and *I haveta open up the ba:nk.*

Donny's utterance *I don' know if it's: po:ssible,* as was noted in the
preceding chapter, specifies the ability condition of requests. The
question arises as to why Donny chose this sort of attack. Brown and
Levinson (cf. their chart on page 137) see this as being a non-coercive
redressive strategy in that it does not presume Marcia's ability to do
what is wanted and, furthermore, expresses a certain pessimism. This
utterance, then, is doing both transactional and interactional work. And
in saying *I haveta open up the ba:nk* Donny is giving a reason for the
FTA, indicating, again, that his request is not ego driven, but is forced
on him by the circumstances he is in. In this respect, he is therefore
doing nothing very different from the responder who gives a reason for
not accepting a request: he explains why he is performing an FTA.

To this, Marcia does not respond, again, presumably, because she
has not found an appropriate way to signal her face-threatening
rejection of the request, forcing Donny to continue. He provides an
additional detail about his destination in saying, *a:t uh: (.) in Brentwood?hh,* again employing a rising tune, which, again, forces a reply
from Marcia. Her response is quite disfluent (containing false starts,
pauses, and an important shift from *but* to *except*) presumably because
she is having some difficulty in formulating her response in some
minimally face-threatening way.

Marcia's saying *I whoa-(.) en I would* looks very much like she tries
out a face-respecting, willingness-based redressive form (*I whoa-(.)*)
before settling on it (*en I would*). The shift from *but* to *except* is
important, for *I would but I've gotta leave in about five minutes* makes a
much weaker claim than *I would except I've gotta leave in about five
minutes.* Utterances of the form "I would do A but for B" give one
reason, possibly among many, for not doing A, but "I would do A
except for B" *L*-Means 'I would do A in every circumstance (that is
relevant and reasonably expectable) other than B,' which pays
significant respect to Donny's positive face. (It is just his bad luck that

111

the one circumstance that precludes Marcia from doing A is the one that obtains.) Finally, as is characteristic of people committing FTA, Marcia offers an explanation for her inability to do as Donny wants.

We may summarize the redressive actions of Donny and Marcia as follows:

- Donny initiates an FTA in telling Marcia that he is having car trouble, for it communicates that he wishes her to help him in some way that will restrict her freedom of action. It is redressed by employing a form that indicates that his action is not ego-driven, but forced on him.

- Donny further redresses his FTA by indicating doubt that Marcia will be able to help him (*I don't know if it's possible*), a move that facilitates rejection by indicating that a rejection is not wholly unexpected, and is nonintrusive for it communicates that he does not presume to know what Marcia's private circumstances are.

- Donny further redresses his FTA by again indicating that his action is not ego-driven (*I haveta open the bank*).

- Marcia redresses her face-threatening response by communicating a willingness in principle to provide him a ride, which pays respect to Donny's positive face, which is enhanced by the suggestion that only one thing – her pressing need to leave for work – precludes her from helping him, and by providing a credible reason (*I've gotta leave in about five minutes*) for her inability to help him.

It seems clear, then, that both initiators and responders are capable of committing FTA and that when initiators perform FTA their utterances contain many of the same elements found in FTA of responders. What ties together these dispreferred initiations and responses is that they both occur when participants are engaging in FTA. Since the approach of Brown and Levinson can handle "dispreferred" initiations as well as responses, it must be preferred to the conversation-analytic account.

### Invitations

Invitations differ from service encounters transactionally in two ways. In an invitation, the initiator proposes that the responder do something with her rather than for her. Secondly, the willingness condition associated with requests is replaced with a condition speaking to whether or not the responder desires to engage in the proposed action, rather than is merely willing to do so. This latter assumption is based on the fact that initiators of invitations very frequently employ utterances containing the verb complexes present+*want* and *would+like* (e.g., *Do you want to come over and watch the World Cup?*, *Would you like to come over for coffee and cake?*). I believe this distinction derives from the fact that compliance with invitations is to some degree more voluntary than compliance with requests, for the latter tend to flow out of an initiator **need** for assistance of some sort and we are under some social pressure to help those in need whereas invitations flow out of an initiator **desire** for social interaction. Thus, in the case of a request it is the willingness of the responder to perform the action that is at issue, not whether or not the initiator actually desires to help.

Invitations differ interactionally from requests in two ways. First, invitations constitute FRA, rather than FTA. My primary reason for saying this, as has been noted, is that responders commonly express appreciation for invitations however they may feel personally about the prospects of spending time with the initiator. (The normal preferred response to any FRA is to express appreciation, which is itself an FRA.) This never happens in the case of requests or other FTA (except in sarcastic responses). Second, the potential threat to the initiator's positive face is much greater than in the case of requests. It is possible to reject a request because one is unwilling to perform the action without necessarily threatening the initiator's positive face. One might reject a request that one take care of someone's cats by saying that one hates cats. This may be an insult to the initiator's cats, but not to the initiator. However, it is very difficult, if not impossible, to turn down an invitation because one is unwilling to accept it without threatening the initiator's positive face, for the action one is rejecting involves being with the initiator.

Let us turn then to a case of a failed invitation. Since I have not discussed this example before, I shall focus on both the transactional and interactional work of the exchange. Let us begin with the opening few lines in (11).

(11)   Drew (1984: 130)
       E: w*<u>W</u>hadiyih <u>d</u>oin.[9]                                      T₁

---

[9]   Underlining represents emphasis.

(0.9)

N: What am I d ⌐ oin?                                    $T_2$

E:                    ⌊ (Cleanin')                       $T_3$

(Mmhm) ?                                                 $T_4$

N: 'h I'm i̱:rening, wouldju ba̱lieve that̲[10] (h).=      $T_5$

E: =Oh: bless it ⌐ s heart.                              $T_6$

N:                 ⌊ In fact I̱: ir- I start'd ir'ning en I'd.I.

Somehow er another ahrning dis kind uv lea̱:ves m̲e:

co:l ⌐ d                                                 $T_7$

E:      ⌊ Yea:h                                          $T_8$

(.)

N: ⌐ °(Y'know)°                                          $T_9$

Initiating an invitation routine with a *Yes-No*-question asking whether someone is doing anything or, as in this case, a *WH*-Question asking what someone is doing, allows testing of the waters before proffering an invitation, in much the way that it does in requesting. Inquiries of both types have come conventionally to be understood as implicitly asking whether the responder is available to do something with or for the initiator as was noted in the case of the baby-sitting example. Thus, the utterance, w*Whadiyih doin, will likely be interpreted along the lines of (12).

(12)  Failed lunch invitation
        Effects:
                Transactional: r commits to do A
                Interactional: threatens r's negative face.
        Initial-state condition: i desires r to do A [T, $<T_1>$]
        Satisfaction condition:
                r able to do A [?]
                        If: ¬ must(r do A′) [?, $<T_1>$]
        Domain(A):
                action(e)
                actor(r)
                at(now)
                with(i)
        Domain(A′):
                action($e_1$)

[10] How one emphasizes a word final voiceless stop is beyond my understanding. I think Drew may have had in mind a released [t].

114

actor(r)
at(now)
$e=e_1$

Note that I treat this opening move (which could be the prelude to a number of different actions) as threatening the responder's negative face. This is because it is intrusive (for it invades the responder's privacy) and because it could prefigure a request. Normally, only persons who are reasonably close to addressees can ask an opening question like this.

In the case of a *Yes-No*-Question like *You doing anything?*, if the responder says *No*, then any initiator who means to make a request of the responder or invite the responder to do something knows that she is available in principle to do something. It is important to recognize, of course, that questions like *You doin' anything?* and *Whatchadoin'?* are *S*-Meaning equivalent to 'You doin' **anything important?**' and 'What, **that is significant**, are you doing?' If the responder says, *Yes*, then the initiator knows that she is not available to do something. If she says something like, *Yes, I'm ironing*, then the initiator must try to determine whether the responder is willing to give up that activity to take up another. The question, *What are you doin?*, could get *Nothing* as a reply, in which case the initiator would also know that the responder is available in principle to do something.

In the case at hand, the responder pauses significantly before speaking and when she does she repeats the question, both of which are dispreferred responses. We cannot know why she has done these things, but the responder may have recognized that the question was not idle – that it implicated a desire for the responder to engage in some activity, something she was apparently not prepared to do – and she was trying to find some way of heading off the initiator. (Or she may have been distracted by her ironing.) The fact that her utterance implicitly inquires about the availability of the responder to do something provides the theoretical foundation for the thesis that the responder's failure to provide some sort of immediate, affirmative response constitutes a dispreferred response.

In the present case, the responder responds ultimately with the statement that she is ironing and implicates in saying, *would you believe that*, that she isn't happy to be doing it. This is made quite explicit later when she says that the kind of ironing she is doing leaves her cold. I shall treat this as implicating that the responder might be able

**115**

to take lunch with the initiator. At turn $T_9$, the net effect on the interaction structure is as is given in (13).

(13)   Failed lunch invitation
       Effects:
               Transactional: r commits to do A
               Interactional: threatens r's negative face
       Initial-state condition: i desires r to do A [T, $<T_1>$]
       Satisfaction condition:
               r able to do A [$\Diamond$T]
                       If: $\neg$ must(r do A') [$\Diamond$T,[11] $<T_1T_7>$]
       Domain(A):
               action(e)
               actor(r)
               at(now)
       Domain(A'):
               action(ironing)
               actor(r)
               at(now)

Though the responder in this case is actually doing something, it is now revealed as being nothing she wants to do and thus is not something that is important to her. Thus, the initiator is entitled to believe that the precondition on the ability condition is possibly true, from which it would follow that the responder may be available (in principle) to have lunch with her.

At this point, the initiator broaches her invitation.

(14)   E: └ Wanna cum down'n ⌐ av a bighta lu:nch witme:?=    $T_{10}$
       N:                                    └ °(        )°    $T_{11}$
       E: =I got s'm bee:r en stu:ff,                          $T_{12}$
          (0.2)
       N: Wul yer ril sweet hon:, uh::m
          (.)
       N: ⌐ l e t- I: ha(v)⌐                                   $T_{13}$
       E: └ or d'yuh'av sum ⌐ p'n el ⌐ se (t')                 $T_{14}$

The initiator frames her invitation with an utterance, *Wanna cum*

---

[11]   The notation "$\Diamond$T" stands for "possibly true."

*down'n av a bighta lu:nch with me:?*, that specifies the responder-desires satisfaction condition, during the uttering of which it appears that the responder begins to say something, but not something that was sufficiently intelligible to be identified. The initiator continues on[12] to offer an inducement, spelling out a desirable property of this lunch (*I got s'm bee:r en stu:ff*). Since inducements to accept invitations tend to occur when the initiator has some reason to believe that there is a nontrivial chance it will be rejected, we may imagine that she heard this potential interruption as prefiguring a dispreferred response.

At this point the initiator's positive face is clearly on the line. After a brief but apparently significant pause, the responder redresses the impending face-threatening rejection by paying respect to the initiator's positive face in saying, *Wul yer ril sweet hon:*. As I have argued, invitations pay respect to the responder's positive face, which is why we find mitigators like *Wul yer ril sweet hon:, uh::* in both preferred and dispreferred responses of invitations (but not in requests). This action communicates to the initiator that the responder values her offer through the reciprocal payment of respect to the initiator's positive face. That the initiator hears this as prefiguring a rejection of the invitation is made clear by the fact that she attempts to frame the rejection in responder-ability terms when she says, *d'yuh'av sump'n else*.

Now, the question arises as to how we might account for the initiator's inference. Adult speakers know that turns comprised of silences, the discourse marker, *well*, and mitigators implicate an impending dispreferred response – they do not need to work it out by engaging in some sort of complex Gricean calculation. The question is what is the mechanism by which the implicature is drawn?

One can accept an invitation by employing an utterance like *I'd love to*, which is equivalent to *Yes, I'd love to*. Thus preferred responses can be initiated by face-respecting utterances. Note, however, that whereas *I'd love to* communicates acceptance, the initiator who hears, *Well, I'd love to*, will expect to hear a following *but*, as in *Well, I'd love to, but . . .* I would suggest, then, that *well*, when it initiates a response to any explicit or implicit inquiry as to whether someone is able to do something, willing to do something, or desires to do something, conventionally implicates a negative response. The same is true of a

---

[12]  The "="-sign indicates that there was no break in the initiator's utterance.

pause. The net effect of the utterance, *d'yuh'av sump'n else,* is represented in (15).

(15)   Failed lunch invitation
      Effects:
            Transactional: r commits to do A
            Interactional: pays respect to r's positive face and
                potentially threatens i's positive face.
      Initial-state condition: i desires r to do A [T, $<T_1 \& T_{10}>$]
      Satisfaction condition:
            r able to do A [?]
                    If: $\neg$ must(r do A'') [?, $<T_{14}>$]
            r desires to do e [?, $<T_{10}>$]
      Domain(A):
            action(have lunch)
            host(i)
            guest(r)
            at(noon)
      Domain(A'):
            action(ironing)
            actor(r)
            at(now)
            $t = t_1$
      Domain(A''):
            action(e)
            actor(r)
            at(noon)

At this point, the responder confirms that there is "something else," but not another lunch engagement or other similar social obligation. Rather, this "something else" is an obligation to her mother-in-law (i.e., an obligation she can't ignore).

(16)   N: ∟ N o :, I haf to uh call Rol's mother. ᵒh I told'er I:'d ca:ll 'er
            this morning=I g⌈ otta
      E: ∟ ᵒ(Ahh.)ᵒ
      N: letter from 'er en (.) 'hhhh A:n'dum
         (1.0)
      N: p.So sh- in the letter she sed if you can why (.) yih know call
         me Sa:turdih mor:ning en I just haven't hhᵒ

E: Mmhm

This explanation (however insincere it may actually be) serves to redress her positive-face-threatening rejection of the invitation.

After a three-minute spate of talk on other matters, the initiator returns to the request routine with talk that suggests that it is getting late (*God what is it. Quarter after eleven?*).

(17)  E: AW:::righ⌈ty I don'know <u>wh</u>at <u>ti</u>:me izit, I- <u>I</u>=
      N:       ⌊ °(allri-)°·
      E: =<u>woke up</u> et s::six this mo:rning⌈ g=
      N:                          ⌊Oh: ⌈my <u>G</u>*od
      E:                                ⌊=<u>God</u> w't izit. Quarter after
         'leven?
      N: Yeah(n)h
         (1.0)
      E: Yea⌈(h°yeh ave got°) ⌉
      N: ⌊The su:n⌋s comin ou(pt).
      E: I kn<u>ow</u> it .
      N: <u>Bee</u>::utiful=
      E: =(Jus') beautiful.
         (0.2)
      N: <u>So</u>: anyway, let uh hhh <u>c</u>all <u>R</u>ol's other, (.) and uh,
         (0.5)
      N: ⌈(Don't)
      E: ⌊Well <u>Give me</u> a <u>bu</u>:zz if you- (.) u*g'mon <u>d</u>own if you- I'd
         <u>li</u>ke tih have yih come down fer . . . .

As Drew (1984: 145) notes,

> "Lateness" is relative to something, and reporting the time can be designed to recall the invitation by implicitly invoking the closeness to lunchtime. Also E initiates her drawing attention to the time . . . in a way that is hearable as beginning to close the call ("AW:::righty"), and thereby occasion the relevance of arrangements talk.

Our excerpt concludes with an utterance explicitly specifying the initial-state condition (*'d like tih have yih come down fer. . .*), after a false start.

This conversation is interesting in a number of ways. Certainly, it should serve as an antidote to a traditional speech-act-theoretic view of invitations that sees them as things that initiators do with single utterances. It also demonstrates the importance of the view that utterances can have both a transactional significance that reflects what they contribute to satisfaction of interaction structure conditions and domain predicates and/or an interactional significance that consists of the respects in which utterances threaten and/or redress the addressee's negative or positive face or pay respect to the addressee's positive face.

## Conclusion

I would like to conclude this discussion by addressing the question whether the interactional effects of acts should be part of a speech-act-theoretic account of conversation or part of some orthogonal, sociolinguistic theory of communication. There are two reasons to believe that the interactional effect must be a part of speech act theory. First, different speech acts have different face-consequences. A request threatens the recipient's negative face by imposing on the recipient's freedom of action. An invitation, on the other hand, seems to pay respect to the responder's positive face. Announcing something to someone (i.e., conveying unrequested information) threatens the recipient's positive face by exposing the recipient as possibly ignorant of something the speaker values. In contrast with announcements, a request for information has the opposite effect of enhancing the addressee's positive face, for it represents the addressee as knowledge-able on some matter of importance to the speaker.

Second, it is possible that a speaker choose to initiate an act not to achieve the transactional effect of the act, but the interactional effect. That is, it is possible for someone in a position of authority (a boot camp sergeant, for instance) to issue an order for her subordinates to march around the barracks less because she wants them to march around the barracks, as opposed to do something else, but to reinforce her superior social position through the negative face-threat associated with the order. Inclusion of the interactional effect along with the transactional effect (Searlean essential condition) is thus critically important to understanding how different types of interactions may differ.

120

# 5

### Indirect speech acts

#### Introduction

In preceding chapters, I have argued that although such terms as requesting, offering, promising, suggesting, and the like, have an undeniable utility to us in informal discussions of what participants are doing in multiturn interactions, they should play no role in accounts of how to go about achieving goals and recognizing the goals of others in interaction. In particular, I have argued that it is a mistake to suppose that the utterances of multiturn interactions should be mapped into actions such as these. Instead, I have claimed that the utterances of such interactions should be mapped into interaction structure conditions and domain predicates reflecting the work they do in the interactions.

However, there exist two classes of utterances which will be thought by some to present significant problems for this theory, namely performative sentences[1] and indirect speech act forms, for in each case, speakers seem to be able to perform actions like making requests, offers, promises, and the like in uttering single sentences. Indeed, Searle (1975) has argued that there exists a set of indirect speech act forms which have developed conventionalized uses as request forms, offer forms, etc.

In this chapter, I shall address the question whether there exists a class of conventionalized indirect speech act forms. I shall argue,

[1]   I shall continue to have little to say about performative sentences. As noted earlier, I believe that their uses are dictated by their literal meanings and context, not their forms.

*contra* Searle (1975) and Morgan (1978), who developed Searle's views in an interesting way, that there can be no mapping (conventionalized relationship) between linguistic forms, **taken as a whole,** and particular communicative actions, whether or not the mapping is mediated by context. I shall further argue that the distinction between direct and indirect actions that the theory of indirect speech acts presupposes is much less useful than a distinction between direct and indirect communication.

What I shall not be doing is arguing that we cannot use single utterances (e.g., *Could you pass the salt?*) by way of communicating a desire for salt, that is, that we cannot perform the communicative action that we informally refer to as "making a request" in uttering a single sentence. What I shall argue is that our ability to do this has less to do with the forms of such sentences than the contexts in which they are used. As we shall see, a single utterance can be used to make a request (using the terminology of traditional speech act theory), only in contexts in which virtually all of the conditions of service encounters are understood by participants to be satisfied. On the other hand, the thesis that the sentences we employ in performing so-called indirect speech acts exhibit significant conventionalization of form is undeniable. However, as I shall show in chapter 6, the sort of conventionalization they exhibit is characteristic of highly colloquial language in general, not of indirect speech act forms in particular, and can be accounted for without supposing a mapping of sentence forms into primary speech acts of the sort that Searle and Morgan envisioned.

## Direct versus indirect speech acts

Austin (1962), recall, argued that a request or order to turn out the lights can be communicated directly, not only by using explicit performative sentences like (1a) and (1b), respectively, but also by employing implicit performative sentences such as (2a) and (2b).

(1)　a.　I request you to turn out the lights.
　　　b.　I order you to turn out the lights.

(2)　a.　Please turn out the lights.
　　　b.　Turn out the lights.

However, Sadock (1970, 1972), Gordon and Lakoff (1971), Green

(1975), and Searle (1975) have noted that we seem to be able to make essentially the same request as is made in uttering (1a) and (2a) by uttering questions like those in (3) or an assertion like (4).

(3)  a.  Could you turn out the lights?
     b.  Would you mind turning out the lights?
     c.  Why don't you turn out the lights?

(4)  I'd like for you to turn out the lights.

A case like (2b) illustrates the point that certain acts can be performed directly using a sentence of a type with which that act is conventionally associated. Thus, we can use a declarative sentence in a direct way to make a literal act (*L*-Act) assertion (*Bill Clinton is President*) or use an interrogative sentence in a direct way to ask an *L*-Act question (*Is Bill Clinton President?*) or use an imperative sentence in a direct way to issue an *L*-Act directive (*Vote for Bill Clinton!*). In these cases, the relationship of the utterance's form and literal meaning to the *L*-Act that is performed in uttering the sentence is conventional – English could logically have dedicated the interrogative sentence pattern to *L*-Act assertions and the declarative pattern to *L*-Act questions.

According to Searle (1975), indirect speech acts arise in cases in which "a sentence that contains the illocutionary force indicators for one kind of illocutionary act" is "uttered to perform, **in addition**, another type of illocutionary act." However, the results one gets employing this criterion depend critically on one's speech act taxonomy. Thus, the sentences of (3) contain the illocutionary force indicators of questions (inversion of the subject and first auxiliary verb), but are used to make requests.[2] Similarly, (4) contains the illocutionary force indicator of an assertion (normal subject-predicate order), but is being used to make a request. And, sentence (5) contains the illocutionary force indicators of an assertion, but could be used to make a promise.

(5)  I will be in my office at noon.

All of the theories of indirect speech acts cited above treat the

[2]  I shall use the traditional language of speech act theory throughout much of this chapter simply to facilitate the discussion.

123

phenomenon as presenting a special problem for speech act theory. However, I shall demonstrate in this and the next chapter that utterances such as these present no problems that do not arise in the attempt to account for the form and content of colloquial, transactionally significant utterances generally. Observe, for instance, that the utterance *Can I have a half pint of the blackberry jam?*, occurring at $T_1$ in (7), is identical in form to $T_1$ in (6) in all of the respects relevant to Searle's and Morgan's theory of indirect speech acts.

(6)  Levinson (1983)
    A: Do you have the blackberry jam?                $T_1$
    B: Yes.                                                 $T_2$
    A: Okay. Can I have a half pint then?     $T_3$
    B: Sure.                                              $T_4$

(7)  Indirect speech act version of (6)
    A: Can I have a half pint of the blackberry jam?     $T_1$
    B: Sure.                                                $T_2$

The only difference in the two conversations is that for the customer felicitously to say *Can I have a half pint of the blackberry jam?* and fully expect the clerk to supply her with the desired jam, she would have to believe that the clerk had the jam in question, something that she appears not to have believed at the outset of conversation (6).

## Three theories of indirect speech acts

There are three theories of indirect speech acts worth special attention:[3] Gordon and Lakoff's theory employing conversational postulates; Morgan's theory employing conventions of use; and the more recent conversation-analytic approach of Levinson. Our focus will be on data like (3) and (4) and the much discussed example (8).

(8)  Can you pass the salt?

Speech acts performed employing sentences like (3), (4), and (8) are said to be indirect because they seem to be intended to perform an action other than that which is most immediately suggested by their

[3] I take the abstract-performative theory to be a dead horse that needs no more beating.

literal meanings. Thus, taking the utterances of (3) and (4) at face value, we might say, for instance, that the speaker of (3a) is requesting information about the ability of the addressee to perform an action, whereas the speaker of (4) is asserting a proposition predicating a desire of the speaker that the addressee perform some action. In each of these cases, therefore, the speaker's intended illocutionary point – that she means to be requesting the addressee to turn out the lights – must be inferred, or so it would seem. The inferences in question are a species of conversational implicature (Grice 1975), for as Searle (1975) showed, it is possible for an addressee to calculate the speaker's illocutionary point in cases such as these by employing common-sense reasoning based on Grice's "Cooperative Principle."

Although the illocutionary points of utterances like (3), (4), and (8) are calculatable, Searle and other early writers such as Sadock (1970, 1972), Gordon and Lakoff (1971), Morgan (1975), and Green (1975) took the position that we do not actually calculate their illocutionary forces but instead (a) associate underlying linguistic representations (logical forms) with them that directly account for their request forces (Sadock and Green), or (b) apply conversational postulates to their logical forms from which their request forces are derived in one inferential step (Gordon and Lakoff), or (c) apply conventions of use that short-circuit the implicature (Searle and Morgan). More recently, Levinson (1983) has offered a theory of short-circuiting that is predicated on the assumption that we have learned to associate certain utterance forms with first members of canonical four-turn request sequences and, for that reason, comprehend their forces immediately.[4] In each of these cases, the authors treated the implicatures as conventionalized in some manner – as a convention of meaning (Sadock, Green, and, though in a very different way, Gordon and Lakoff) or a convention of use (Searle and Morgan, and, though in a very different way, Levinson).

### Gordon and Lakoff

Gordon and Lakoff, who gave the first account of indirect speech acts, argued that there exists a set of "conversational postulates" such as

---

4    Actually, Levinson rejects the notion of a speech act, as we have already noted. However, the actions he and other conversation analysts concern themselves with have the same names as those speech act theorists use. The difference is that conversation analysts see them as communicative actions which are fundamentally social in nature, rather than as linguistic actions.

those in (9), where Q is of the form 'FUT(DO(b,R)),' that are functions from literal meanings to literal meanings, in which the input is the literal meaning of an utterance (if we assume (counterfactually) that the logical forms of utterances contain performative prefixes indicating the literal act they perform) and the output is what we might call a "performative logical form" that determines the utterance's illocutionary force.

(9)  a.  SAY(a,b,WANT(a,Q))$\star \rightarrow$ REQUEST(a,b,Q)
     b.  ASK(a,b,CAN(b,Q))$\star \rightarrow$ REQUEST(a,b,Q)
     c.  ASK(a,b,WILLING(b,Q))$\star \rightarrow$ REQUEST(a,b,Q)
     d.  ASK(a,b,Q)$\star \rightarrow$ REQUEST(a,b,Q)
     where Q is of the form FUT(DO(b,R)) [b will do act R]

The basic idea is that if an utterance by a speaker entails the proposition on the left-hand side of an arrow (*I want you to take out the garbage* – cf. (9a)), it implicates a proposition with the logical form on the right-hand side of the arrow (*I request that you take out the garbage*). By the asterisks, Gordon and Lakoff meant to signal a dependence of these postulates on a mutual recognition by speaker and hearer that the speaker of an utterance entailing the left-hand side of one of these postulates did not mean the utterance to be taken literally. They did not say how exactly this mutual recognition was to be achieved.

The principal strength of Gordon and Lakoff's approach is that it can capture certain very important semantic generalizations. Arguably, *Will you open the door?*, *Would you open the door?*, and *Do you want to open the door?* would all be mapped into the input condition of postulate (9c), thereby capturing the generalization that they are making essentially the same type of request – a willingness-based request.

The connection between the approach of Gordon and Lakoff to the analysis of indirect speech acts and my view of the transactional significance of utterances should be clear. According to Gordon and Lakoff, an utterance can be used to perform an indirect request if it specifies a felicity condition on requesting. According to DSAT, the transactional significance of an utterance reflects what it contributes to instantiation of interaction structure domain predicates and satisfaction of interaction structure conditions. This feature of Gordon and Lakoff's position is therefore preserved and generalized in my DSAT account. It is also exploited in a number of artificial intelligence

126

approaches to language understanding (Allen 1983, Cohen and Perrault 1986, and Perrault and Allen 1980).

The position of Gordon and Lakoff is not unflawed. As Morgan (1978: 278f, fn. 5) has pointed out, Gordon and Lakoff's approach suffers from the major defect that there seem to be utterance-types that are semantically very similar to conventionalized request forms that do not seem to have the same indirect speech act potential. Searle (1975) claimed, for instance, that a sentence like (10) can be uttered to make a request, but a sentence like (11) has "a formal and stilted character that in almost all contexts would eliminate it as a candidate for an indirect request."

(10)   Do you want to hand me the salt?

(11)   Is it the case that you at present desire to hand me the salt?

The approach of Gordon and Lakoff cannot distinguish the indirect speech act potential of these two cases because their account is wholly semantically based.

Still another difficulty with the position of Gordon and Lakoff is that there are utterance-types that do not in any direct way specify classical felicity conditions on requests but can be used to make requests, such as those in (12) and (13).

(12) Have you got Embassy Gold please? (Levinson 1983: 361)[5]

(13)   a.  I'll have a large pineapple.
       b.  I'll take a large pineapple.

However, as we shall see in the next chapter, the pragmatic stratum I propose for English maps utterances like those in (13) into the initial-state condition of interaction structures. The approach of Gordan and Lakoff could easily be extended to cases like these.

### Searle and Morgan

According to Searle (1975:76), who took a more syntactic line than did Gordon and Lakoff, certain forms have become "conventionally

---

[5]   From an unpublished diploma dissertation by Sinclair (1976), a source I have not had access to. This utterance was the first turn of a two-turn, successful request sequence.

established as the standard idiomatic forms for indirect speech acts. While keeping their literal meanings, they will acquire conventional uses as, e.g., polite forms for requests."[6] There are two features of this claim worth highlighting. The first is that the forms are idiomatic or colloquial in nature, but are not idioms. The second is that the forms in question are polite forms.

In Morgan's (1975) development of Searle's insight, he argued that such forms arise when the implicative relationship between utterances like those in (3), (4), and (8) and their respective intended illocutionary points gets short-circuited, somewhat after the manner of an idiom like *Break a leg!* Morgan argues that this sort of short-circuiting arises when the relationship between someone's employing a certain means (saying *Break a leg!*) to achieve a certain purpose (to wish an actor well) on a particular occasion (as an actor leaves for the theater or goes on stage) gets obscured.

Morgan's view, like Gordon and Lakoff's, allows us to account for the fact that speakers construe sentences like (3), (4), and (8) as requests without supposing that they engage in complex calculations or that they have request meanings (in the sense of *L*-Meaning). Moreover, Morgan makes a convincing case that short-circuiting must surely be the device at work in the emergence of many conventional expressions such as *Break a leg!*

A three-stage process seems to be involved in the emergence of idioms like *Break a leg!*. At Stage 1, the implicature is attached to the meaning of the utterance in the sense that the meaning of the utterance plays a role in the calculation of its force. At Stage 2, the implicature comes to be directly associated with a particular sentence or sentence form even though it is still calculatable in principle. At Stage 3, the historical association of the implicature with the meaning of the utterance is lost (i.e., the implicature is no longer calculatable) and the association between the implicature and the sentence or sentence form becomes fully conventional. An expression like *Break a leg!* has reached Stage 3. If the expression of good will to another at parting is a kind of speech act, then *Goodbye* would count as a Stage 3 speech act. However, as Lycan (1984) has pointed out, few of the standard examples of indirect speech

---

6   It is quite wrong to suppose that indirection in the performance of speech acts inevitably leads to greater politeness. There is nothing particularly polite about saying *I need the salt* as a way of requesting the salt, but it is quite indirect. However, I will argue in chapter 8 that indirection does have a great deal to do with politeness, even if not with being polite.

acts have progressed beyond Stage 2. The reason for this may be that Stage 3 examples exist primarily in cases where a very simple message is being conveyed in a very specific type of context. This is true of *Break a leg!* and *Goodbye*, of course. There are few types of speech acts that are as simple as these. This is an exceedingly important point.

Lycan (1984) has offered a taxonomy of indirect speech acts that mirrors Morgan's account of the three stages in the development of indirect speech acts. There are Type-1 cases like (14) which (p. 174) "have perfectly straightforward literal uses that require no stage-setting, and when they are used with indirect force, we feel the conveyed force depends pretty squarely on the literal content. By the same token, hearers do not compute these sentence's indirect forces conventionally or automatically; multiple contextual factors are needed in the determination." It is clear that Type-1 indirect speech acts are Stage 1 implicatures, i.e., are calculatable and do not involve a convention of use.

(14) a. It's cold in here.
     b. Are you tall enough to reach the top shelf?
     c. I wonder what time it is?

Type-2 cases are the most widely discussed and include examples like (3), (4), and (8) or

(15) a. Would you take out the garbage?
     b. Could you take the kids to school?

These are the cases that Searle and Morgan have claimed are calculatable but have indirect force in virtue of a convention of use and are therefore Stage 2 implicatures.

Lycan goes on to say that we must recognize a third class of indirect speech acts which consists of cases in which the utterances in question have **only** indirect force. The paradigmatic case, first cited by Gordon and Lakoff (1971), is (16).

(16) Why paint your house purple?

According to Lycan, this sentence "cannot be understood as an ingenuous **or** disingenuous request for information about the hearer's state of mind" (p. 164). He agrees, then, with Gordon and Lakoff, who say (p. 96) that (16) "always conveys" (17).

(17)  Unless you have some good reason for painting your house purple, you should not paint your house purple.

A question that arises is whether or not Lycan's Type-3 indirect speech acts are cases of Morgan's Stage 3 implicatures, i.e., of implicatures that are not calculatable and necessarily therefore involve a convention of use. If so, then they are best treated as a species of minor sentence type.

Though Morgan does not explicitly say so, his approach presupposes the existence of production rules of the form of (18), one for each syntactic form that has associated with it some indirect speech act.

(18) On an **occasion** of type O, when a speaker intends (**purpose**) to cause the addressee to perform some action A for the speaker, the speaker can say (**means**) *Could you do A?*

To flesh this proposal out, we would need to say what O is.

The principal strength of the approach taken by Searle and Morgan over that of Gordon and Lakoff is that they see a connection between the use of an utterance and its form and are therefore in a position to distinguish the different illocutionary force potentials of the pairs like (10) and (11). A major problem with their approaches is that there are a large number of different polite request forms each of which will require a different production rule, for they are form-specific in character. As a consequence, they will miss an important generalization that Gordon and Lakoff's account captured, namely that utterances that specify the same felicity condition will *ceteris paribus* have the same use. Another difficulty is that, like Gordon and Lakoff, neither Searle, nor Morgan, provides an explicit account of how the conventions they speak of depend on context.

### Levinson

Recall that Morgan took the line that it is a convention of use that $T_1$ in conversation (19) will be construed as having the illocutionary force of a request and he argued that such conventions of use arise as the means for performing a particular communicative action become more specific.

(19)   Levinson (1983: 361)
      S: Have you got Embassy Gold please?             $T_1$
      H: Yes dear ((provides))                           $T_2$

According to Morgan, the short-circuiting involved was a short-circuiting of a reasoning process.

Levinson would agree that $T_1$ will be construed as a request and that a process of short-circuiting is involved, but appeals to a quite different process of short-circuiting to account for it. He argues that sentences like $T_1$ come to be recognized as requests by a process that drops out the second and third turns of four-turn request sequences.

Four-turn request sequences which are initiated by *Yes-No* Questions asking whether or not the addressee possesses a desired object are certainly very common. Conversation (6) illustrates such a case. On Levinson's view, we get from four-turn conversations like (6) to two-turn sequences like (19) by dropping out turns $T_2$ and $T_3$. Obviously, such short-circuiting would occur only when the addressee of $T_1$ can be expected to have the extra domain knowledge required to fully understand what is wanted (i.e., whether this particular customer wants a single pack or a carton, which might, of course, be clear from the amount of money the customer has displayed).

Levinson (1983) claims that a conversation like (6) consists of two sequences – a pre-request sequence initiated by the utterance *Do you have the blackberry jam?* followed by a request sequence initiated by the utterance *Can I have a half pint then?* He argues that a primary desideratum of requesting is the avoidance of what are called "dispreferred responses" – in this case, rejections – and that, therefore, we employ a question form like *Do you have the blackberry jam?*, for a dispreferred (negative) response to an information question of that sort is less face-threatening than a dispreferred (negative) response to a request form like *Can I have a half pint of the blackberry jam?*

As Jacobs and Jackson (1983b) have correctly observed, however, Levinson's elision theory will be able to account for only a very small subset of classical indirect request forms. It cannot, for instance, handle indirect requests like *Can I have a half pint of the blackberry jam?* The problem is that Levinson cannot show in such a case that there is a canonical **pattern** of four-turn request sequences in which utterances of the form *Can I have. . .?* occur as first turns. The same is true of forms like (20) that specify the ability and willingness conditions.

(20)   a.  Could you gimme a half-pint of the blackberry jam?
       b.  Would you gimme a half-pint of the blackberry jam?

In fact, Levinson's account covers so little territory, it cannot be said to be a genuine competitor to the accounts of Gordon and Lakoff and of Searle and Morgan. What is right about Levinson's account, however, is his attempt to bring accounts of indirect speech acts into line with accounts of more ordinary conversational practices.

## What utterances do

We are said to have an indirect speech act when the speaker employs an utterance with the illocutionary force indicators of one sort of act (usually, sentence type indicators) but means to perform some other act. Thus, *Can you pass the salt?* is said to be an indirect request because the utterance has the illocutionary force indicators of a question, but the utterance is being used to make a request. However, as Good (MS) has pointed out, the illocutionary forces of many indirect speech acts "are so transparent that to call them 'indirect' seems perverse" (p. 6). Anyone who has tried to teach the Searlean distinction to undergraduates will find, I think, that students have a very hard time grasping how it is that *I want a drink of water* or *Can I have a drink of water?* constitute **indirect** requests. In this chapter and in somewhat more detail in chapter 8, I shall offer a very different approach to indirect communication that is better founded theoretically and is of greater utility.

I have taken the position here that people can do either of two things with an utterance insofar as interaction structure conditions and domain predicates are concerned. They can posit values or request that values be posited. An utterance[7] like *I'd like a beer* posits the values "one" and "beer" for the "num" and "object" predicates of the domain of a thing-request and the value "true" for the initial-state condition (relative to this assignment of values to the num and object predicates). An utterance like *Would you like a beer?* also posits the

[7]   Of course it is speakers, not utterances, that do things. I shall however use this stylistically simpler way of writing.

132

values "one" and "beer" for the "num" and "object" predicates of the domain, but requests a value ("true" or "false") for the initial-state condition (relative to this assignment of values to the num and object predicates). If one person says *I would like something to drink* to another, he posits the value "true" for the initial-state condition of a thing-request and restricts the class of objects (things) to potables. In that context, *Would you like a beer?*, assumes that the initial-state condition is true for some instantiations of the "num" and "object" predicates, and asks whether the instantiations "one" and "beer" do make it true.

The thesis that what utterances (people) do is posit and request values for interaction structure conditions and domain predicates is essential for a straightforward computational approach to the generation and understanding of illocutionarily significant utterances, that is, utterances having transactional (interaction structure) significance. It also helps to shed light on issues that arise in connection with so-called indirect speech acts.

Within DSAT, it is argued that communicative interactions arise out of the initiator being in some initial state. The initiator may desire that the responder do something for the initiator (service encounters) or do something with the initiator (invitation interactions) or do something that will benefit the addressee (suggestion) or agree to wager a sum of money on the outcome of some sporting event (bet). In each case, there is a goal state – respectively, that the responder commit to doing something for the initiator or to doing something with the initiator or to doing something that benefits the addressee or to wagering money with the initiator – which is closely linked to the initial state. I shall take the position that if a person has a particular goal (e.g., obtaining money from the responder), then she will choose to initiate a type of interaction that has as its transactional effect the appropriate goal state (the responder commits to handing over the money) and which has acceptable interactional and social costs. Thus, she might choose to request a loan, rather than a gift, in order to maximize her chances of getting the money, and minimize the threat to her positive face and to her addressee's negative face. She might choose to request either a loan or gift over threatening the responder with bodily harm to avoid unwanted social costs (e.g., being arrested).

I shall further argue that we recognize another person's goal by recognizing what sort of interaction the initiator means to engage us in. This parallels exactly the traditional speech-act-theoretic position that we recognize people's goals by recognizing what speech act they are performing, as I noted in chapter 3. And, finally, I shall take the position that the key to recognizing what sort of interaction the initiator means to engage the responder in lies in identifying the initiator's initial state. Thus, I recognize that I should give you a beer by recognizing that you want a beer and that you expect me to satisfy this desire.

This way of looking at interactions yields an interesting approach to the identification of indirect speech act forms. As I have said, if I say *I'd like a beer* to you in your home in a circumstance in which it can be assumed that you have beers in your fridge, you will assume that I am positing the value "true" for the initial-state condition relative to the values "one" and "beer" for the "num" and "object" predicates of the domain of the thing-request interaction structure.[8] I would say the same of utterances like *I'll have a beer* or *I'll take a beer* if said to a bartender or to anyone who has just said something like *Can I get you anything to drink?*

Now, according to the traditional view, an utterance like *Can you reach the salt?* can be used either to request information (a direct speech act) or to request that the addressee get the box for the speaker (an indirect speech act). The question arises as to how addressees recognize the intent of the speaker.

There are, in fact, not one, but two distinct interpretations of a value-requesting utterance like this. In a context in which the speaker is attempting to determine whether the kitchen arrangements he has made for someone confined to a wheelchair are suitable and **it is clear that the speaker has no need for the salt** (i.e., the initial-state condition of the thing-request interaction structure is not true for the speaker for a domain in which the object predicate is instantiated with the value "salt"), but the speaker does **have an information deficit** with respect to the truth or falsity of the proposition, "You can reach the salt," the utterance will be understood as a request for information, i.e., a request that the addressee return the value "true" (= *yes*) if the value of "You can reach the salt" is true or the value "false" (= *no*) if this proposition is false. I shall refer to this as a "pure" information question, i.e., a question asked solely to gain information. The interrogative form of the utterance on this interpretation is due to the fact that it is value-requesting.

---

[8]   In other circumstances, the speaker might be conveying information, rather than requesting a beer.

Second, consider a context in which the speaker is eating and therefore might need the salt. Suppose, first, that the salt is up on a shelf behind the table and the speaker cannot be assumed to know whether the addressee can easily reach the salt. In this circumstance, the utterance *Can you reach the salt?* is not a pure information question but is requesting whether the value for the ability condition (i.e., "r is able to reach and pass the salt") of the thing-request interaction structure is true or false, and, at the same time, implicating that the initial-state condition is true (i.e., that the speaker desires the salt). In this circumstance, the speaker is requesting a value for the ability condition of the thing-request interaction structure and positing a value (albeit indirectly) for the initial-state condition. This is the second value-requesting reading for *Can you reach the salt?* The interrogative form of the utterance on this interpretation is also due to the fact that it is value-requesting.

Then, of course, there is the value-positing, indirect request reading. This reading arises in a context in which the speaker is eating and therefore might need the salt and it is clear that the addressee is physically able to reach the salt and pass it to the speaker. In this context, the speaker does not have an information deficit of any sort concerning the addressee's salt-reaching and passing abilities, and the utterance will be heard as communicating a desire for the salt, i. e., as positing the value "true" for the initial-state condition of the thing-request interaction structure relative to a domain in which the instantians for the object predicate is "salt." In this case, the interrogative form of the utterance is due to the fact that the speaker means to show deference to the addressee.

Thus, there are two readings for the utterance, *Can you reach the salt?*, in which it indirectly implicates a desire for salt, one in which the speaker cannot be expected to know whether the addressee is able to pass the salt (in which case the utterance requests a value for the ability condition of the thing-request interaction structure) and one in which he can. However, the implicature in question is quite automatic: **if an utterance by an initiator either posits a value or requests a value for any condition or domain predicate of an interaction structure, then it posits the value "true" for the initial-state condition of that interaction structure.** Should the utterance be consistent with more than one interaction structure (as would be true of an utterance like, *You doin' anything tonight?*, which could be prelude either to a request or invitation) then it automatically posits

135

the value "true" for the initial-state condition of each such structure. In this case, the addressee would assume that the speaker **either** wants the addressee to do something for her **or** with her.

In sum, there are actually three, not two interpretations of utterances like, *Can you reach the salt?* In the next chapter, I shall discuss how utterances like these are mapped into elements of interaction structures (in the case of the second and third readings) and in chapter 8, I shall develop further the DSAT approach to indirect communication.

## A cognitive approach to indirect speech acts

The thesis that conventions of use arise as a result of some sort of short-circuiting process is a historical thesis. Morgan suggested how short-circuiting might evolve in several cases, but did not, of course, provide attested cases involving indirect speech acts (with the exception of *Goodbye*). And Levinson has provided no historical evidence of short-circuiting either. I would like to cite an actual request routine that evolved between a colleague and me that comes a bit closer to providing historical evidence of short-circuiting, but evidence that points to a quite different mechanism of "short-circuiting" than those proposed by Morgan and Levinson. My discussion will also provide an illustration of how indirect speech acts are handled in DSAT.

At some point in the past, a colleague B and I (M) must have had a conversation along the lines of (21), where the event referred to at $T_1$ (the talk or faculty meeting, etc.) would normally end at around 5:00 p.m.

(21) Hypothetical conversation (the talk in question would have been a late afternoon talk)
    B: Are you going to the talk/faculty meeting/etc today? $T_1$
    M: Yeah, why do you ask? $T_2$
    B: I need a ride home. Could you give me one? $T_3$
    M: Where do you live? $T_4$
    B: Clintonville. $T_5$
    M: Sure, that's not far out of my way. $T_6$

(I specifically recall only my inquiry about where he lived, which is the only part of this conversation that is material to my argument.) Later on, we had a series of conversations identical in form to (22).

(22)   Actual B and M ride-requests
      B:  Are you going to the talk/faculty meeting/etc. today?   $T_1$
      M: Yeah, do you need a ride home?   $T_2$
      B:  Yeah, could you give me one?   $T_3$
      M: Sure.   $T_4$

We have an informationally richer context in the case of (22) than in the case of (21), for the question of where B lived had been answered and my willingness in principle to take this indirect way home had been established. The importance of this cognitive context is clear. Had another colleague or a student asked me, *Are you going to the talk today?*, it is most unlikely that I would have replied *Yeah, do you need a ride home?*

This sort of request routine might have evolved into a classical instance of an indirect speech act like (23) though it never did.

(23)   Hypothetical conversation
      B:  Say, could you give me a ride home after the talk/faculty
           meeting/reception, etc. today?
      M: Sure.

Since my willingness in principle to give this colleague rides home had been established, all he needed to know to employ an indirect request like this is that I was, in fact, going to this talk or faculty meeting.

These examples illustrate the critically important fact that **the more we know, the less we have to say.** But, of course, if we are to exploit this fact, we must move to a cognitively based account of conversational interactions such as that provided in DSAT. I would like to suggest that after the first ride-request interaction, B and M each stored a particularized ride-request interaction structure along the lines of (24).

(24)   B and M ride-request interaction structure
      Effects:
              Transactional: r commits to do A
              Interactional:
                      threatens r's negative face
                      potentially threatens i's positive face.
      Initial-state condition: i desires r to do A
      Satisfaction conditions:

137

r is able to do A
    If:

           possess(r, car) [T, <Contextual Given>]
           be-at(r, $p_1$, 5:00 p.m.) [?]
    r is willing to do A [T, <Contextual Given>]
Domain(A):
    action(ride)
    provider(r)
    receiver(i)
    instrument(car)
    depart-time(5:00 p.m.)
    depart-place($p_1$)
    CAMPUS-LOCATION($p_1$)
    arrive-place(B's-Clintonville-Home)

Given this representation, and assuming that it was psychologically salient during the period these conversations took place, it is quite easy to see why M might hear utterances making a reference to his being at some campus location in late afternoon as a possible ride-request, for two sets of domain predicates bear on this, "depart-time(5:00 p.m.)" and "depart-place($p_1$) & CAMPUS-LOCATION($p_1$)," both of which bear on the truth of the uninstantiated precondition, "be-at(r, $p_1$, 5:00 p.m.)."

It is only if we assume that B and M had a stored interaction structure along the lines of (24) that we can explain why M was so easily able to recognize B's goal and therefore was in a position felicitously to say, *Yeah. Do you need a ride home?* Notice, now, that all that would need further be assumed to account for the classical indirect speech act form (23) is that B also believe that the value of the precondition "be-at(r, $p_1$, t)" of the ability condition was true (i.e., believe that M was going to be at the talk or faculty meeting at the time in question). In that circumstance, both the ability and willingness conditions could be assumed to be true, and all that B would need to do at that point is signal his desire for a ride. Virtually any indirect speech act request form could be used in such a circumstance, including *I need a ride home after the talk today, Could I have a ride home after the talk today?, Could you give me a ride home after the talk today?, Would you give me a ride home after the talk today?), How about a ride home after the talk today?*, for each of these, in this context, would equally communicate B's desire for a ride home.

Similarly, a request like *Can you pass the salt?* would normally be made by one dining partner to another where it is clear that the addressee is willing to do salt-passing (a normal consequence of an agreement to dine together) and able to do salt-passing (as would be true of most persons, of course). In such a circumstance, all that the speaker need do is identify what it is that she wants and it hardly matters how she does this so long as what she says (or does) involves a reference to salt consistent with wanting it, such as *I need the salt, Would you pass me the salt?, How about the salt?, The salt, please,* as well as *Can you pass the salt?* (or just pointing to the salt).

The point that speech act theorists have missed is that context is more important than form or literal meaning in our ability to use single utterances to do so complex a thing as requesting people to do things for us. All that is required of the utterance is that it posit values for all interaction structure conditions and domain predicates not contextually instantiated (including, instantiated as a result of prior interactions).

## The question of conventionalization

Recall that Searle and Morgan took the position that only certain linguistic forms have indirect speech act potential. As I understand this position, a sentence like *Can you reach the salt?* can be used while dining (the occasion) to request the salt because sentences having that form, namely the form "*Can you* [action predicate]," are conventionally understood as communicating requests.

The view of Searle and Morgan is quite seriously defective, if it is taken to mean that it is forms like "*Can you* [action predicate]," **taken as a whole,** that are conventionally associated with making requests, for as I noted in chapter 2, we can use sentences of the form *Can you do A?* to perform a wide variety of acts. I repeat the examples for ease of reference.

(25)  a. Can you reach that book? [Request]
      b. Can you eat more cake? [Offer]
      c. Can you come over tonight? [Invitation]
      d. Can you get off my fucking foot? [Menacing Request Threat]
      e. Can you clean and jerk as much as Sandy? [Question]

139

Sentences (25a)–(25d) all specify the ability condition on some interaction and are fully colloquial.[9] Given the account of Searle and Morgan, they must all be said counterfactually to have indirect request potential. Obviously, what the speaker is doing in each case depends on the *L*-Meaning of the action predicate and the context. From this it clearly follows that we do not have a simple knee-jerk association of particular forms and particular speech acts in the case of sentences like (25a)–(25d) of the sort that Searle's and Morgan's analysis, and that of Levinson's as well, suggests we have. Nevertheless, there is clearly something about the forms of (25a)–(25d) that is conventionalized.

Within DSAT, the most natural assumption is not that there is a conventional association of these forms and particular speech acts, but between a conventional association of these forms and elements of interaction structures. What is wanted, then, is some device that is capable of mapping these forms into the interaction structure conditions they specify. Given such an account, we would have the best feature of Gordon and Lakoff's account (for a connection is seen between the utterances in question and felicity conditions, i.e., conditions on interaction structures) and the best feature of the account of Searle and Morgan (for the forms of these utterances are treated as involving conventionalization of form for use) without suffering the defects of either account. In the next chapter, I provide such a mapping for a representative class of forms found in requests and other similar types of interactions.

9   Sentence (25e) differs from the others in that the presence of *can* does not result from the fact that the utterance specifies the ability condition of DSAT interaction structures. Instead, this utterance is semantically compositional, with *can* being a modal realization of the same predicate that underlies the adjective *able*.

# 6

# *Conventions of use*

## Introduction

The strongest argument that has been given in support of the thesis that indirect speech acts involve conventions of use – a pairing of a context of use and a purpose with a particular linguistic form – has been that close paraphrases of indirect speech act forms do not seem to have the same force as their models. Thus, although *Do you want to open the door?* can be used to request someone to open a door, *Is it your present desire to open the door?* normally cannot, or so it is claimed.

That there is conventionalization of form for function in the case of typical indirect speech act forms is demonstrated by the fact that (a) the conventional meanings of many such forms are arguably not compositional functions of the usual meanings of their parts, that (b) such sentences exhibit severe restrictions on combinations of auxiliary elements and main verbs that cannot be accounted for semantically, and that (c) there is no univocal semantic correlation between the sentence type of the utterance and the transactional work it does. Thus, in a case when a speaker says *Can I have a hot chocolate?* in a cafe by way of placing an order for a hot chocolate, (a) the meaning of the whole utterance is not a compositional function of the meanings of the words that comprise it (certainly not if *have* is said to mean "possess"), (b) the verbs that can be employed in the slot occupied by *have* are restricted to *have* and *take* when the utterance is being used in thing-request service

141

encounters (encounters in which what is wanted is some thing or routine service like a massage or haircut), and (c) the utterance is being used in a value-positing, as opposed to a value-requesting way (where the interrogative form is being used to show deference to the addressee). In short, the speaker is not asking whether or not she can possess hot chocolate when she says *Can I have a hot chocolate?*, but rather (as we shall shortly see) she is communicating that she wishes to select hot chocolate from among some set of options available in that context.

Utterances like these raise three very interesting, interrelated problems. The first is what semantic representation should be assigned to such utterances? The second is how are they generated? The third is how do addressees go about interpreting such utterances? In this and the next two chapters, I propose answers to these questions and illustrate them with an account of colloquial forms used in request interactions. The heart of my proposal is that we employ a device that maps semantic features, pragmatic meaning features (derived from interaction structure conditions and domain predicates), and politeness, style, and register features into linguistic features that determine the forms of the utterances. The device that effects this mapping I will call the "pragmatic stratum."

Within this framework we account for utterance generation and understanding in the same terms. In generation, the input is a set of semantic features, interaction structure-specific meaning features, and discourse, politeness, style, and register features that is mapped into a set of linguistic features. In understanding, these same linguistic features are mapped into the corresponding semantic features, interaction structure-specific meaning features, and discourse, politeness, style, and register features from which the addressee would recover not just the intended transactional significance of an utterance but also its intended interactional significance.

What I am proposing here is novel and I have no illusions concerning the ultimate correctness of the details of the account of the data I shall be considering. However, I submit that the approach is sufficiently sound to warrant the attention of computer scientists, pragmaticians, semanticians and others who have an interest in providing formal and/or computational accounts of conventions of use, including how they are generated and understood.

## The nature of the problem

The data of (1), all of which can be used to make requests in isolation and occur in multiturn request sequences, exhibit some of the evidence for conventionalization sketched above.

(1)   a. I'd like a hot chocolate.
      b. I want a hot chocolate.
      c. I need a hot chocolate.

Observe, for instance, that it is difficult to say what the *L*-Meaning of (1a) is. The principal problem lies in the modal *would*, which occurs in cliticized form in this utterance.

There are hypothetical or conditional occurrences of *would* in which it is accompanied by a conditional clause or other conditional adverbial, as (2) illustrates.

(2)   a. I would like a hot chocolate if it weren't so bitter.
      b. I would want a hot chocolate were I not so warm.
      c. I would need a hot chocolate if I were cold.

Indeed, if such a conditional adverbial is not present in sentences such as these, the result is normally an unacceptable sentence or one that is felt to be incomplete as (3) illustrates.

(3)   a. *I would like a hot chocolate. [*would* is the same *would* as in (2a)]
      b. *I would want a hot chocolate.
      c. *I would need a hot chocolate.

The exceptions to this latter generalization are examples like (1a), colloquial utterances which instantiate the initial-state condition of interaction structures. The point is that *would* is not hypothetical or conditional in this sentence, which is not to say, of course, that it is not historically related to conditional *would*.

Let us refer to the *would* we find in (2) and (3) as the conditional modal *would* and to the *would* we find in (1a) as the initial-state condition modal *would*. Normally, the former must occur with a conditional clause or phrase but the latter must normally occur without such a clause or phrase. While (2a) is perfectly grammatical and makes perfectly good sense, no one would use it to place an order for hot chocolate.

There are exceptions to the claim that utterances like (1a) do not occur with conditional clauses, as the data of (4) evidences.

(4)  a. I would like a hot chocolate if you don't mind.
    b. I would like a hot chocolate if it's not too much trouble.

However, in these cases the *if*-clause is a politeness conditional: it does not articulate a condition on the speaker's having a desire for hot chocolate and it is normally understood that the success of the request (or other communicative action) is not contingent on the addressee not minding or not finding the act requested to be too much trouble (especially in retail contexts). In these cases, the *if*-clause is what Geis and Lycan (forthcoming) call a "nonconditional conditional" and seems to be present in order to redress the negative face-threat associated with the request.

We have strong evidence then that the initial-state condition *would* of (1a) and (4) is different in conventional meaning from the conditional modal *would*. Secondly, we find that in utterances instantiating the initial-state condition, *like* occurs only with *would* (cf. (5)) whereas neither of the other verbs in (1) (also initial-state condition verbs, I will argue) can occur with *would* in requests (cf. (6)).

(5)  a. #I will like a hot chocolate.
    b. #I could like a hot chocolate.
    c. #I might like a hot chocolate. (infelicitous used actually to place an order for hot chocolate)
    d. #I like a hot chocolate.

(6)  a. #I would want a hot chocolate.
    b. #I would need a hot chocolate.

None of the sentences of (5) or (6) would make a natural request initiation. The point is not that these sentences are ungrammatical or even nonsensical, but simply that they are not used in interactions in which (speaking informally) we make requests, invitations, proposals, or perform other communicative actions sharing the same initial-state condition.

What we have here is a pragmatic co-occurrence relationship: when the initial-state predicate "desire" is being lexicalized with *like*, as opposed to *want* or *need*, for some politeness reason, the auxiliary is restricted to *would*. We need therefore some way of mapping pragmatic meaning elements – in this case, the initial-state predicate "desire" – and certain politeness features into linguistic features (e.g., those required to generate *would* with *like*) if we are to account for these facts.

The question arises as to what sort of meaning representation should be assigned to an utterance of a sentence like (1a). I submit that in so far as this utterance has *L*-Meaning at all, it is identical to its *S*-Meaning when being used in service encounters and invitations, and therefore its propositional content is identical to that of the initial-state condition. This is in accord with the supposition that the point of saying (1a) is to instantiate this condition (i.e., posit the value "true" for this condition). According to this view, the propositional content of (a) is as is represented in (7), where "i" is a designated discourse referent[1] (variable) referring to the initiator of a interaction.

(7)   $(\exists i)(\exists t)(\exists y)(\text{desire}(i, y, t)$ & hot-chocolate$(y)$ & num$(y, 1)$ & $\text{at}_{\text{time}}(t, \text{now})$

As we have seen, a datum like (1a) illustrates two of the properties of colloquial request forms: their conventional meanings are either obscure or, at least, are not compositional functions of the normal meanings of their parts, and they evidence pragmatic co-occurrence relations holding between auxiliary elements and main verbs. Examples (1b) and (1c), however, differ from (1a) in that they are, or, at least, seem to be, semantically compositional. Thus, if I say I want a hot chocolate then it will be understood that I have a present desire for a hot chocolate or if I say I need a hot chocolate and I have spoken truthfully, it will be true that I need a hot chocolate. However, in the case of utterances like these, when they are being used in service encounters and other similar interactions by way of specifying the initial-state condition, *want* and *need* are restricted to occurring in the present tense and this restriction is pragmatic. Forms like those in (8) would not normally occur in service

---

[1] The notion "discourse referent" is drawn from Discourse Representation Theory. I begin to use it now to anticipate my demonstration of how DSAT can be incorporated in this theory.

encounters or invitation routines in English in efforts to assert that the initial-state condition holds.

(8)   a. #I wanted a hot chocolate.
       b. #I would want a hot chocolate.
       c. #I could want a hot chocolate.

In Italian, on the other hand, when the verb lexicalizing the initial-state condition occurs, it seems to be either in the imperfect tense (*volevo*), as in (9), or in the conditional mood (*vorrei*), as in (10), not the present tense (*voglio*).[2] Thus, we find the forms (Gavioli and Mansfield 1990):

(9)     Eh volevo sapere se avevate: "The sun's net" di: George Mackay Brown. (I wanted to know if you have "The Sun's Net" from George Mackay Brown)
(10)   Vorrei sapere se avete "Practica de español para extranjeros". (I would want to know if you have "Practica de español para extranjeros".)

This very striking difference between Italian and English provides strong support for the thesis that conventions of use, not conventions of meaning, are at work here.

Forms like (1b) and (1c) are clearly different in *L*-Meaning. However, we must not assume therefore that the speaker's selection of one over the other is always or even normally predicated on this meaning difference *per se*. Since, normally, we want what we need and need what we want, we are free to represent our desire for something as our wanting it or our needing it. If I want to build a saw horse, I will need some two-by-fours. When I go to a hardware store to get these two-by-fours, I could say either *I want five three-foot two-by-fours* or *I need five three-foot two-by-fours*. Either would be accurate and the *L*-Meaning difference between them would normally be largely irrelevant transactionally to utterance choice. In such a case, I argue, it is the difference in their interactional effects, rather than their difference in *L*-Meaning that determines which verb will be selected.

A child who wants a new bike might say either *I want a new bike* or *I*

[2]   I am indebted to Michela Shigley-Giusti for pointing out these facts to me. It is her understanding that Italian is moving increasingly in the direction of the imperfective form.

*need a new bike* to her parent but most children learn early on that the latter is the more effective form. Saying *I need a new bike* suggests that one's desire for a bike arises out of a bike-deficit of some sort over which one has no control (e.g., the old bike no longer works properly) whereas saying *I want a new bike* suggests that the desire for the bike is ego-motivated. For this reason, *I want a new bike* sounds a good deal pushier than *I need a new bike*; it suggests something on the order of "my wish is your every command."

Three questions arise at this point.

- What pragmatic features (interaction structure-specific meaning features and politeness, style, and register features) are critical to distinguishing the different forms of (1)?
- What factors go into a speaker's choice of one form over others?
- How can the relevant pragmatic features be mapped into linguistic features?

The first question can be pursued to some degree employing the standard techniques of linguistic research, including distributional analysis, as we have seen. Thus, there is syntactic evidence supporting the thesis that (1b) and (1c) form some sort of class, for they both are restricted to the present tense in colloquial service encounters, whereas (1a) occurs with the modal *would*. And there is semantic evidence supporting a grouping of (1a) and (1b), for they employ verbs that are much closer in meaning than either is to (1c). Once we have grouped conventionalized forms into different sets based on pragmatic evidence of the sort discussed above, we can then turn to consider what features should be posited by way of defining these classes.

Though we can make progress in understanding what pragmatic distinctions are relevant to conventions of use of the sort illustrated by (1a)–(1c), the features we use to define the relevant classes will need interpretations as to their psychosocial significance (i.e., as to their conditions of use). Determining what the psychosocial significance of style and politeness features is will require a great deal of empirical research (observation of the choices people make in particular contexts of use) and experimentation. This sort of research has not been done, nor will it be easy to do. However, if we are to make progress on the third question – the question of how features of context are mapped into linguistic forms – we must postulate some sort of interpretation here. I trust that it will be understood that the interpretations I assign to politeness features are therefore speculative.

The device I shall employ to effect the mapping of semantic features, interaction structure-specific meaning features, and politeness, style, and register features into linguistic features is an inheritance hierarchy,[3] that is a rooted tree in which there are two types of branchings from mother features to daughter features – exclusively disjoined branchings[4] and inclusively disjoined branchings.[5] Any given feature can have two or more mothers, from which it follows that branches can cross each other. Associated with any pragmatic feature can be a set of linguistic realization rules and/or semantic realization rules. In a pragmatic inheritance hierarchy, the features are pragmatic features, the linguistic realization rules map these pragmatic features into grammatical features, and the semantic realization rules map these features into discourse referents and associated predicates (conditions). The hierarchy is said to be an inheritance hierarchy because a feature inherits its own realization rules and any realization rules associated with any ancestor feature.

In a computational model of utterance generation, the pragmatic stratum lies at the interface between the utterance planner and the grammar in that it maps the output of the planner into linguistic features. Manifestly, the form and content of the pragmatic stratum will be determined in part by assumptions about what planner output features and what grammar features will be available. In developing the present pragmatic stratum, I assumed the existence of a systemic grammar (cf. Halliday 1985), for that was what was available in my computational work. However, any type of grammar that employs features and is capable of integrating syntactic, semantic, and pragmatic information (which is, of course, the strength of systemic grammar) can be employed. I have assumed a planner of the sort described in Patten, Geis, and Becker (1992). Since relatively few readers will be familiar with systemic grammar, I shall employ relatively transparent grammatical features of the sort that might be

---

[3] I am indebted to my former colleague Terry Patten for instructing me as to the value of inheritance hierarchies in accounting for compiled linguistic, including pragmatic, knowledge. Michael Halliday in his work on systemic grammar was the originator of this approach.

[4] In the case of exclusively disjoined branchings, the mother node is a system feature (as opposed to a pragmatic feature) and only one of its daughters is selectable.

[5] In the case of inclusively disjoined branchings, the mother node is a pragmatic feature and the daughter nodes may be either system features or pragmatic features. Any number of daughters can be selected.

found in a phrase-structure grammar in the realization rules presented here. It should be understood, however, that the only implementation that has been tested computationally is the systemic implementation.

We can model the effect of mapping linguistic features into interaction structure-specific meaning features by employing the Discourse Representation Structures (DRS) of Discourse Representation Theory (Kamp and Reyle 1993, Asher 1993), a dynamic semantic theory capable of dealing with pragmatic phenomena.

Discourse Representation Theory (DRT) is one of several approaches to the theory of meaning (especially of what I am calling "*L*-Meaning") that are dynamic in the sense that they see the meaning of an utterance as being a function from contexts to contexts (Asher 1993: 63). From this perspective, the meaning of a specific utterance is treated as a function from the context that exists prior to the occurrence of the utterance in the discourse to the context that results from its occurrence.

DRT is primarily a theory of utterance interpretation, as opposed to utterance production. It is assumed that associated with any conversation is a Discourse Representation Structure (DRS) which is constructed via a set of Discourse Construction Rules that map utterances into the elements that comprise DRSs, specifically, discourse referents and discourse conditions (cf. Kamp and Reyle 1993: 63ff). Let us illustrate this with several examples drawn from Kamp and Reyle.

According to Kamp and Reyle (p. 64), the first of the two sentences of (11) is to be assigned the DRS representation of Figure 3.

(11)  Jones owns Ulysses. It fascinates him.

In this DRS, in which it is assumed that the variables "x" and "y" are existentially quantified, "x" and "y" are discourse referents and "Jones(x)," "Ulysses(y)," and "x owns y" are discourse conditions. It is built up by recursively applying discourse construction rules, including, in particular, a rule for proper nouns, to the phrase structure representation associated with the sentence, *Jones owns Ulysses*.

In the case of the second sentence, *It fascinates him*, we find two definite pronouns. These are respectively linked to the discourse referents "x" and "y" by pronoun-specific discourse construction rules. The result is the DRS of Figure 4.

```
┌─────────────────┐
│    x  y         │
│                 │
│  Jones(x)       │
│  Ulysses(y)     │
│  owns(x, y)     │
└─────────────────┘
```

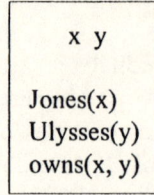

Figure 3.   The DRS for *Jones owns Ulysses*

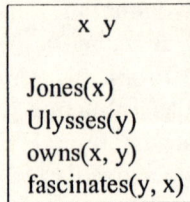

```
┌─────────────────┐
│    x  y         │
│                 │
│  Jones(x)       │
│  Ulysses(y)     │
│  owns(x, y)     │
│  fascinates(y, x)│
└─────────────────┘
```

Figure 4.   The DRS for discourse (11)

Discourse referents introduced in antecedents of conditional sentences cannot serve as anaphors for subsequent definite pronouns and definite noun phrases. Consider

(12)   If John caught a fish, he ate it. *It was a redfish.

In sentence (12), the first *it* is in the scope of the conditional operator and (speaking quite informally) can refer back to *a fish*. The second *it* is not in the scope of the conditional and it cannot refer back to *a fish*. Because of this difference in how the two *its* are treated, it is necessary to distinguish the discourse referents inside the scope of the conditional from those that are outside. I shall follow Kamp and Reyle in representing a conditional like that in (13) after the manner of Figure 5.

(13)   Sandy eats eggs. If Terry cooks fish, Kim eats steak.

DRS 3 consists of a **main** DRS containing the discourse referents "x" and "y" and two **inner** DRSs linked by the conditional operator "⇒" in which we find the discourse referents "w," "z", "u," and "v." These latter discourse referents cannot serve as anaphors for a

150

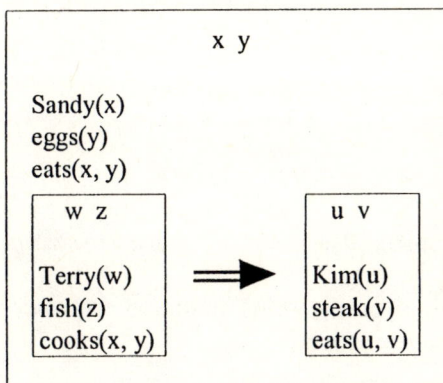

Figure 5.   The DRS for discourse (13)

subsequent definite pronoun unless they are in the scope of a related conditional operator.[6]

In preceding chapters, representations were provided that can easily be converted to DRS. Compare representation (14), for instance, with DRS (6), which is the DRS for the sentence, *I want a hot chocolate.*

(14)   Initial-state condition: i desires o
       Domain(o):
              object(hot chocolate)
              num(1)

As in the case of (7), I will employ the designated discourse referent "i." I will take the DRS of Figure 6 to represent the *S*-Meaning of utterances like *I'd like a hot chocolate, I want a hot chocolate,* and *I need a hot chocolate* when occurring in typical service encounters.

## A mini-treatment of communicative actions

My focus here shall be on service encounters in which initiators are attempting to cause another person to provide them with some thing. However, many of the forms employed in service encounters of this type occur in utterances employed in other types of interactions. In (15a) and (15b) we find present+*want* and *would like* realizing the

---

[6]   In the minidiscourse, *If John caught a fish, he ate it. It would have been a redfish,* would functions to bring the second *it* under the scope of the original conditional operator.

```
┌─────────────────────┐
│        i, y         │
├─────────────────────┤
│  desires(i, y, now) │
│  hot-chocolate(y)   │
│  num(y, 1)          │
└─────────────────────┘
```

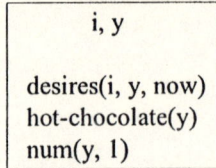

Figure 6.   The DRS for *I want a hot chocolate*

initial-state condition predicate of invitation sequences and of information exchanges, respectively.

(15)   a.   I want you to come to a party next week.
      b.   I would like to know what their names are.

In general, forms available to the initiator are also available to the responder. Note that we have responder utterances corresponding to each of the forms in (1):

(16)   a.   Would you like a hot chocolate?
      b.   Do you want a hot chocolate?
      c.   Do you need a hot chocolate?

The sentences of (16) would traditionally be referred to as offers. However, in DSAT, where the notion "offer" has no official status, they are treated simply as responder uses of the initial-state condition. Ideally, we would want to account for both (1) and (16) with the same pragmatic net (inheritance hierarchy). However, since the focus of my research has been almost exclusively on initiator utterances (because it is the initiator of such encounters who has the most interesting politeness choices), I am not in a position to guarantee that this is fully possible (though it clearly is to some degree).

    Let us assume that interactions are differentiated with respect their goals. Since service encounters and invitation interactions both have as a goal that the responder perform some action, they will be grouped together (under the feature "goal=action") and differentiated from information exchanges (goal=information). Goal=action interactions are then differentiated into invitation interactions and two types of service encounters, thing-requests and action-requests, under the

152

system feature "S_SERVICE-ENCOUNTER." These divisions are given in Figure 7.

The subnet of Figure 7 contains two types of features – pragmatic features, which are contained in ordinary rectangles, and system features, which are contained in the rectangles with rounded ends. System features cannot serve as the output of the planner (i.e., are not preselectable pragmatic features) and serve to dominate a set of nodes only one of which is selectable. On the other hand any number of pragmatic or system features dominated by a pragmatic feature can be selected. Given this part of the net, to generate a thing-request, one must preselect "thing-request."

Of special importance to us here is the distinction between thing-requests (e.g., *I want a hot chocolate* or *Could you give me a hot chocolate?*) and action-requests (i.e., *Leave now!* or *Could I ask you to take this to the office?*), for the distinction has syntactic consequences in that thing-requests must contain a verb and an object (and may also contain an indirect object if the utterance is resp-centric, as in *Give me a hot chocolate*). Thus, any time the feature "thing-request" is preselected, the net dictates that the verb will be transitive. The linguistic realization rule "VP[transitive]," in which "transitive" is a head feature, guarantees this. In utterance generation anything that appears in a sentence must be stipulated to occur either through pragmatic or semantic preselections. There are no optional constituents. Thus, preselecting the feature "thing-request" will cause there to be a transitive occurrence of relevant verbs (e.g., *want, need, like, have, take, give, pass*, etc.).

## Politeness

The level of politeness of a form is a function of a large number of factors including the nature of the interaction in which the participants are engaged, the discourse role of the speaker (Init or Resp, for the initiator and responder, of course), the relationship of the speaker to the addressee along social power and social distance dimensions, the way in which the speaker goes about redressing any face-threats associated with the actions in the interaction, and the level of formality employed. I shall assume here that three factors are at work in making politeness choices: the social power relationship between the initiator and the responder, the social distance between the initiator and the responder, and the degree

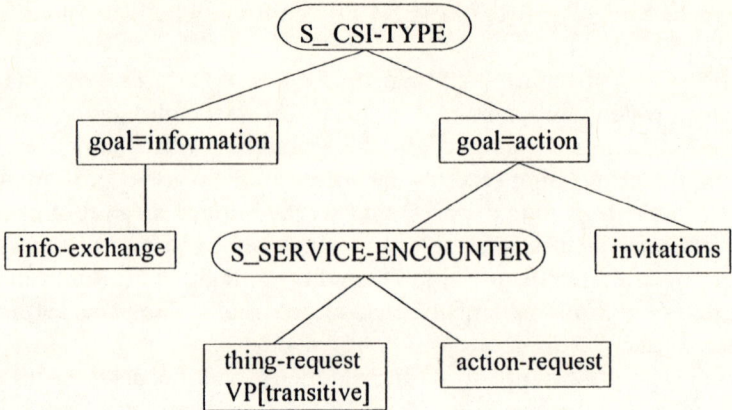

Figure 7.   The interaction structure net

to which the someone committing an FTA means to redress the face-threats.

Certain forms represent the initiator as having greater social power than the responder and will be referred to as "init-up" forms. The contrasting feature is no-init-up. I would argue, for instance, that the initiator who says (1a) or (1b) (i.e., uses *would like* or present+*want*) suggests that simply communicating a desire for something is sufficient in the context to cause the addressee to provide what is wanted. This is appropriate when the initiator has greater social power than the responder. Thus, a boss could say, *I want you to finish this report today*, as opposed to, *I need for you to finish this report today*, without engendering resentment in an employee in most cases. But the employee who frames a request to the boss with init-up forms like *I want a raise* or *I want a larger office*, as opposed to *I need a raise* or *I need a larger office*, runs some risk of giving affront to his boss. (As is so often the case with language use, however, intimates may often use power forms without giving offense, at least in routine requests. Thus, in some circumstances, init-up forms are available among equals who are intimate.)

A second distinction I shall draw is between resp-up and no-resp-up forms. I shall argue that present+*want* and present+*need* forms (no-resp-up) show less respect for the responder than does the vestigially conditional resp-up *would like* form. Note that *I want a raise* and *I need a raise* are more assertive than *I would like a raise*. Similarly,

154

note how peremptory an invitation like *I want you to come over for dinner tonight* sounds in contrast with *I'd like for you to come over for dinner tonight*. I presume that the more power a person enjoys in a given context, the more free she is to say, *I want NP*. (But, again, choice of such a form between intimates can be a sign of intimacy.)

A third distinction I shall draw on concerns forms that show deference (and will be interrogative if the initiator is the speaker) and those that do not. A deferential init-speaker utterance (*Can I have a hot chocolate?*) is one that treats the responder as having an option whether to satisfy some need of the speaker, where a non-deferential form (*I'll have a hot chocolate*) does not. Similarly, *Would you give me a hot chocolate?* is deferential in that it suggests that the addressee could refuse while *Give me a hot chocolate* is not.

The politeness choices just discussed are presented in Figure 8, where the mother nodes of these separate branchings is a system feature which is itself a daughter of the root node of the stratum as a whole.

It should be noted that each of these politeness features is used to define a contrast between two classes of forms and therefore has a relative, as opposed to an absolute interpretation. I shall assume that init-up, no-resp-up, and no-deference are default values, that is that initiators, in the default circumstance, do not display politeness – that "being polite" is something that speakers must **choose** to do. As we shall see, this has some interesting implications concerning which forms are said to be the more basic ones.

*Orientation*

In addition to the politeness options of Figure 8, the initiator has orientation options, which themselves have politeness implications. There are two basic orientations – an init-centric orientation exhibited by the utterances of (1) and thing-specific utterances like *I'll have/take a hot chocolate,* and a resp-centric orientation exhibited by forms like *Give me a hot chocolate* or *Could you give me a hot chocolate*. All other things being equal (which they rarely are), resp-centric utterances, in which the subject is *you* if the initiator is the speaker (except in the imperative), are more polite than init-centric utterances, in which the subject is *I* when the initiator is the speaker. The basic orientation choices are given in Figure 9. The features "init-centric" and "init-oriented" are default choices.

155

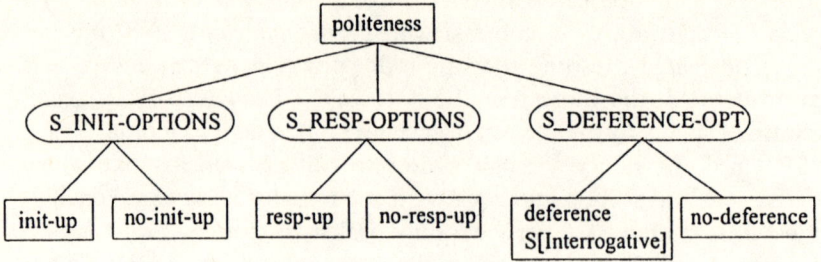

Figure 8.   The politeness net

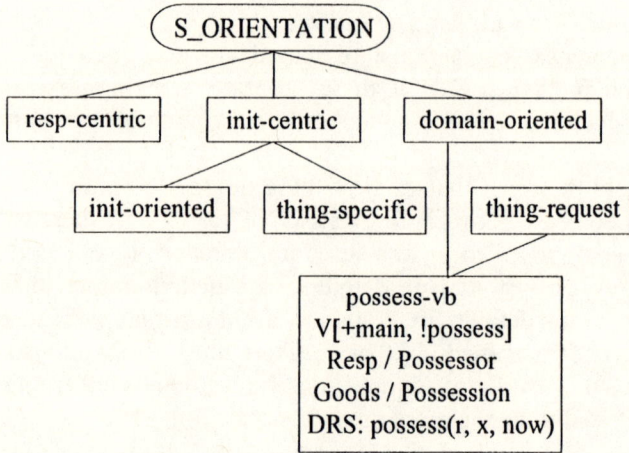

Figure 9.   The orientation net

### INIT-CENTRIC FORMS

I shall take the position here that each of the utterances of (1) instantiates the initial-state condition and shall refer to such utterances as being init-centric. This assumption allows us to account for the fact that their subjects refer to the initiator no matter whether the initiator or the responder is speaking: in both *I'd like a hot chocolate* and *Would you like a hot chocolate?*, *I* and *you* both refer to the same discourse participant, namely the initiator, the person who will be receiving the hot chocolate. In this, they are like the forms, *I'll have/ take a hot chocolate* and *Can I have/take a hot chocolate?*, which are also init-centric.

This assumption will also allow us to account for the fact that the verbs in these sentences enjoy certain implicative relationships. There is, for instance, an implicative relationship between *like* and *want* (we normally want what we like and like what we want) and an implicative relationship between *need* and *want* (we normally want what we need and (think we) need what we want). There is also an implicative relationship between forms like *I'll have/take a hot chocolate* and *I want/ would like/need a hot chocolate*. We account for these implicative relationships automatically by mapping each of these forms into the initial-state condition.[7] No Gricean reasoning or axioms are required, an essential feature of any computational approach to implicature, for Gricean reasoning (assuming, surely counterfactually, that it could ever be made explicit enough to be implemented computationally) would involve a multistep chain of reasoning inconsistent with rapid language processing (by machines or humans).

Among the init-centric forms, it is necessary to differentiate init-oriented forms (*I want/would like/need a hot chocolate*) from thing-specific forms (*I'll have/take a hot chocolate*). This is necessary because the two sets of forms exhibit quite different syntactic properties and pragmatic co-occurrence relations, have substantially different DRS discourse conditions associated with them (as we shall see), and occur in somewhat different slots in conversations.

*Init-oriented utterances*    Although we have deferential, value-positing uses of thing-specific forms like *Can I have a hot chocolate?* (versus the non-deferential *I'll have a hot chocolate*) and resp-centric forms like *Would you give me a hot chocolate?* (versus the non-deferential *Give me a hot chocolate*), we do not have deferential, value-positing variants of (1). Thus, we would never say any of the forms in (17) in a value-positing, deferential way (i.e., by way of placing an order for hot chocolate).

(17)   a.   Would I like a hot chocolate?
       b.   Do I want a hot chocolate?
       c.   Do I need a hot chocolate?

There do exist value-requesting uses of sentences like these, but we do not use such utterances to place orders in retail stores (and so they are

[7]   This would presume a pointer from the feature "init-centric" to the initial-state conditions of all interaction structures.

157

not instances of init-oriented sentences). I would argue that the decision by the initiator to employ an init-oriented utterance reflects so ego-centric an orientation as to be inconsistent with a significant redress of the face-threat (except to the degree that employing the form *would like* allows).

We may reasonably expect that the factors of social power and social distance would be critical to a speaker's choice between these forms. Except when responding to inquiries specifically about what one wants, which would license forms that might otherwise be impolite, the speaker who uses *would like* or present+*want* communicates that he enjoys power over or is an intimate of the addressee. The speaker who uses present+*need*, on the other hand, suggests that the addressee is superior in power to or is an equal of the speaker.

I shall therefore treat an initiator who chooses *would like* or present+*want* as acting out a presumption of intimacy or power (init-up), whereas the speaker who chooses present+*need* makes no such presumption (no-init-up). Treating *would like* and present+*want* as realizations of the feature init-up and present+*need* as a realization of no-init-up is consistent with the fact that *would like* and present+*want* are more similar in meaning to each other than either is to present+*need*, but that is not my primary reason for doing so.

As we saw earlier, there is a compelling syntactic reason for linking present+*want* to present+*need*. If we can say that they form a pragmatic class, we can account for the fact that they both occur in the present tense in the forms of interest to us. In treating (1a) and (1b) as forming a class apart from (1c), we were focusing on how the initiator represents himself (or is represented by the responder) in the interaction. However, (1b) is like (1c) and different from (1a) in how the initiator represents the responder's position in the interaction. The initiator who says (1b) or (1c) is treating the responder with less respect than is the initiator who employs the vestigially conditional form (1a). Note, in this connection, that (18a) is a bit more natural than (18b) and (18c), which, I suggest, follows from the fact that the aggressive character of present+*want* and present+*need* is inconsistent with the mitigating expression *if you please*.

(18)  a.  I would like a hot chocolate, if you please.
     b.  ?I want a hot chocolate, if you please.
     c.  ?I need a hot chocolate, if you please.

In my view, (1a) sufficiently defers to the responder to be a species of deferential form. However, since the deference feature has consequences for sentence type, I shall employ the feature "resp-up" for this form and "no-resp-up" for the other forms.

I shall assume that the lexicon of the language is organized in the form of a thesaurus, much like Roget's International Thesaurus, and that the verbs *like, want, need, desire,* and some others as well, are in the class defined by the thesaurus feature "!desire." I shall further assume that the linguistic realization rules of the pragmatic stratum can consist of thesaurus features like "!desire," unifications (e.g., Init/Experiencer),[8] politeness features (e.g., init-up and no-init-up), style features (e.g., formal and informal), register features (e.g., thing-request), and node-admissibility conditions (e.g., VP[+modal]), and that there is a DRS realization rule "desire(x, y, now)," which works in conjunction with the unification rules to associate arguments with argument positions of discourse conditions. Given these assumptions, we may summarize what has been said about init-centric sentences in the subhierarchy of Figure 10.

In this and subsequent networks, if lines from two or more features converge at a point, this means that each of the parent features must be preselected for the daughter feature to be selected. Some of these might, of course, be defaults, and need not be expressly preselected. Given this network, if we preselect the features "init-oriented," "init-up," and "resp-up" this will force selection of "cond-desire" and the sentence that ultimately results will have a modal as the head of the predicate, for "+modal" will be treated as a head feature.

The linguistic realization rules associated with the "init-oriented" stipulate that there will be a main verb that is in the semantic class named by "!desire" ("!" serves as a prefix for thesaurus features). There are two additional syntactic stipulations, each associated with the two different subclasses of init-oriented sentences. One subclass consists of cases in which the predicate is headed up by a modal (the *would like* case) and a second in which the predicate is headed up by a non-past finite verb (present+*want/need*). The combination of the

---

8   The unification "Init/Experiencer" unifies the pragmatic, Init role, with the semantic, Experiencer role. These unifications play an important role both in utterance generation and utterance understanding. The person referred to by the discourse referent "i" has the Init role inherently with the person referred to by "r" having the Resp role. The semantic and syntactic roles used here are those of the systemic grammar implementation. Obviously those who hold to different conceptions of semantic roles/themes would want to formulate these unifications somewhat differently.

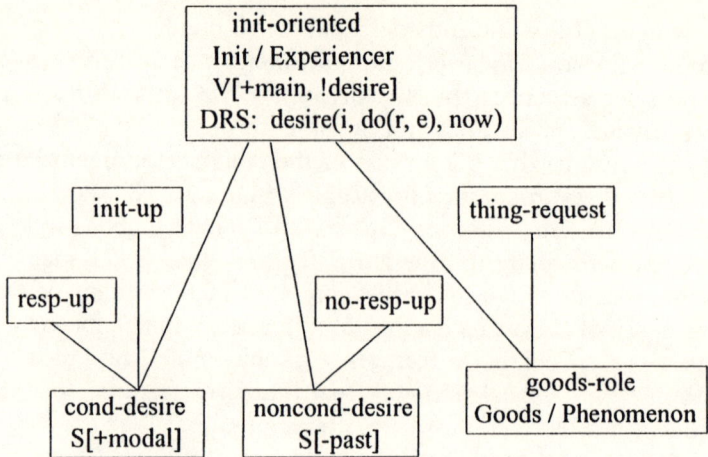

Figure 10.   The init-oriented net

realization rules associated with the pragmatic features "init-oriented" and "cond-desire" is to be interpreted as restricting the predicate to a modal and main verb, thereby forcing a predicate structure like that of Figure 11.

The combination of init-oriented and no-resp-up forces a predicate structure in which there is only one verb, a finite main verb. In designing the pragmatic stratum, I am assuming, as one must in working in utterance generation, that no constituent may appear in an utterance unless it is stipulated to occur via some pragmatic or semantic choice. Thus, there will be no intervening aspectual verbs in any sentence generated through this part of the stratum.

In the subhierarchy of Figure 10, we also find a unification rule "Init/ Experiencer" that unifies the pragmatic role of "Init" (an interaction structure discourse role associated with the DRS discourse referent "i") with the semantic role of "Experiencer" and a rule unifying the register-specific pragmatic "Goods" role with the semantic role "Phenomenon," where "Goods" are understood in relevant contexts to be transferables (often sellables) or, in the case of reified actions, as doables (e.g., massages and haircuts). These unifications are critical to language understanding, as well as generation. Thus, in the systemic grammar the Phenomenon role is unified with the surface syntactic Object role, so this unification and the one in the subnet given above effect a link between what is the goods of a transaction with the syntactic object of the verb in init-oriented sentences.

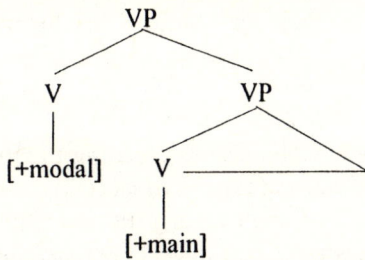

Figure 11. The subtree for *would like* predicates

Let us assume further that the thesaurus contains the lexical information in (19) for the main verbs we have been considering, and (20) and (21) for the modals *can, could, will,* and *would.*

(19)   !desire {[Experiencer –], [– [Phenomena]}
     a.   *like*: +main, informal, init-up, resp-up
     b.   *desire*: +main, formal, init-up, no-resp-up
     c.   *want*: +main, informal, init-up, no-resp-up
     d.   *need*: +main, informal, no-init-up, no-resp-up

(20)   !volitional
     a.   *would*: +modal, resp-up
     b.   *will*: +modal, no-resp-up

(21)   !ability
     a.   *able*: +adjective, . . .
     b.   *could*: +modal, resp-up
     c.   *can*: +modal, no-resp-up

In (19), we find the thesaurus feature "!desire" and "[Experiencer –]" and "[– [Phenomena]," which identify the thematic roles (using systemic roles) of the logical subject and logical object, respectively. These are the semantic equivalent of syntactic subcategorization rules. I presume that the grammar is capable of unifying these thematic roles with surface syntactic roles: in the case of (1), the grammar will have to unify the Experiencer role with the Subject role and the Phenomenon role with the Object role.

Also note that I treat the *will/would* and *can/could* distinctions as being like the distinction between *want* and *need*, namely as a no-resp-up/resp-up distinction. This seems right, for forms like *Would you open the door?* and *Could you open the door?* display more respect for the responder's positive face than do *Will you open the door?* and *Can you open the door?*

In the case of utterance generation, feeding the pragmatic stratum (cf. (22)) the feature "init-speaker" (which is necessary to cause the Init role to be realized as *I*, instead of *you*) and "thing-request," and setting the Goods role equal to whatever *a hot chocolate* is said to mean in the system being used, will result in generation of *I want a hot chocolate*, for the features init-oriented, init-up, and no-resp-up are defaults, as noted earlier.

(22)   a.   init-speaker
        b.   thing-request
        c.   Goods = {a hot chocolate}

(The declarative form of the sentence must be dealt with by stipulating that init-speaker, init-oriented forms are necessarily declarative.) Adding "resp-up" to the above input file will give us *I would like a hot chocolate*. Adding "no-init-up," instead, would yield *I need a hot chocolate*. I have designed the pragmatic stratum in this way because I see the initial-state condition as being the ur-condition for any communicative interaction and see the utterance that most closely instantiates this condition as the best candidate for a default form. As this example illustrates, if properly designed, the pragmatic stratum, working in concert with a feature-driven grammar, can accomplish utterance-generation in the case of conventionalized forms with the stipulation of very few pragmatic features.

If the pragmatic stratum is to effect a mapping between pragmatically determined elements of DRS representations and syntactic forms, there must be some way of associating DRS construction rules with elements of the stratum. I shall assume that there exists a parser that, given a sentence like *I want hot chocolate*, will set the syntactic object role to the value "hot-chocolate," that is, to a particular linguistic form. Since the lexicon stipulates that the logical argument of !desire predicates has the Phenomenon role, the grammar will be forced to unify the Object role with the Phenomenon role. The pragmatic stratum will, in turn, unify the Phenomenon Role with the Goods role. This accounts for the fact that whatever discourse referent and DRS condition is associated with the surface object *hot chocolate* in some commercial or gratis transaction will be construed as the Goods in that transaction.

These unifications conspire with the representation "desire(i, y, now)" to effect assignment of the predicate "hot-chocolate" (the Goods in this interaction) to a discourse referent "y," which, given the thesaurus representation "[– [Phenomena]" in (19) and the unification "Goods/Phenomenon," will be a DRS constituent that plays the pragmatic "Goods" role. In general, we may assume that pragmatic, as well as semantic, roles will play a significant part in effecting assignments of discourse conditions to particular discourse referents.

In the case of *I* and *you*, forms that refer to participants of communicative interactions, the pragmatic stratum plays a critical role in construction of the DRS, for it is important to know whether a given occurrence of *I* or *you* refers to Init or Resp. The pragmatic stratum stipulates, as presently designed, that if we have an init-oriented sentence the Init role is unified with the Experiencer role (which will itself be unified with the syntactic Subject role). The following DRS construction rules are required.

(23)  a.  In any utterance in which some constituent plays the Init pragmatic role, insert the designated discourse referent "i" into the DRS (where "i" is modeled by the individual who is Init in the discourse).

   b.  In any utterance in which some constituent plays the Resp pragmatic role, insert the designated discourse referent "r" into the DRS (where "r" is modeled by the individual who is Resp in the discourse).

Given the DRS condition associated with init-oriented utterances (namely, "desires(i, y, t)") and these DRS construction rules, the init-oriented sentences of (1) will be mapped into the DRS of Figure 6 above.

There are two very important payoffs within the system being advanced here. First, bits of utterances that evidence conventions of use are vastly easier to generate than those bits that do not, for in the former case short-cuts are available that are not available in semantic generation. In order to generate the *I want* part of *I want NP*, all we need to say is that the sentence is an init-speaker, thing-request utterance. The pragmatic stratum supplies the additional features, "init-centric," "init-oriented," "init-up," and "no-resp-up," as defaults. Generating the "NP" part is a great deal more difficult for that must be done semantically.

There is also a substantive payoff in utterance understanding. When fed a form like *I would like NP*, for instance, *would* would be paired initially both with the conditional modal *would* and with the initial-state condition modal *would* of (20a), and *like* would be paired initially with a representation appropriate to its ordinary conventional meaning, where it is loosely paraphrased by "positively evaluate," and the representation in (19a). This results in four surface combinations: both the conditional and initial-state *would*s would be paired with both the !desire and !positively-evaluate instances of *like*. Of these, only the pairing of initial-state *would* and !desire *like* or conditional *would* and !positively-evaluate *like* will result in a well-formed DRS. However, the conditional modal *would* would require some sort of completing conditional phrase or clause, which is not present, and the pairing of the conditional modal *would* and !positively-evaluate occurrence of *like* will therefore fail. This leaves us with only the correct interpretation according to which *would* is the initial-state *would* and *like* is the !desire *like*.

Utterance understanding is greatly facilitated in any context, as in a retail sales context, in which the utterance employs a referential expression that refers to something that counts as Goods, as would be true of *hot chocolate* in the retail context, for that will entail that we have a thing-request thanks to the unification of Goods with Phenomenon. This will force the !desire reading of *like* and the initial-state reading of *would* in the case of *I would like a hot chocolate*. And, it is worth emphasizing again that since the pragmatic stratum maps all of the sentences of (1) into the same DRS (in the case of thing-requests), we do not require inferencing of any sort to account for the implicative relationships that hold between these forms. This represents a significant advance over Gricean accounts (which presuppose computationally expensive reasoning) and allows us to capture generalizations of the sort that motivated the Gordon and Lakoff account of indirect speech acts. However, no meaning postulates are required.

*Thing-specific forms*     Thing-specific utterances like (24) and (25), like those of (1), are ego-centric when spoken by the initiator, from which one might conclude that they too are init-oriented and serve to signal a speaker desire for something.

(24)  a.  I'll have a hot chocolate.
      b.  I'll take a hot chocolate.

(25)  a.  I'll have a haircut today.
      b.  I'll take a back rub today.

However, there is good reason to believe that they play a more specialized role in conversations than do the other init-oriented utterances.

As the data of (26) reveal, the init-oriented forms we just considered do not necessarily presume that the responder has what is desired (i.e., is able to provide what is wanted).

(26)  a.  I'd like four widgets. Do you have any?
      b.  I want four widgets. Do you have any?
      c.  I need four widgets. Do you have any?

On the other hand, as the oddness of forms like (27) and (28) shows, thing-specific utterances clearly do presume the availability of what is wanted.

(27)  a.  #I'll have four widgets. Do you have any?
      b.  #I'll take four widgets. Do you have any?

(28)  a.  #I'll have a haircut. Do you offer them?
      b.  #I'll take a back rub. Do you do them?

Similarly, init-oriented forms do not presume the willingness of the responder to satisfy a request.

(29)  a.  I'd like four widgets. Would you give'm to me?
      b.  I want four widgets. Would you give'm to me?
      c.  I need four widgets. Would you give'm to me?

Thing-specific forms like (30) and (31) do.

(30)  a.  #I'll have four widgets. Would you give'm to me?
      b.  #I'll take four widgets. Would you give'm to me?

(31)  a.  #I'll have a haircut. Would you give me one?
      b.  #I'll take a back rub. Would you give me one?

Thing-specific forms differ from init-oriented forms in another way. As we have noted, we sometimes employ the interrogative form, not to request information (a value-requesting use), but for politeness reasons (a value-positing use). If the initiator knows that the responder is willing and able to satisfy a desire for a hot chocolate, the initiator can say *Would you give me a hot chocolate?* or *Could you give me a hot chocolate?*, not to inquire redundantly about something the initiator already knows, but to display deference by way of redressing the face-threat associated with the request in suggesting that the responder has an option whether or not to comply with the request. Similarly, an utterance like (32) can be used in a value-positing, deferential way when the willingness and ability of the responder to satisfy the request is a given.

(32)   Can I have a hot chocolate?

Similar cases with *take* require special contexts. I think one might be able to use (33) in a value-positing, deferential way in a bakery where a set of cookies is sitting on a plate in easy reach of the customer and marked for sale.

(33)   Could I take three of these?

Declarative (value-positing) thing-specific forms, unlike init-oriented forms, normally occur in contexts in which options are made available to the initiator from among which the initiator is invited to choose. They are a very commonly used form in frozen yoghurt stores and other contexts in which what is offered for sale is fully evident to the initiator. When this sort of information is not evident at the outset of a request sequence, such forms do not initiate requests. They can, however, occur after this information is made evident.

As was noted on page 86 of chapter 4, thing-specific forms are restricted to what I am calling thing-requests in which the objects of the verbs *have* and *take* refer to things (cf. (24)) or reified actions (cf. (25)), but not with action predicates generally (cf. (34)).

(34)   a.   *I'll have your cutting my hair today.
       b.   *I'll take your rubbing my back today.

This represents a register restriction.

In cases in which the object is a thing, *have* clearly doesn't mean "possess" – (35) is not equivalent in meaning to (24a).

(35)   I'll possess a hot chocolate.

Even less plausible is the idea that *have* means "possess" in the case in which the object refers to a reified action. Note that (36) is quite nonsensical.

(36)   *I'll possess a back rub.

Instead, *have* and *take* mean something like "select" in thing-specific forms, as one might expect from the fact that they tend to be used only when what is available is known and it is known that one can have what is wanted. This constitutes a clear case of a discourse restriction on use of *have* and *take*. The relevant discourse context can be characterized as one in which a certain class of objects or services are routinely made available or have come to be known to be available, which are, of course, the sorts of contexts in which we could use *select*. Note how similar the forms of (37) are transactionally.

(37)   a.   I think I'll select the red one.
      b.   I think I'll take the red one.
      c.   I think I'll have the red one.

I shall take the position here that (37b) and (37c) would be favored over (37a) in informal speech contexts and that (37b) and (37c) differ in politeness. In my view, initiating a request with *take* is rather pushier than would be using *have* and I shall therefore treat *take* as being an init-up form and *have* as a no-init-up form.

That conventionalization of form for function is involved in thing-specific forms couldn't be clearer. The *have*-form is not semantically compositional unless we say that *have* has !select as one of its conventional meanings and even if we do say this, then we shall be forced to say that both *have*-forms and *take*-forms predicate **future** actions (selectings) by the initiator, when in fact, the actions in question are being performed through uttering the sentences. In short, *I'll have the red one* means not "I will select the red one at some future time" but something more like "I hereby select the red one." Thus, if we are to account for these forms in a compositional semantics we must say both that *have* and *take* mean !select here and that *will* is to be interpreted as referring to the time of utterance. These are not promising hypotheses.

A second reason to believe that these forms are pragmatically conventionalized is that they exhibit pragmatic co-occurrence relations between auxiliary elements and main verbs. The verbs *have* and *take* are restricted to occurring with the modal *will* in declarative, value-positing utterances like (24) and (25). The forms in (38) and (39) cannot be used in a value-positing utterance in which the speaker means to identify what it is she desires when doing requesting.

(38)　a.　#I can have a widget.
　　　b.　#I would have a widget.
　　　c.　#I might have a widget.

(39)　a.　#I can take a widget.
　　　b.　#I would take a widget.
　　　c.　#I might take a widget.

On the other hand, when we have an interrogative form like (32) the modal is restricted to *can/could* and *may/might* in cases in which the utterance is used in a value-requesting way (as when the speaker is unsure whether the desired thing or action is available) or in a deferential, value-positing way (i.e., when the speaker knows the desired thing or action is available but is using the interrogative form to redress the face-threat). The data of (40) and (41) illustrate this point.

(40)　a.　Can/Could I have that?
　　　b.　May/Might I have that?
　　　c.　#Will/Would I have that?
　　　d.　#Shall/Should I have that?
　　　e.　#Must I have that?

(41)　a.　Can/Could I take that?
　　　b.　May/Might I take that?
　　　c.　#Will/Would I take that?
　　　d.　#Shall/Should I take that?
　　　e.　#Must I take that?

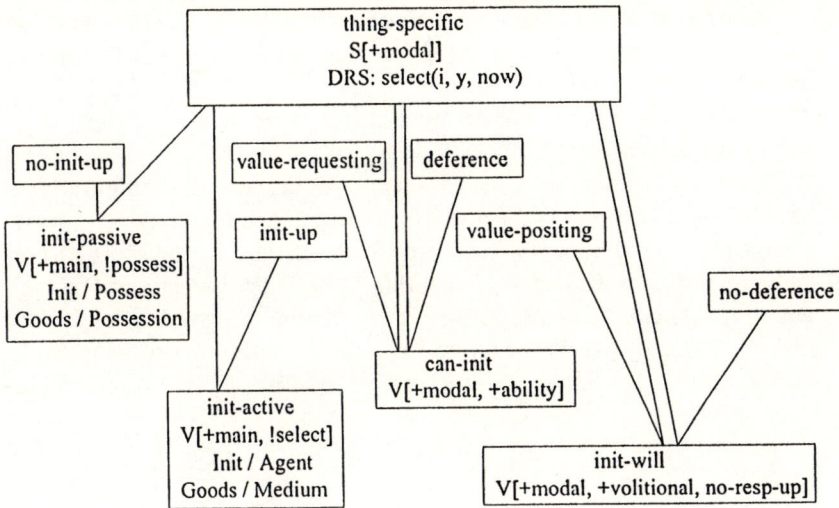

Figure 12. The thing-specific net

The above observations (excepting those involving *may* and *might*) are captured in Figure 12.

We shall also need thesaurus representations (20) and (21) and (42) and (43).

(42)  !select {[Agent –], [– [Medium]}
    a.  *take*: +main, init-up, informal
    b.  *select*: +main, init-up, formal

(43)  !possess {[Possessor –], [– Possession]
    a.  *have*: +main, no-init-up, informal
    b.  *get*: +main, [+past-part], informal

The claim being made is that *take* is in the subnet of the thesaurus defined by !select, while *have* is in the subnet defined by !possess. I am not saying that *have* means "possess" in thing-specific sentences. Indeed, I would argue that it makes no sense to ask what *have* means or, for that matter, what *will* means in a sentence like *I'll have a hot chocolate*. What matters in the case of an utterance exhibiting pragmatic conventionalization is what the utterance **as a whole** means, and that is determined in this case by the DRS realization rule "DRS: select(i, y, now)" found in Figure 12.

The verb *have* of *I'll have a hot chocolate* is linked in the thesaurus to the *have* of *I have a broken foot* for syntactic reasons, for the two *haves* have the same syntactic properties. Neither tolerates the passive construction, as ⋆*A hot chocolate will be had by me* and ⋆*A broken foot is had by me* evidence.

The stratum restricts all thing-specific utterances to configurations like the trees of Figures 11 and 13, for these are the smallest phrase structures consistent with the stratum. According to this part of the stratum, *I'll have NP*, will be generated via the preselections of (44), with "no-deference" and "no-resp-up" being supplied as defaults, and *I'll take NP* will be generated via the preselections of (45), with "no-deference," "init-up," and "no-resp-up" being supplied as defaults.

(44)  a.  init-speaker
     b.  thing-specific
     c.  value-positing
     d.  no-init-up

(45)  a.  init-speaker
     b.  thing-specific
     c.  value-positing

We get the forms *Can I have NP?* and *Can I take NP?* simply by adding the preselection "deference" to these lists. In value-requesting occurrences of the latter utterances, the feature "value-requesting" would occur in place of "value-positing" and "deference" would be irrelevant (and have a null effect even if preselected).

The section of the thesaurus for the !select class of verbs treats its objects as playing the Medium role, which is a semantic role. The Medium role is unified in the pragmatic stratum with the pragmatic role of "Goods" and with the surface Object role in the grammar. We might illustrate how this works by considering a case in which a customer comes into a store and says *I'll take a hot chocolate*. In this case, *a hot chocolate* (or more precisely the subtree associated with it) will be set equal to the Object role. Since we have both the modal *will* and the verb *take*, the only parsing that will survive in this register will be one in which the Object role is unified with the Medium role in the grammar and the Goods role in the pragmatic stratum, which is consistent with the fact that hot chocolate counts as a sellable. The

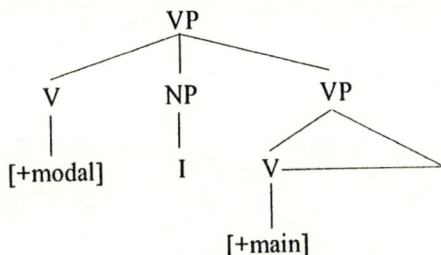

Figure 13.   The subtree for deferential thing-specific utterances

parsing according to which this utterance predicates a future act of acquiring hot chocolate would be excluded on register grounds in that in this context, we are concerned with present acts of selecting, not future acts of acquiring things *gratis*, which is what *I'll take a hot chocolate* suggests on a literal interpretation. In the case of *I'll have a hot chocolate* or *Can I have a hot chocolate?*, "a hot chocolate" will be set equal to the Object role. The Object role will be unified with the Possession role in the grammar and with the Goods role in the pragmatic stratum. In either case, as in the case of *I'll take a hot chocolate*, the resulting DRS will be that of Figure 14.

The function of thing-specific utterances is to instantiate the initial-state condition with respect to certain domain predicates, and, as a consequence, the speaker will be understood as placing an order when they are value-positing (i.e., when the clerk is reasonably sure that the customer is not suffering an information deficit, as will be clear in many contexts, of course). This "understanding" is facilitated by the fact that the pragmatic stratum maps thing-specific utterances into the pragmatic feature, "init-centric," which, in a computational implementation, would point to the initial-state condition.

I draw attention again to the fact that declarative (*I'll have a hot chocolate*) and interrogative (*Can I have a hot chocolate?*) value-positing thing-specific sentences, though they have dramatically different conventional meanings, will have precisely the same transactional effect in certain contexts of use, and this fact can be accounted for given the present pragmatic stratum without appealing to some sort of (inevitably informal and therefore problematic) Gricean calculation. This follows, as noted, from the fact that they are both init-centric

$$\boxed{\begin{array}{l} \text{i, y} \\[4pt] \text{hot-chocolate(y)} \\ \text{num(y, 1)} \\ \text{select(i, y, now)} \end{array}}$$

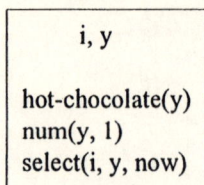

Figure 14.   The DRS for *I'll take hot chocolate*

utterances. This account is consistent with the fact that the transactional effects of such utterances are instantly recognized, which is of psychological and computational importance and should, I would argue, be of importance to a theory of conversational competence. Instant recognition of the intent of a speaker is evidence, I would argue, of computation, but little or no calculation in Grice's sense of the term.

### RESP-CENTRIC UTTERANCES

Resp-centric forms like (46)–(49) are forms specifying interaction-structure satisfaction conditions.

(46)   a.   Give me a hot chocolate.
      b.   Will you give me a hot chocolate?
      c.   Would you give me a hot chocolate?

(47)   a.   Open the door.
      b.   Will you open the door?
      c.   Would you open the door?

(48)   a.   You can give me a hot chocolate.
      b.   Can you give me a hot chocolate?
      c.   Could you give me a hot chocolate?

(49)   a.   You can open the door.
      b.   Can you open the door?
      c.   Could you open the door?

Note that all of these forms, including the interrogative forms, can be used *sui generis* to make so-called "indirect requests," from which it follows that they have value-positing uses.[9] However, if the initiator is in doubt as to the willingness or ability of the responder to perform some act, then the initiator could use the interrogative forms in a value-requesting way as well. In the former case, we are dealing with deference forms, that is, questions intended to show deference, as was true of value-positing, thing-specific utterances like *Can I have a hot chocolate?*.

The forms in (46) and (48) involve thing-requests. As in the case of init-oriented and thing-specific utterances, we have resp-centric utterances in which reified actions are the "things" in question. The sentences of (50) provide evidence of this.

(50)  a.  Give me a back rub.
      b.  Could you give me a haircut today?
      c.  Would you give me a ride to the airport?

In these forms, as in the case of (46) and (48), *give* seems to mean "provide," either "provide for compensation" (i.e., "sell") or "provide gratis" if uttered to a friend who is one's host. And *give* could be replaced by *provide* in most such utterances with essentially the same transactional results though the resulting utterances would be heard as being relatively formal in style.

Resp-centric forms fall into two major classes, resp-willingness cases like (46) and (47) and resp-ability cases like (48) and (49). There is unquestionably a meaning difference between these two classes of forms that would be of transactional significance when the initiator is confident in the ability of the responder to perform some action, but not his willingness, or conversely, and chooses to inquire about it. However, there are other circumstances in which the choice between these two classes of forms must be based on politeness considerations, specifically when the willingness and ability of the responder to perform some action are both evident and the utterance

---

[9]  I shall take the position here that though an utterance may employ a resp-centric form, when any resp-centric utterance is being employed in a value-positing way, it actually instantiates the initial-state condition. The basic idea is that when an utterance is value-requesting and resp-centric the initiator is genuinely trying to determine whether the responder is willing or able to do what is wanted. However, when the initiator has reason to believe that the responder and initiator have a mutual belief that the responder is willing or able to do what is wanted, any resp-centric utterance will be interpreted as communicating a desire for something, that is, will be interpreted as instantiating the initial-state condition. In this circumstance, the choice of a resp-centric form would reflect a politeness choice to frame the utterance in an exo-centric fashion.

will therefore be value-positing. In either case, whether for politeness reasons or because one is in doubt about the responder's willingness or ability to do what is wanted, either the feature "resp-ability" or "resp-willingness" must be preselected.

As in the case of init-oriented and thing-specific forms, we find significant conventionalization of form for function in the case of resp-centric forms, especially in thing-requests. First note that the verb of choice is *give*, rather than any of its close paraphrases (e.g., *provide*, *transfer*, etc.) even though the transaction may be commercial (in which case no gift is involved). Second, the range of modals that can occur in such sentences is highly restricted. We get *can* and *could* and *will* and *would*. Forms like those in (1) do not occur as colloquial request forms.

(51)  a.  #May you give me a hot chocolate?
      b.  #Might you give me a hot chocolate?
      c.  #Shall you open the door?
      d.  #Should you open the door?

Finally, of course, there is the fact that we get value-positing, interrogative resp-centric forms and a resp-ability, value-positing declarative form (49a) that is highly conventionalized. In Figure 8 above, I associated the interrogative form with the pragmatic feature "deference." This accounts for value-positing uses of the interrogative forms of (46)–(49). The imperative form of (47a) and declarative form of (49a) will be treated as no-deference forms. Certainly they are the least polite of the forms in their respective classes.

The contrast between the *realis* modals (*will/can*) and the *irrealis* modals (*would/could*), though of semantic importance in many types of sentences, is not of semantic importance in the case of value-positing, deferential, resp-centric utterances. As we saw in the case of *would like*, *would* is clearly not hypothetical in meaning in forms like (46c) and (47c) if an entailment of *would*'s being hypothetical is that it must occur with an actual or contextually understood conditional adverbial, as is the case with clear cases of semantically hypothetical *would*. Sentences like (46c) and (47c) are clearly not elliptical for forms like those in (52) and (48c) and (49c) are not elliptical versions of forms like those in (53).

(52)  a.  Would you give me a hot chocolate if I had enough money/
          I asked politely/etc.?

174

  b.  Would you open the door if your arm weren't broken/I
      were to need you to/etc.?

(53) a.  Could you give me a hot chocolate if I had enough money/I
      asked politely/etc.?
  b.  Could you open the door if your arm weren't broken/I were
      to need you to/etc.?

In the thesaurus representations of (20) and (21), I treated the
distinction between *would/could* and *will/can* as involving a face-redress
contrast, with the former being resp-up forms and the latter no-resp-
up forms. I based this on my intuition that the *can* and *will* forms seem
to take for granted the compliance of the responder whereas the
corresponding *could* and *would* forms leave this open.

This intuition is supported by the fact that hedge items like *possibly*
and *perhaps* seem very slightly more natural in utterances with the
relatively more hedged modal *could* than with *can*, as the contrast in
naturalness of the pairs in (54) and (55) suggests.

(54) a.  Could you possibly give me a hot chocolate?
  b.  Can you possibly give me a hot chocolate?

(55) a.  Perhaps I could give you three.
  b.  Perhaps I can give you three.

I would explain this (admittedly quite subtle) difference as due to the
fact that utterances that don't mix levels of politeness (or style, for that
matter) sound more natural than those that do.

In order to account for the basic patterning of resp-centric
utterances, we need the subnet in Figure 15. In order to account for
the fact that *give* is the verb of choice in resp-centric thing requests (cf.
the pragmatic feature "provide-vb"), we must provide the lexical
representation of (56) for !provide verbs.

(56) !provide {[Agent –], [– Medium, Recipient]}[10]
  a.  *provide*: formal
  b.  *give*: informal

---

[10]  The notation "[– Medium, Recipient]" is meant to indicate the predicate takes, in
      addition to the Agent argument, a Medium argument (i.e., logical object of a certain
      type) in second argument position and a Recipient argument in third argument position.

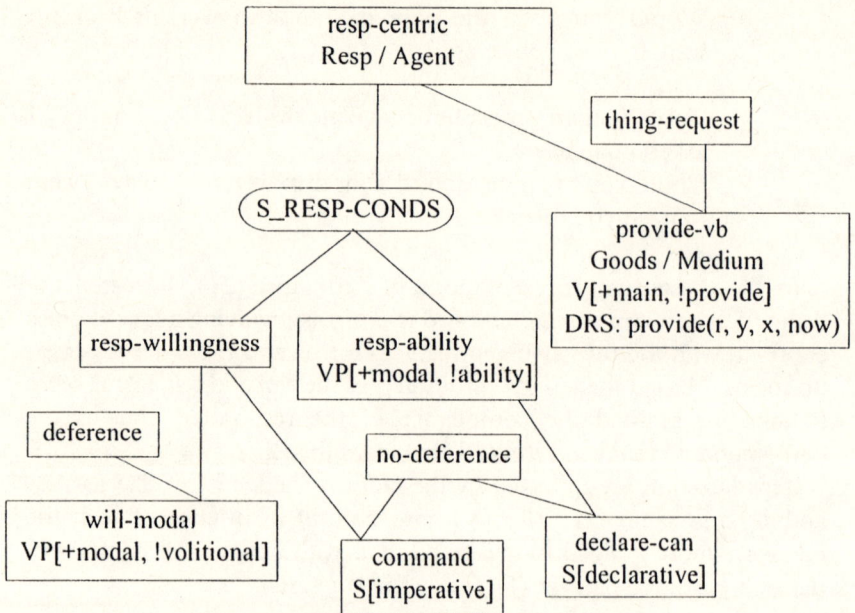

Figure 15. The net for resp-centric utterances

Thus, when we hear an utterance like *Could you give me a hot chocolate?*, since one of the possible thesaurus entries for *give* is (56b), we have a surface form consistent with the realization rules of provide-vb. This entails that the utterance, on this interpretation, will be a resp-centric thing-request. It is important to note that no inferencing will be required to recognize that the initiator wants the responder to provide her with some thing, whether the utterance is understood in a value-requesting or deferential, value-positing way.

## SUMMARY

I offer now a summary of the value-positing (i.e., indirect speech act) forms treated in this section and a list of the minimal input preselections (other than init-speaker, value-positing, and thing-request, which are shared by all) required to handle them, assuming that init-oriented, init-centric, init-up, no-resp-up, and no-deference are defaults.

(57)   a.   I want NP. {nil}
       b.   I need NP. {no-init-up}

   c.   I would like NP. {resp-up}
   d.   I'll take NP. {thing-specific}
   e.   I'll have NP. {thing-specific, no-init-up}
   f.   Can I take NP? {thing-specific, deference}
   g.   Could I take NP? {thing-specific, resp-up, deference}
   h.   Can I have NP? {thing-specific, no-init-up, deference}
   i.   Could I have NP? {thing-specific, no-init-up, resp-up, deference}
   j.   Give me NP. {resp-willingness}
   k.   Will you give me NP? {resp-willingness, deference}
   l.   Would you give me NP? {resp-willingness, resp-up, deference}
   m.  You can give me NP. {resp-ability}
   n.   Can you give me NP? {resp-ability, deference}
   o.   Could you give me NP? {resp-ability, resp-up, deference}

As noted earlier, form (57a) is being treated here as the most basic request form and (57j) as the most basic resp-centric form. This goes against the standard view that (57j) is a direct request form while (57a) is indirect. However, there is no credible concept of directness that favors the view that (57j) is the most direct request form.[11] The fact that we have a special sentence type in the case of (57j) is irrelevant, for, as Austin noted, imperative forms can be used to do things other than make requests. The claim that (57a) is more basic than (57j) is based on the fact that the simplest inheritance hierarchy for request forms (I have been able to devise) favors such a view and the fact that it most directly instantiates the ur-condition of service encounters (and other interactions), namely the initial-state condition.

Those who are troubled by this result should perhaps consider that all of the forms in (57) are equally automatically generated in utterance production and none of these forms requires inferencing in any form in order for their transactional and interactional significance to be recognized. They are equally conventionalized request forms.

## Domain-oriented utterances

One additional class of utterances requires treatment if we are to account for typical instances of thing-requests of the sort we have

---

[11] I shall discuss the DSAT distinction between direct and indirect communication in chapter 8.

considered in previous chapters, namely, such init-speaker questions like those in (58), which are often used to initiate thing-requests.

(58)  a.  Do you have hot chocolate?
      b.  Do you have Marlboro Lights?

These utterances, which I shall term "domain-oriented" utterances, are normally value-requesting when interrogative and value-positing when declarative, and involve efforts of participants to cause the domain to be sufficiently saturated that the request can be acted on.

The verb of choice in domain-oriented utterances is *have*, which is not to be confused with the *have* of thing-specific utterances. As we saw in chapter 2, *have* can be taken in at least three ways in sentences like (58), depending on the nature of the object. If the object refers to a sellable (a hot chocolate), then it will be taken as asking whether the clerk has this sellable available for sale now. Should it refer to a useable (a rest room), it will be heard as asking whether the clerk has available a rest room for the use of the questioner. In my view, when the participants are in a retail sales register and the customer employs an utterance like (58a), *have* will be taken to mean 'possess,' but it will be recognized that the customer has initiated a retail sales thing-request interaction and thus that the customer wants to purchase a hot chocolate. According to this analysis, we do not actually have to associate a special sense with the verb *have* to account for the have-for-sale uses.

The subjects of domain-oriented utterances are determined by who is speaking, as in other cases. In Figure 9, I noted that domain-oriented thing-request utterances will branch to the feature "possess-vb." This will result in an utterance which contains the verb *have*. Note that the DRS predicate associated with this sort of occurrence of *have* is "possess(r, x, now)." In addition, we must have the following thesaurus information.

(59)  !possess {[Possessor –], [– Possession]}
      a.  *have*: domain-oriented, informal
      b.  *got*: domain-oriented, casual

## Utterance form

The fragment pragmatic stratum sketched above accounts primarily for the pragmatic co-occurrence relationships between auxiliary elements and verbs, and for sentence type in many cases. One omission is the stipulation that init-speaker init-oriented utterances must be declarative.[12] We will also need a semantic treatment of sentence type to account for value-requesting uses of thing-specific and resp-centric utterances and for all domain-oriented utterances.

## Subjects and objects

I turn now to consider the issue of how subjects and objects are generated in pragmatically conventionalized forms. The net being offered here contains no resp-speaker forms. However, were we to have such forms, (60) would account for occurrences of *I* and *you* in subject position in a grammar (such as the systemic grammar that the computational implementation of PGB employs) in which features like "speaker-subject" and "hearer-subject" immediately determine the forms of first and second person pronoun subjects.[13]

(60) a. (((resp-centric ∨ domain-oriented) & resp-speaker) ∨ (init-centric & init-speaker)) ⇒ (speaker-oriented {S[speaker-subject]}))

   b. (((resp-centric ∨ domain-oriented) & init-speaker) ∨ (init-centric & resp-speaker)) ⇒ (hearer-oriented {S[hearer-subject]}))

The features "speaker-subject" and "hearer-subject" force the grammar to generate the respective forms *I* and *you* in subject position no matter what semantic roles (Agent, Experiencer, Possessor, etc.) have come to be unified with the subject. This is admittedly highly ad hoc treatment of *I* and *you*. However, I would argue that the subjects and objects of utterances with interaction structure implications, when they refer to participants, are so pragmatically predictable that it would not be cost-effective to generate them semantically.

The critical cases in which we must care about indirect objects in a

---

[12] If we construe the nets given above as init-speaker nets, then the feature "S[+declarative]" could be placed with the feature "init-oriented." I suspect that we must provide two partially intersecting nets for initiators and responders, but am not in a position to prove this.

[13] I employ here a Boolean notation rather than the sort of graphical representation I have been employing. In "speaker-oriented {S[peaker-subject]}," "speaker-oriented" is a pragmatic feature and "S[peaker-subject]" is the linguistic realization rule. If this feature is selected, the subject of the sentence will be *I*.

study of pragmatically conventionalized forms are those occurring in utterances like (61).

(61)  a.  Could you give me a hot chocolate?
      b.  Could you give a hot chocolate to me?

Thus, some sort of treatment of Dative Shift is required.

We need concern ourselves with two cases – cases in which the recipient of the action is the initiator and cases in which someone in the conversation other than the initiator (who plays the Other role in the discourse) is the recipient. In the latter case we would get forms like those in (62).

(62)  a.  Could you give Sandy a hot chocolate?
      b.  Could you give a hot chocolate to Sandy?

I treat this as a distinction between "init-recipient" and "other-recipient" forms, with the difference between them coming down to whether it is the Init or Other role that is unified with the semantic Recipient role. The feature "init-recipient" is the default, and the realization rule associated with it gives rise to an objective, first person singular pronoun. When the recipient is someone other than Init (i.e., is "Other"), its lexical content is supplied semantically. The subnet of Figure 16 is responsible for these unifications.

In order to account for Dative Shift, we need a pragmatic trigger. I shall assume that forms like (61a) and (62a) result in informal speech situations. Figure 16 also claims that when there is a recipient of some action ("act-recipient" has been preselected), then in informal speech situations, the indirect object occurs in object position (which is forced by the grammar feature "recip-med"); otherwise not. The features "recip-med" and "med-recip" are grammar features that trigger different unifications in the syntax. In the case of "recip-med," the Medium (the semantic object) is unified with the surface Object and in the case of "med-recip," the Recipient is unified with the surface Object. The person of the pronoun is determined by the subnet of Figure 17. The nets in Figures 16 and 17 combine to determine the actual form of the pronoun, *me* or *you*, in these cases.

In utterance recognition, if our parser is presented with an utterance like *Give me a hot chocolate?*, the syntactic Object role will be set equal to *me*. The grammar will unify the Object role with the Recipient role

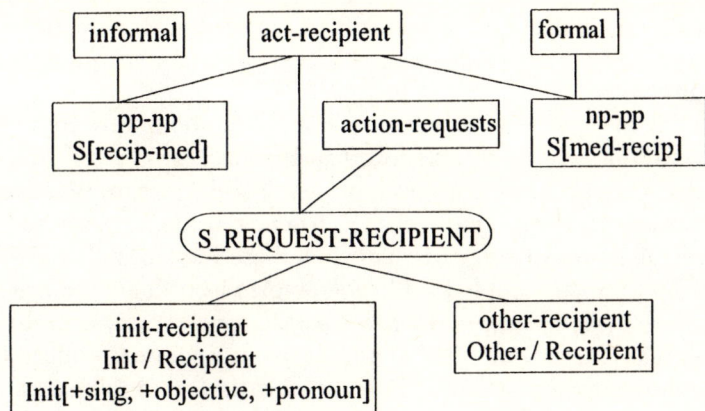

Figure 16.   A pragmatic treatment of indirect objects

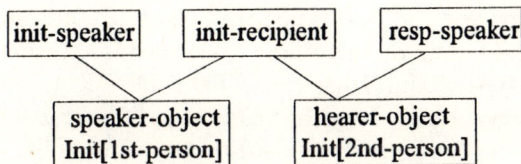

Figure 17.   Indirect object pronouns

(via recip-med) and the subnet of Figure 16 will unify the Recipient role with the Init role. DRS construction rule (23) will cause the introduction of the discourse referent "i" and it will be tied to the variable "x" in "provide(r, y, x)" thanks to the unifications just mentioned and the association of semantic roles with arguments in the thesaurus representation of *provide*-class verbs found above.

## Conclusion

It is worth noting, I think, how the present account of conventionalized request (and similar) forms differs from prior accounts. First, it does not presuppose a direct mapping from utterance forms as a whole into uses, as in Morgan's approach. Instead, it is **pragmatically compositional** in that a particular utterance form is generated by a particular combination of pragmatic features (init-oriented, thing-specific, domain-oriented, resp-ability, resp-willingness), style (formal versus informal), politeness ((no-)init-up, (no-)resp-up, (no-)deference), and register features (thing-request), with different forms resulting from different combinations of features.

Within the present framework, we are able to capture important generalizations not capturable in other approaches. We can account for the fact, critical in the account of Searle and Morgan, that certain paraphrases of so-called indirect speech act forms do not seem to have the same illocutionary force potential as these forms. Within DSAT, we account for this simply by allowing a form like *Would you open the door?*, but not *Is it your present desire to open the door?*, to be produced by the pragmatic stratum. Just as a form that cannot be produced by a generative grammar is treated as ungrammatical, a form that cannot be linked by the pragmatic stratum to elements of any interaction structures will not be perceived (immediately, at least) as having transactional and interactional significance. If these noncolloquial forms are to have transactional or interactional significance with respect to some specific interaction in a given circumstance, this will have to be the result of reasoning from their *L*-Meanings and the context, which sometimes happens. Thus DSAT accounts for the principal observation underlying Searle's and Morgan's accounts in that it directly links elements of linguistic form and politeness choices, something presupposed by their accounts, but not provided, and does these things in a fully explicit manner.

This pragmatic stratum also accounts for the primary observation that motivated Gordon and Lakoff's account of indirect speech acts, namely, the fact that colloquial utterances that instantiate felicity conditions tend to have illocutionary significance. This falls out of the association of the basic orientation features – especially the features "init-oriented," "resp-ability," and "resp-willingness" – with particular combinations of auxiliaries and verbs. However, as our account of thing-specific forms (e.g., *I'll take a hot chocolate*) shows, we can account for the significance of utterances that actually do not instantiate traditional Searlean felicity conditions (in any transparent way) with equal ease.

DSAT is also able to account for additional generalizations, such as the fact that the *will* and *would* and *can* and *could* consistently differ in politeness whether they occur in thing-specific (*Can/could I have a hot chocolate?*) or resp-centric (*Can/could you give me a hot chocolate?*) forms and that *will* and *can* seem to be less polite than their conditional or subjunctive counterparts. We can also account for such syntactic facts as that *need* and *want* occur in the present tense, while *like* does not, when occurring in utterances realizing the initial-state condition.

It is not difficult to see why conventions of use and the pragmatic stratum that accounts for them are so vital in utterance understanding. There are an infinite number of sentences, and thus an infinite number of possible *L*-Meanings. There are also an infinite number of possible utterance meanings in context (*S*-Meanings). Given the great importance of utterances having interaction-structure-specific significance for goal recognition (a topic we shall take up in the next chapter), it is not surprising that we have developed direct means for virtually instantaneous recognition of the *S*-Meanings of transactionally significant utterances.

# 7

*The structure of conversation*

## Introduction

Anyone who examines ordinary conversation must be struck by its apparent organization. Conversation (1), for instance, provides quite compelling evidence in support of the view that conversations (often, if not almost always) consist of sets of turns in which the parties seem to be engaged in doing some particular thing (engaging in an invitation interaction, as in (roughly) $<T_5 \ldots T_{10}>$, an information exchange, as in (roughly) $<T_{11} \ldots T_{17}>$, or service encounter, as in (roughly) $<T_{18} \ldots T_{22}>$), and that the utterances that comprise turns seem to come in pairs (e.g., $<T_3, T_4>$, $<T_5, T_6>$, and $<T_7, T_8>$, among many others).

(1)  In a prior conversation, M invited J to go to a basketball game with him (which was agreed to) and had suggested that J come over early so that they could play computer games before going to the basketball game (which was only tentatively agreed to).

| | |
|---|---|
| J:  <<Ring of telephone>> | $T_1$ |
| M: Hello? | $T_2$ |
| J:  Mike? | $T_3$ |
| M: Yeah. | $T_4$ |
| J:  **Whatayadoin?** | $T_5$ |
| M: Not much. | $T_6$ |
| J:  I was gonna come over. | $T_7$ |
| M: Okay. | $T_8$ |

| | |
|---|---|
| J: Play some games. | $T_9$ |
| M: Sure. | $T_{10}$ |
| J: *Okay*..well I'll be over.uh..**whuh..which number is that apartment?** | $T_{11}$ |
| M: A. | $T_{12}$ |
| J: (unhuh) | $T_{13}$ |
| M: Right on the corner. | $T_{14}$ |
| J: *Okay*..well I mean **what..what's the number there?** | $T_{15}$ |
| M: Oh 1078. | $T_{16}$ |
| J: 1078 *okay*. | $T_{17}$ |
| M: **Hey..why don't you pick up some diet soda?** | $T_{18}$ |
| J: Okay..what () kind? | $T_{19}$ |
| M: I don't care. | $T_{20}$ |
| J: Pepsi is that okay? | $T_{21}$ |
| M: Yeah. | $T_{22}$ |
| J: *Okay*. | $T_{23}$ |
| M: Arright. | $T_{24}$ |
| J: Bye. | $T_{25}$ |
| M: Bye. | $T_{26}$ |

In fact, one can argue that this conversation consists of something on the order of seven sequences – a summons-response sequence $<T_1-T_2>$, a sequence in which the parties establish their identities $<T_3-T_4>$, a sequence in which J invites himself over to M's place $<T_5$ through OKAY..*well I'll be over* in $T_{11}>$, a sequence in which J requests information from M <from *uh..whuh..which number is that apartment?* at $T_{11}$ through $T_{17}>$, a sequence in which M requests something of J $<T_{18}-T_{22}>$, a pre-closing sequence $<T_{23}-T_{24}>$, and a closing sequence $<T_{25}-T_{26}>$.

Evidence of the existence of multiturn sequences and of specific pairs can be obtained by examining the several occurrences of *okay* that we find in this conversation. First, note that *okay* at $T_8$ provides an affirmative response to the self-invitation occurring at the immediately preceding turn, and $T_{19}$ provides an affirmative response to the request initiation occurring in the immediately preceding turn. On the other hand, the occurrence of *okay* at $T_{11}$ does not constitute an affirmative response to the immediately preceding turn, for this latter turn proposes nothing that *okay* could affirm. The same is true of the occurrences of *okay* in turns $T_{15}$, $T_{17}$, and $T_{23}$. Rather than pairing up with the immediately preceding turn, these occurrences of *okay* seem to constitute signals by the speaker that he is satisfied that the work of the sequence is accomplished (which turns out not to have been true in the case of *okay* in $T_{15}$).

There is, then, some evidence that conversations are sequentially organized, or, at least, that we can impose a sequential organization on them. The question arises as to what the significance of sequential organization is. According to conversation analysts, it is its most important single structural property.

## The CA view of the structure of conversation

According to Heritage (1984: 245)

> Conversation analysis is ... primarily concerned with the ways in which utterances accomplish particular actions by virtue of their placement and participation within sequences of actions. It is sequences and turns-within-sequences which are thus the primary units of analysis.

And Schegloff (1988: 61) claims that "parties to real conversations are always talking in some sequential context," where a "sequential context" is taken by him to be the (p. 61) "more or less proximately preceding and projectably ensuing talk," and, in an attack on the utility of "linguistic resources" such as syntactic form and prosody in the analysis of conversation, he argues (Schegloff 1984: 34):

> Most centrally, an utterance will occur someplace sequentially. Most obviously, except for initial utterances, it will occur after some other utterance or sequence of utterances with which it will have, in some fashion, to deal and which will be relevant to its analysis for coparticipants. Less obviously, but more importantly, it (and here initial utterances are not excepted) may occur in a structurally defined place in conversation, in which case its structural location can have attached to its slot a set of features that may overwhelm its syntactic or prosodic structure in primacy.

Although these passages suggest that CA is concerned with the sequential organization of utterances, it would be more accurate to say that their actual focus is on the sequential organization of actions. It is not so very different in this respect from traditional speech act theory despite the vigorous protestations of conversation analysts against the value of speech act theory in the analysis of conversation. Indeed, conversation analysts employ essentially the same terms as speech act theorists for many actions, e.g., "request," "offer," "invitation," and the like, but unlike speech act theorists like Searle, have not provided us with sets of necessary and sufficient conditions for identifying such actions. One major difference between CA and speech act theory is that CA recognizes actions having to do with conversation management, such as "closing initiation" (e.g., $<T_{23}-T_{24}>$ in (1) above). But the CA approach to actions shares one fundamental defect with speech act theory, namely proponents of CA have provided no explicit mapping or, for that matter, even a hint of an explicit mapping of actions into verbal and nonverbal behaviors.

Despite the fact that conversation analysts constantly refer to "actions in interaction," to use a phrase Schegloff is fond of employing,[1] he and others have vigorously criticized speech act theory. Schegloff has argued, for instance, that speech act theory cannot account for how Russ interprets his mother's utterance at $T_1$ in conversation (2).

(2)  Schegloff (1988: 57) – Family dinner
    MOTHER: 'z everybody (0.2)=washed for dinner?
    GARY:    =Yah.
    MOTHER: Daddy 'n I have t- both go in different directions, en I wanna talk ta you about where I'm going (t'night).
    GARY:    Is it about us?
    MOTHER: mm hmm
    RUSS:    *I* know where you're go'in,
    MOTHER: Where.
    RUSS:    To the uh (eighth grade) =
    MOTHER: = Yeah. Right.
    MOTHER: Do you know who's going to that meeting?    $T_1$
    RUSS:    Who.                                        $T_2$
    MOTHER: I don't kno:w.                               $T_3$
    RUSS:    Oh: : . Prob'ly Missiz McOwen ('n detsa) en prob'ly Missiz Cadry and some of the teachers. (0.4) and the counsellors.    $T_4$

---

[1]  In, for instance, a talk before a NATO Advanced Workshop on discourse analysis in Maratea, Italy, in the Spring of 1993.

According to Schegloff, Russ construes *Do you know who's going to that meeting?* as a pre-announcement, where a pre-announcement[2] is understood as an action that prefigures an announcement. He maintains that this is an interpretation that speech act theory cannot account for.

Schegloff (1988: 61) argues that "what a rudimentary speech act theoretic analysis misses, and I suspect a sophisticated one will miss as well, is that parties to real conversations are always talking in some sequential context," where a "sequential context" is taken by him to be the (p. 61) "more or less proximately preceding and projectably ensuing talk." He then goes on to say that (p. 61)

> although it could be argued that speech act theory can incorporate another category of speech act like "pre-announcement" and establish its felicity conditions and incorporate the result into future analysis, this is not the same as incorporating sequential connectedness itself. Here the outlook is not hopeful, for speech act theory has inherited from traditional philosophy the single act or utterance as its fundamental unit.

The thesis that one needs the sequential concept of "pre-announcement" to account for this conversation is very far from being true. Consider scenarios (3)–(5), where I refers to the identity of the people going to the meeting.

(3) The indirect *Wh*-Question interpretation
    Contextual premises:
      a. Sp(eaker) does not know I.

---

[2] The notion of a "pre-sequence" (e.g., pre-announcement, pre-request, pre-offer, etc.) figures large in recent work in conversation analysis. Levinson (1983: 346f) gives the following general characterization of how pre-sequences are related to the sequences they prefigure, where the pre-sequence consists of turns $T_1$ and $T_2$ and the prefigured sequence consists of $T_3$ and $T_4$.

(1)  a. $T_1$ (Position 1): a question checking whether some precondition obtains for the action to be performed in $T_3$.
$T_2$ (Position 2): an answer indicating that the precondition obtains, often with a question or request to proceed to $T_3$.
$T_3$ (Position 3): the prefigured action, conditional on the "go ahead' in $T_2$.
$T_4$ (Position 4): response to the action in $T_3$.
     b. *distribution rule*: one party, A, addresses $T_1$ and $T_3$ to another party, B, and B addresses $T_2$ and $T_4$ to A.

Notice the reference to actions in (1a) and (1b). In many cases, the actions in question are identical to speech-act-theoretic actions. One wonders what the fuss is actually about.

    b.  Sp needs to know I.
    c.  Sp believes Ad(dressee) may know I.
Example conversation:
    MOTHER:  I need to phone the people going to that meeting.
                 Do you know who's going to be there?
    RUSS:     Yeah, Missiz McOwen, Missiz Cadry, . . . .

(4)  A direct *Yes-No*-Question interpretation, non "pre-announce-ment" reading
Contextual premises:
    a.  Sp does not know I.
    b.  Ad needs to know I.
    c.  Sp does not know whether or not Ad knows P.
Example conversation:
    MOTHER:  I want you to phone everyone who is going to that meeting. Do you know who's going to be there?
    RUSS:     No.
    MOTHER:  Well, you better find out.

(5)  The so-called "pre-announcement" interpretation.
Contextual premises:
    a.  Sp knows I.
    b.  Ad needs to know I.
    c.  Sp does not know whether or not Ad knows I.
Example conversation:
    MOTHER:  I want you to phone everyone who is going to that meeting. Do you know who's going?
    RUSS:     No, who?
    MOTHER:  Missiz McOwen, Missiz Cadry, . . ..

As these scenarios make clear, how an utterance like *Do you know who's going to that meeting?* is **intended** to be interpreted depends on the *L*-Meaning of the utterance and which of the sets of premises (3)–(5) is believed by the speaker to be true. How it **will** be interpreted will depend on the *L*-Meaning of the utterance and which of the sets of premises (3)–(5) is believed by the addressee to be true. We can expect to have failures in communication, as is true of the case at hand, when speaker beliefs are inconsistent with addressee beliefs.

In these crafted scenarios, Mother and Russ have the same beliefs, and the interactions are successful in that the speaker achieves her conversational goal. Notice that there is nothing about these exchanges that the notion "pre-announcement" would assist us in accounting for. Note, specifically, that the so-called "pre-announcement" reading happens when conditions (5a)–(5c) hold. We do not need to refer the sequential location of the utterance at all. We need, instead, to know what the contextual presuppositions of the participants are.

We have here a quite clear contrast between a text-oriented approach to interactions and a cognitive approach. The text-oriented approach sees conversational structure in terms of sequences of actions (or utterances) without regard to the presuppositions of the speaker (i.e., without regard to the cognitive context, including the special properties of the interaction structure being interacted). The DSAT account is concerned not with the nature of the actions participants perform, but with their transactional and interactional significance, which will always reflect both the context, viewed as a set of propositions (usually shared), and the nature of the interaction structure being interacted.

We can account for the misunderstanding between Russ and Mother only if we adopt a cognitive approach, for the misunderstanding arises because they have different sets of beliefs. The actual context at $T_1$ (and what Mother believes is true) is:

(6)  a.  Sp does not know P.
     b.  Sp needs to know P.
     c.  Sp believes Ad may know P.

For reasons best known to Russ, Russ acts as if he believed:

(7)  a.  Sp knows P.
     b.  Ad needs to know P.
     c.  Sp does not know whether or not Ad knows P.

Notice that every single presupposition of (7) is in conflict with (6).

There are other difficulties with the CA approach to conversational structure, not the least of which is the fact that Schegloff's claim that the "structural location [of an utterance] can have attached to its slot a set of features that may overwhelm its syntactic or prosodic structure in primacy" is quite hopelessly inexplicit. The notion "structural location" is not defined; we are not told how different structural locations are individuated; nor are we told what the possible "features" of structural slots are. The prospects of an explicit treatment of the notion "structural location" are not good.

The conversation analytic emphasis on the primacy of sequential order is realized especially through their concept of the **adjacency pair** (Schegloff and Sacks 1973). Adjacency pairs are constituted (Heritage 1984: 246) of a sequence of two utterances that are adjacent, though not necessarily immediately consecutive, produced by different speakers, ordered as a first pair part and a second pair part, and typed so that a particular first pair part must be followed by a particular range of second pair parts.

Now, a given turn can contain a single pair part of an adjacency pair or parts of two adjacency pairs. Turn $T_1$ in conversation (8) contains the second part (*Yeah, I think so*) of a Question-Answer pair initiated in turn $T_1$ and the first member (*You want me to watch him?*) of a second, Offer-Acceptance adjacency pair.

(8)  Jacobs and Jackson (1983a: 299)
     C: Hey Debbie. Are you going to be free from 1:30 to
         2:30?                                  $T_1$
     D: Yeah, I think so. You want me to watch him?      $T_2$

The second turn of an adjacency pair need not follow the first immediately. There are cases in which the paired actions are interrupted by what Schegloff (1972b) has called an Insertion Sequence. In (9) the Request-Rejection pair consisting of turns $<T_2, T_3>$ interrupts the Question-Answer pair $<T_1, T_4>$.

(9)  Merritt, (1976: 333)
     A: May I have a bottle of Mich?                      $T_1$
     B: Are you twenty-one?                           $T_2$
     A: No                                         $T_3$
     B: No                                         $T_4$

Even in this sort of case, the pair-wise organization of the actions that are said to comprise conversation is maintained, for after the intrusive sequence has run its course, the relevant and expected next action (to $T_1$) occurs.

The existence of insertion sequences suggests that speakers must retain more than just the immediately preceding item in memory in formulating responses. Thus, it might be argued that B must remember what was **said** at turns $T_1$–$T_3$ in order to know how to respond at turn $T_4$. However, simply storing representations of the transactional and interactional significance of utterances in interaction structures, as we did in chapter 3, would achieve the same effect. Typically insertion sequences are comprised of inquiries as to whether preconditions on satisfaction conditions hold (as in the case of *Are you twenty-one?* in (9), where a precondition on the willingness of a bartender to serve alcohol to a customer is that the customer be of legal age) or are domain-oriented. Obviously, some sort of "step-down" recursive procedure in which unverified preconditions and uninstantiated domain predicates critical to affirmation of some satisfaction condition are attacked is required. What is not required in a cognitive account is reference to the notion "adjacency pair" or "insertion sequence."[3]

The question arises as to when a pair of actions does and does not constitute an adjacency pair in a given conversation. How, one might ask, does A recognize that *Are you twenty-one?* is not an answer to his question in conversation (9)? In my view, for a theory of conversation to be taken seriously, it must offer up a plausible answer to this question. So far, the best conversation analysts have been able to do is provide lists of types of adjacency pairs and stipulations of what sorts of actions are paired with what other sorts of actions in pairs of a given type, e.g., answers are paired with questions, acceptances or rejections are paired with requests (or offers or proposals), denials or confessions are paired with accusations, etc., without providing any real insight into how participants recognize which particular actions are paired with which other particular actions in particular conversations. What is needed are statements like (10) if the concept of an adjacency pair is to be of any empirical interest.

(10)   Two actions $A_1$ and $A_2$ constitute an adjacency pair of a certain type $T$ if and only if $A_1$ has property $P_i$ and $A_2$ has property $P_j$.

I do not mean to suggest that conversation analysts have no criteria. It is just that their criteria are not sufficiently explicitly stated to be tested. What is true of the notion "adjacency pair" is also true of "insertion sequence" and all other CA sequential structural notions.

---

[3]   I say more about this later.

That conversation exhibits sequential organization is clear. However, it does not follow from this fact that conversations are structured sequentially. Internally, utterances are sequentially organized in that they are produced one word at a time, but it does not follow from this that sequential organization (i.e., word order) is the only or even the most important aspect of the structure of sentences. The same is true, I would argue, of conversation.

## A cognitive approach to discourse structure

The text-based approach to conversation of conversation analysis contrasts sharply with the cognitive approach of DSAT. However, if DSAT is to provide an adequate account of communicative interactions it must be embedded in some sort of dynamic account of conversation – either a computational model of utterance generation in which DSAT interaction structures are continuously updated or some sort of dynamic semantic theory or (ideally) both.

The representations provided in chapter 3 are very similar to those employed in the computational implementation of Patten, Geis, and Becker (1992), henceforth PGB. The basic idea behind this implementation was that associated with any domain predicate is a slot that holds the value for that predicate and that associated with any satisfaction condition is a slot that holds such values as "true," "false," "possibly true," etc. It was assumed that the parties to a particular interaction will normally engage in efforts to determine values for these domain predicates and satisfaction conditions and that the structure of any conversation would reflect the internal structure of interaction structures. Thus, we would normally expect the preconditions of a given satisfaction condition to be addressed before, not after the conditions they are subordinate to unless an utterance specifying a satisfaction condition receives a dispreferred response. Thus, it is unlikely that an initiator would say *Do you have your car with you today?* after receiving a positive response to the question, *Can you give me a ride home today?*

In PGB, we simulated utterance generation of one of the parties to a relatively complex conversation without appeal to such notions as "adjacency pair" and "insertion sequence." The conversation in question, which was crafted out of naturally occurring, taped interactions with travel agents, was (11).

(11)   Patten, Geis, and Becker (1992) conversation
      A: May I help you?
      C: Do you have any flights to Miami on the 26th?
      A: How many seats are you looking for?
      C: One.
      A: What time can you leave?
      C: Some time in the afternoon.
      A: Let me look. . . I'm not finding anything then. . . Can you
          leave earlier?
      C: If I have to.
      A: I've got a seat on an 11: 00 a.m. flight on Treetop Airlines.
      C: That'll be good.
      A: When can I bring you back?
      C: On the morning of the 30th.
      A: Well, all I'm showing is a 10: 00 p.m. flight.
      C: Do you have anything the night before?
      A: I can put you on that 10: 00 p.m. flight.
      C: That'll be okay.
      A: The round trip fare will be $295.
      C: Okay.

This conversation is quite complex in that *Do you have any flights to Miami on the 26th?* has two second pair parts, a dispreferred completion, *I'm not finding anything then,* and a later, preferred completion, *I've got a seat on an 11: 00 a.m. flight on Treetop Airlines,* the first being interrupted by two insertion sequences (initiated by *How many seats are you looking for?* and *What time can you leave?*) and the second by one (*Can you leave earlier?*).

At no time did our utterance planner create an adjacency pair type of architecture to keep track of where it was in utterance planning. Instead, it employed a quite standard AI planning technique. The utterance, *Do you have any flights to Miami on the 26th?*, a domain-oriented utterance quite like *Do you have hot chocolate?*, was "heard" as specifying a precondition on the ability condition of the flight-bookings interaction structure.[4] Since an efficient search for a flight meeting the conditions "arrive-place (Miami)" and "depart-date(12/26)" presupposes knowing the de-

---

[4]   Somewhat different terminology was used in PGB from what I am using here.

parture time and sometimes the number of seats,[5] our planner was designed to attempt to instantiate these domain predicates before attempting to find a flight meeting the customer's needs. Thus, the planner went into a "Need-Determination" phase in which it attempted to find values for "depart-time" and "seats" predicates. On successfully executing this program, it then moved into a "Need-Satisfaction" phase in which it both searched for flights meeting the needs of the speaker and reported the results. On reporting failure to satisfy the needs of the customer (cf. *I'm not finding anything then*), the planner was forced to return to Need-Determination to get new values for the depart-time predicate. It then returned to the Need-Satisfaction program and on achieving success, reported back to the customer (cf. *I've got a seat on an 11:00 a.m. flight on Treetop Airlines.*). At no point was reference made to the structural location of any utterance (or utterance-action) in a sequence of utterances (or utterance-actions). Such a reference was unnecessary and would, in fact, have been a considerable hindrance.

In addition to being embedded in a computational implementation like that of PGB, DSAT interaction structures can also be embedded in dynamic semantic theories such as DRT by way of accounting for the progress of conversations. We have seen how the pragmatic stratum can map elements of pragmatically conventionalized utterances into DRS discourse referents and discourse conditions. In what follows in this chapter, I propose to sketch how suitably modified DSAT interaction structure representations can be incorporated in DRS by way of accounting for goal-achievement in conversation.

## DRT revisited

Asher (p. 64) notes that among the interpretations of DRS that have been given are that "(1) the DRS is a level of 'logical form,' (2) the DRS is a 'partial model' of what is said in the discourse, or (3) the DRS is a 'mental representation' of the content of a discourse formed by a recipient of it." He himself takes the line that DRS can be all three things.

---

5   Whether travel agents ask how many seats are desired before searching for flights seems sometimes to depend on whether they think it will be difficult to find seats on relevant flights, as was true when I did my taping. Obviously, at peak travel times, it will be easier to find one seat than four or six.

In this chapter, I shall take the position that the DRS is a cognitive representation of the content of a conversation and, as such, includes both *L*-Meaning and *S*-Meaning representations, for only if we make this assumption can we account not only for what is said, but what is implied (Grice 1975). What I shall argue is that DRS must contain (modified) interaction structure representations if they are to account for how we use and understand utterances in interactions.

DSAT interaction structures constitute a part of the shared background knowledge of participants. DRS representations of DSAT interaction structures must be treated differently from representations of what is said, for the discourse referents of DSAT interaction structures cannot serve as anaphors of pronouns, even indefinite pronouns, until they are explicitly introduced. Observe, for instance, that should Terry call Sandy and say, *My car is stalled,* Sandy could not say, *I'll give you one,* meaning, 'I'll give you a ride,' even if Sandy and Terry were both to recognize that Terry meant to cause Sandy to commit herself to giving Terry a ride and what Terry said implicates that *I need a ride* is true. The discourse referent "e" associated with the discourse condition (domain predicate) "ride(e)" of the ride-request interaction structure is not made accessible to discourse pronouns as a result of Terry's saying, *My car is stalled.* Had Terry said, *I need a ride,* then Sandy obviously could say, *I'll give you one.*

I shall assume here that shared background knowledge, including DSAT interaction structures, are injected into DRSs as inner DRSs of the main DRS. As a result, the discourse referents of interaction structures will not be accessible to anaphoric pronouns unless they are explicitly injected into the main DRS. I shall also assume that implicated propositions derived from the interaction structures of inner DRSs also occur as inner DRS.

Interestingly, it appears that discourse referents introduced in prior conversations can serve as the antecedents for definite noun phrases, if not definite pronouns. Recall that conversation (6) on page 124 of chapter 5 began with *Do you have the blackberry jam?*[6] In order to account for the presence of the definite noun phrase *the blackberry jam,* we must assume that the speaker believed that she and her addressee explicitly shared knowledge of some particular blackberry jam. Thus, a discourse referent "x" and the discourse condition "blackberry-jam(x)" must have been part of the main DRS as this conversation began.

[6]  In certain circumstances, *it* would be possible here – say, on the third successive day the customer had come in looking for precisely the same thing.

In the normal case, the DRS for an utterance is provided by DRS construction rules that recursively associate elements of DRS representations (discourse referents and conditions) with the elements of syntactic structures. Thus, there are DRS construction rules that map common noun phrases, pronouns, verbs, verb phrases, and quantifiers, etc. into DRS discourse referents and conditions. Such rules can be expected to handle virtually all term expressions, including those that occur in pragmatically conventionalized utterances of the sort we discussed in chapter 6. However, it would be a mistake to attempt to employ ordinary DRS construction rules for the conventionalized parts of such utterances, including the auxiliaries and main verbs of such utterances and sentence types in cases in which participants are showing deference. Instead, the pragmatic stratum provides the DRS construction rules for such forms through the DRS realization rules associated with particular pragmatic features.

The claim that DRS must contain DSAT interaction structures if DRT is to be able to account for conversational interaction is based on the fact that we cannot easily account either for goal achievement or for interaction-structure-specific implicatures unless it does.

## *Incorporation of interaction structures in DRS*

I shall assume that each party to a conversation maintains a DRS for that conversation that and, in many cases, the two DRSs will be the same and therefore constitute what is usually called the "common ground" (Stalnaker 1978). However, the notion "common ground" is very much a fiction, and to some degree a harmful one, for adopting it precludes accounts of misunderstandings arising because participants bring different contextual assumptions into a conversation or draw different inferences from what is said. Recall, for instance, the miscommunication between Mother and Russ in the conversation treated earlier in this chapter. Were we to assume that there actually is a common ground, we could not account for this misunderstanding (if that is what it was). In this chapter, I shall focus primarily on the responder's side of interactions and will provide responder DRS. I shall also restrict my attention to the transactional side of the interaction. In chapter 8, where we shall be concerned with utterance generation, the focus will shift to the initiator and to both interactional and transactional considerations.

197

As I have previously noted, at the outset of a given interaction sequence, the responder will normally not know what particular interaction the initiator means to engage her in. I have argued that we recognize people's goals by recognizing what interaction they mean to engage us in (I recognize that you want money from me through recognizing that you have initiated a thing-request interaction, where money is the goods) and that we recognize what type of interaction the initiator of a sequence means to engage us in by mapping *S*-Meaning representations of successive utterances into elements of candidate interaction structures until a unique interaction is identified. At the point the responder has identified what interaction the initiator means to engage her in, she will inject the interaction structure DRS associated with that interaction into the main DRS as an inner DRS.

As I suggested earlier, it will be necessary to modify interaction structure representations for use in DRS. I shall assume that associated with any interaction is a **goal state**, which corresponds closely to the transactional effect of interaction structures, and that a given interaction's goal state can be achieved only if it can be deduced from relevant contextual assumptions, what is said, and the interaction structure DRS, given conventional rules of inference. I shall assume that the interaction structure DRS for a given interaction contains a goal-state conditional, the antecedent of which consists of the conjunction of the satisfaction conditions and the consequent of which is the goal state. I do not include the initial-state condition as a condition on achievement of the goal state because injection of an interaction structure DRS presupposes identification of the specific interaction the initiator means to engage the responder in and that, in turn, entails recognition that the initial-state condition of the interaction is true. Associated with each of the satisfaction conditions is a conditional, the antecedent of which consists of a conjunction of that condition's preconditions and the consequent of which is the condition itself. In addition, the interaction structure DRS will, of course, contain pertinent discourse referents and discourse conditions corresponding to the domain predicates of interaction structures.

Given this way of interpreting DSAT interaction structures, once it has been determined that all of the preconditions of a satisfaction condition are true, it will follow (via *modus ponens*) that the satisfaction condition is true. Once the satisfaction conditions have been determined to be true, it will follow (again via *modus ponens*) that the goal state has been achieved.

198

## THING-REQUESTS

In order to account for thing-requests in DRT, I shall employ the interaction structure DRS schema of Figure 18. According to this representation, the initiator ("i") desires that the responder ("r") perform the action ("e") of providing someone ("x") with one or more ("n") objects ("y") at some time ("t"), often "now," where r plays the provider role, i the beneficiary role, x the receiver role, and y the goods role. These discourse referents are subject to two conditions: that the responder be able to do this thing, which is itself subject to the precondition that she have this thing, and that the responder be willing to do this thing, which may be subject to preconditions as well. The DRS of Figure 18 can be injected into the main responder DRS of some conversational interaction if and only if the responder believes that the initiator desires that she provide him with some thing either because he has asserted or implicated that he does. This DRS is quite appropriate for general personal requests, as when a guest requests a glass of water from a host. However, it is insufficiently particularized to handle retail sales service encounters, where there is a precondition on the willingness condition that the customer commit himself to paying for what is ordered.

I have argued that in any context, things are known by their utilities in that context and that in a retail store, for instance, things are classified, among other things, as sellables (what is sold in the store) and useables (things like water fountains and restrooms that customers may use), among other (less salient) things, and that when a clerk hears an affirmative reference to some sellable (i.e., a reference to a sellable **consistent** with a desire to purchase it), he will inject the retail sales specific DRS schema of Figure 19 into the main DRS. This DRS contains the discourse condition that the clerk be willing to provide what is desired and that this is subject to the condition that the customer commit to paying for it. I shall assume that something from the context will make evident that the customer is willing to pay for what is desired. I suspect, for instance, that most clerks assume that if the customer communicates a desire for some sellable she implicates that she is willing to pay for it (should she take possession of it).

Suppose then that a customer walks into a cafe, sits down, and the following conversation ensues.

199

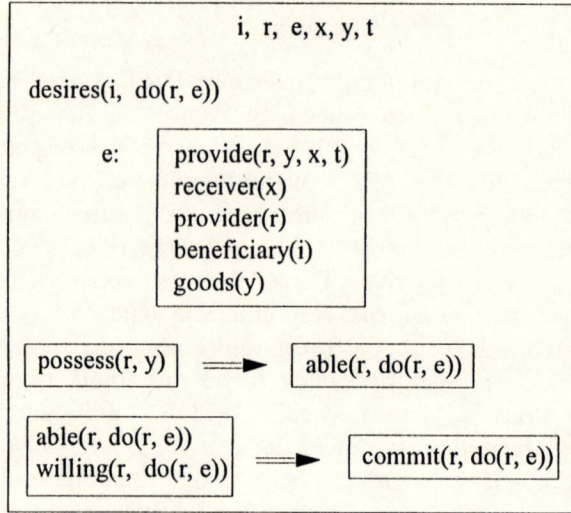

Figure 18.   The thing-request interaction structure schema

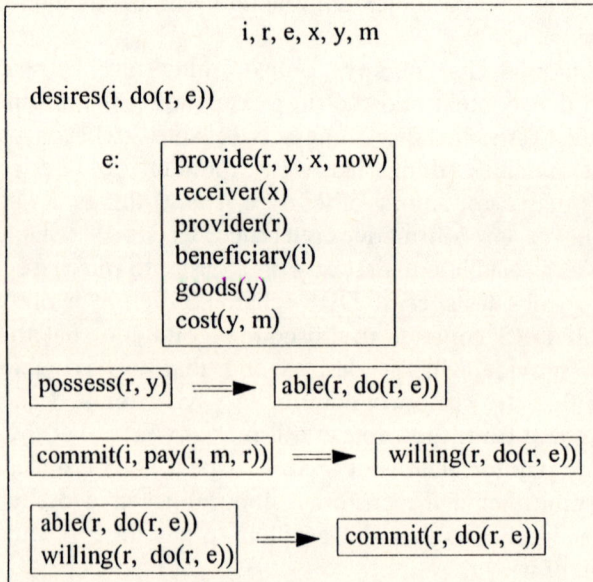

Figure 19.   The retail sales interaction structure schema

200

(12)   Merritt (1976,:337)

| | | |
|---|---|---|
| CUSTOMER: | Do you have hot chocolate? | $T_1$ |
| CLERK: | mmhmm | $T_2$ |
| CUSTOMER: | Can I have hot chocolate with whipped cream? | |
| | | $T_3$ |
| CLERK: | Sure ((leaves to get)). | $T_4$ |

The utterance, *Do you have hot chocolate?*, is value-requesting, of course, and I employ the notation "possess(u, v) = T v F," by way of indicating that the inquiry is a *yes-no*-question, where the discourse referent "u" is subject to the condition "clerk(u)" and "v" is subject to the conditions "hot-chocolate(v)" and "num(v, 1)."[7] Since hot chocolate is a sellable in this context, the clerk will infer that the customer desires hot chocolate,[8] and once this is recognized, a suitably particularized version of DRS schema 19 will be injected into the main DRS.[9] The resulting DRS is that portion of Figure 20 that precedes the clerk's response. As this DRS indicates, the clerk seems to have inferred that the customer was willing to pay for the hot chocolate (though we do not know why), and was therefore willing to provide it. I believe that in most cases of requests for products with fixed prices, a customer's asserting or implicating a desire for some thing implicates a commitment to paying for it. This implicature is placed in inner DRS as an extension[10] of the inner retail sales DRS as is the resulting entailment that the clerk is willing to provide the hot chocolate.[11]

---

[7]   To simplify my DRSs, I shall often assume that transactions are to occur at the time of interaction.

[8]   The pragmatic stratum would be responsible for this implicature.

[9]   In this conversation, the clerk did not immediately provide hot chocolate after hearing *Do you have hot chocolate?* I take this to be due to the fact that the clerk did not believe that a complete specification of what was wanted had been made. I represent this fact by supposing that requests for hot chocolate contain the condition "with(y, w)," where "w" is some condiment (or "nil") with the understanding that until "w" is specified, "y" will be understood as not fully specified. This is analogous to flight-bookings in which a flight is understood not to be fully specified until the origin, destination, departure time, arrival time, and number of seats predicates are specified.

[10]   This is necessary to distinguish what is said from what is implied.

[11]   The fact that conversations proceed sequentially creates the problem for DRS that implicatures and entailments that depend at least in part on DRS interaction structures will necessarily be discontinuous. In a computational implementation, the mode of implementation of DSAT that I prefer, such problems do not arise for how DSAT interaction structures are instantiated is in no way affected by the sequential character of conversations. It is a wholly non-text-oriented mode of representation.

Customer: *Do you have hot chocolate?*

z, u, v, n

customer(z)
clerk(u)
hot-chocolate(v)
num(v, 1)
possess(u, v) = T v F

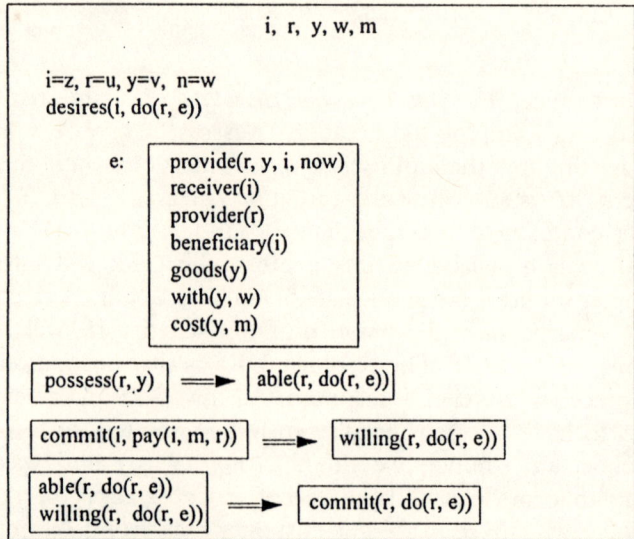

> i, r, y, w, m
>
> i=z, r=u, y=v, n=w
> desires(i, do(r, e))
>
> e: | provide(r, y, i, now)
> receiver(i)
> provider(r)
> beneficiary(i)
> goods(y)
> with(y, w)
> cost(y, m)
>
> possess(r, y) ⟹ able(r, do(r, e))
>
> commit(i, pay(i, m, r)) ⟹ willing(r, do(r, e))
>
> able(r, do(r, e))
> willing(r, do(r, e)) ⟹ commit(r, do(r, e))

commit(i, pay(i, m, r))

willing(r, do(r, e))

Clerk: *mmhmm*

possess(u, v)

able(r, do(r, e))

commit(r, do(r, e))

Customer: *Can I have hot chocolate with whipped cream?*

whipped-cream(n)
with(v, n)
select(i, v) = T v F

Clerk: *Sure (leaves to get)*

select(i, v)

able(r, do(r, e))

commit(r, do(r, e))

Figure 20.   The hot chocolate DRS

202

Once the customer's question is answered affirmatively, it follows that the clerk does possess hot chocolate (cf. "possess(r, y)") and therefore that the clerk is able to provide the hot chocolate (cf. "able (r, do(r, e))") to the customer and, further, that the clerk is committed to providing the hot chocolate (cf. "commit(r, do(r, e))") to the customer. The resulting DRS is that portion of Figure 20 that precedes the customer's second utterance.

Note that the representation I have given seems to entail that the transactional work of this interaction is completed, for the goal state is achieved, but this is clearly not the case, for (or it seems), the clerk does not immediately turn to get the hot chocolate and (for sure) the customer goes on to request that whipped cream be added to the hot chocolate. In order to account for this conversation, I think we must assume that there must have been an understanding that hot chocolate can be ordered with condiments of some sort and that until it is determined whether or not the customer wants a condiment with her hot chocolate, the transaction is not finished. In a computational implementation, one could account for this by associating an obligatory "condiment" slot.[12] In a DRS-style representation of requests for hot chocolate, we might employ the predicate "with(y, w)," where "w" is the "condiment" discourse referent. This is equivalent to saying that there is some thing w that y occurs with. What that "w" is must be determined in the interaction.

The customer goes on to say, *Can I have hot chocolate with whipped cream?* As I noted in the previous chapter, this use of *have* has a meaning more closely related to that of *select,* than *possess.* In fact the pragmatic stratum maps this utterance into (13), which is injected into the DRS.

(13)   select(i, v) & with(v, n) & (whipped-cream(n) = T v F)

In a computational implementation, *Can I have hot chocolate with whipped cream?*, when the clerk says, *Sure,* he implicates that he is able to provide the customer with hot chocolate with whipped cream, and since he has implicated a willingness to do so, he implicates a commitment to do so.

---

[12]   What ancillary predicates occur with any "providable" depends, of course, on the nature of the providable.

## RIDE-REQUESTS

We turn now to consider successful and unsuccessful ride-requests and in the process show how so-called indirect speech acts can be accounted for. The basic ride-request DRS schema is given in Figure 21. Before examining particular instances of ride-requests, I should perhaps say what the division of labor of the ability and willingness conditions is. Given how the preconditions on these two conditions are stated, any rejection of the request that concerns the destination of the drive will be construed as a willingness-based rejection.[13] On the other hand, a colleague with whom one works who rejects a ride-request because she is working late will be taken as giving an ability-based declination. Though she is perhaps at the place of departure at the time of the interaction, she will not be there at the proposed time of departure. She will be in her office. Recall that we interpreted Marcia's saying she couldn't give a ride to Donny because she had to leave for work shortly as signifying that she could not be where Donny needed her to be at the desired time.

By way of illustrating use of this DRS schema let us first examine the series of conversations – hypothetical and actual – we considered in connection with the question of how so-called indirect speech acts arise. We need, first, to consider conversation (14) and the DRS given in Figure 22.

(14) Hypothetical conversation (the talk in question would have been a late afternoon talk)

| | | |
|---|---|---|
| B: | Are you going to the talk/faculty meeting/etc. today? | $T_1$ |
| M: | Yeah, why do you ask? | $T_2$ |
| B: | I need a ride home. Could you give me one? | $T_3$ |
| M: | Where do you live? | $T_4$ |
| B: | Clintonville. | $T_5$ |
| M: | Sure, that's not far out of my way. | $T_6$ |

[13] Though there are a number of reasons why someone might not be willing to give another a ride, I posit just the precondition that the responder not find the destination to be inconvenient because I believe it to be the only willingness-based precondition that is routinely addressed in conversation. It might be argued that inquiries about the destination of the ride are pure domain-oriented inquiries, but if that were true, we would expect that responders might agree to the request before inquiring as to the destination of the ride.

i , r, e, x, p$_d$, p$_a$, t$_d$, y
desires(i, do(r, e))

e:
provide(r, y, i)
provider(r)
receiver(i)
ride(y)
depart-time(t$_d$)
depart-place(p$_d$)
arrive-place(p$_a$)
instrument(x)
car(x)

possess(r, x)
be-at(r, p$_d$, t$_d$) $\Longrightarrow$ able(r, do(r, e,))

-inconvenient(p$_a$, r) $\Longrightarrow$ willing(r, do(r, e))

able(r, do(r, e,))
willing(r, do(r, e)) $\Longrightarrow$ commits(r, do(r, e))

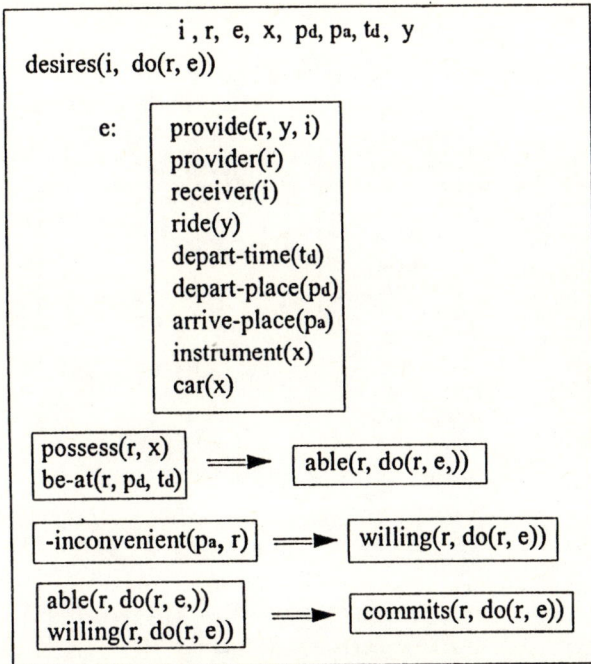

Figure 21. The ride-request DRS

B's first utterance is simply mapped into a representation of its conventional meaning, for it has no particular context-specific *S*-Meaning (transactional significance). However, the talk in question has some context-relevant properties concerning the location and time of the talk which constitutes part of B and M's shared background knowledge.

On affirming that he was going to the talk, M then asks the reason (g) for which B's question was asked. (The representation of the *L*-Meaning of this utterance is not to be taken particularly seriously.) B's utterance, *I need a ride home*, provides sufficient evidence for M to recognize that B means to engage him in a ride-request interaction, and the ride-request DRS is injected into the main DRS. B appears to have assumed that M did possess a car (and have it with him). I include this contextually presupposed discourse condition in the ride-request DRS. One consequence of this utterance is that B's first utterance will be reheard as (an *S*-Meaning) inquiry about whether M will be at the place from which the ride will commence at the time B desires that it

205

$$x, z, f, q, c, l, p, t_b, t_e, l_t$$

M(x)
B(z)

**B:** *Are you going to the talk today?*

do(x, f) = T v F

f:
> attend(x, t)
> talk(t)
> from($t_b$, $t_e$)
> $t_b$, $t_e$ ε today
> 4:00pm($t_b$)
> 5:00pm($t_e$)
> talk-location($l_t$)
> Cunz($l_t$)

**M:** *Yeah.*

do(x, f)

*Why do you ask?*

reason(q)
ask(z, x, (do(x, f) = T v F), q) = T

**B:** *I need a ride.*

ride(c)
need(z, c)

> $i$, $r$, $e$, $y$, $x$, $p_d$, $p_a$, $t_d$
>
> i = z, r = x, e = g, c = y, $p_d$ = $l_t$, $p_a$=p, $t_d$ = $t_e$
>
> desires(i, do(r, e))
>
> e:
> > provide(r, y, i, $t_d$)
> > provider(r)
> > receiver(i)
> > ride(y)
> > depart-time($t_d$)
> > depart-place($p_d$)
> > arrive-place($p_a$)
> > instrument(x)
> > car(x)
>
> possess(r, x)
>
> | possess(r, x) be-at(r, $p_d$, $t_d$) | ⟹ | able(r, do(r, e,)) |
>
> | -inconvenient($p_a$, r) | ⟹ | willing(r, do(r, e)) |
>
> | able(r, do(r, e,)) willing(r, do(r, e)) | ⟹ | commit(r, do(r, e)) |

be-at(r, $p_d$, $t_d$)

able(r, do(r, e))

Figure 22.   The B and M ride-request DRS

commence, for that is its significance relative to the ride-request service encounter and M's affirmative response to this initial question will therefore be interpreted as implicating that he would be at the place in question (Cunz Hall) at 5:00 p.m., the time of the end of the talk. This in turn implicates that M was able to provide the desired ride, for the two preconditions on the ability condition are satisfied.[14]

B's utterance, *Could you give me one?*, will be mapped into the ability condition of the ride-request interaction structure by the pragmatic stratum, as in Figure 23, the continuation of Figure 22. Though M has already implicated an ability to provide this ride, it could never-theless still be true that there is some context-specific ability-based reason why he could not do so – perhaps a prior plan to go to dinner with someone immediately after the talk. In this case, however, M responds with an inquiry as to where B lives, which is relevant to the precondition "¬inconvenient($p_a$, r)," of the willingness condition, not to the ability condition (given how I am interpreting the ability and willingness conditions).[15] After discovering where B lives, which provides the destination of the ride in question, M responds to the earlier question, *Could you give me one?*, affirmatively. This I take to implicate that the destination is not inconvenient to him and that he is therefore willing to provide the ride. However, M goes on to say, *That's not far out of my way*, which makes this explicit. Since both the ability condition and willingness condition are satisfied, B is entitled to assume that M has committed himself to providing the ride though he does not make an explicit commitment to do so (perhaps saying something like, *Sure. Yeah. I'll give you a ride*). Accordingly this conclusion must be a part of the inner ride-request DRS, for it is an implicature of it and of what was said.

Recall that there were a number of subsequent conversations between B and M that took the form of (15):

(15)   Actual conversation type
       B: Are you going to the talk today?                    $T_1$

[14] At this point it is worth pointing out that the DRS tracks both the *L*-Meanings and the *S*-Meanings of each utterance. The *L*-Meanings are contained in the main DRS and the *S*-Meanings are contained in inner DRSs, all of which are to be interpreted as extensions of the ride-request DRS. Thus, they employ the discourse referents of the ride-request DRS.

[15] One might reasonably argue that it is at this point that the ability of M to provide this ride is actually implicated, for in turning to inquire as to the destination of the ride, M could be taken as having conceded an ability to provide the ride.

B: *Could you give me one?*

able(x, do(x, g)) = T v F

g: | provide(x, c, z) |

M: *Where do you live?*

live(x, p) = T

B: *Clintonville*

Clintonville(p)

| Clintonville(pa) |

M: *Sure*

able(x, do(x, g))

| willing(r, do(r, e)) |

*That's not far out of my way.*

-inconvenient(p, x)

| commit(r, do(r, e)) |

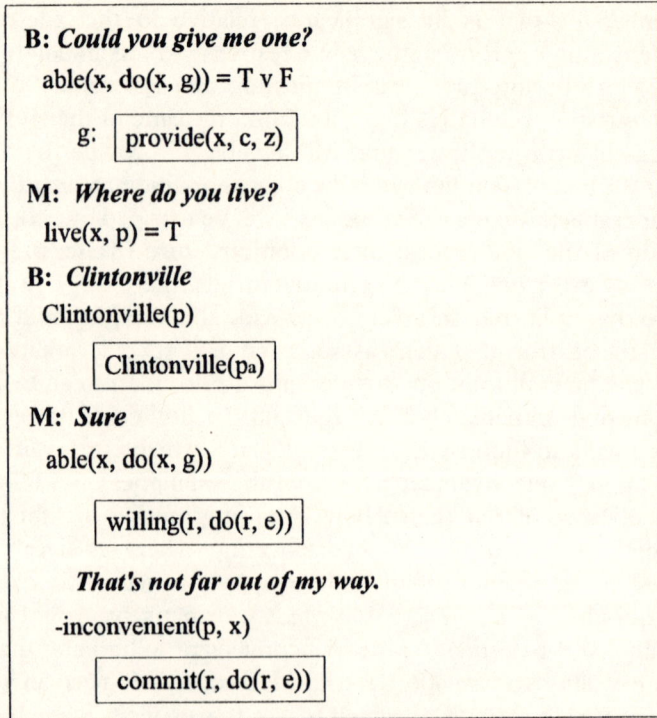

Figure 23.   The B and M ride-request DRS, continued

M: Yeah, do you need a ride home?                    $T_2$
B: Yeah, could you give me one?                      $T_3$
M: Sure                                               $T_4$

As I argued earlier, this conversation is odd in that normally an inquiry like *Are you going to the talk today?* by one colleague in a university to another would not be followed with a question like *Do you need a ride home?*. In order to account for this, we must assume that B and M each maintained a shared, particularized ride-request DRS along the lines of that in Figure 24.

B's asking whether M would be at the talk on the day in question makes this particularized DRS salient, therefore implicating that he may desire a ride. M's affirming that he would be at the talk implicated an ability to provide the ride since the precondition on the ability condition was satisfied. Since his willingness in principle to

---

i , r, e, x, pd

desires(i, do(r, e)))

e:
| provide(r, y, i, 5:00 p. m.) |
| --- |
| provider(r) |
| receiver(i) |
| ride(y) |
| depart-time(5:00 p. m.) |
| depart-place(pd) |
| arrive-place(B's-Clintonville-home) |
| instrument(x) |
| car(x) |

willing(r, do(r, e))

| be-at(r, pd, 5:00 p. m.) | ⟹ | able(r, do(r, e,)) |

| able(r, do(r, e,)) | ⟹ | commit(r, do(r, e)) |

---

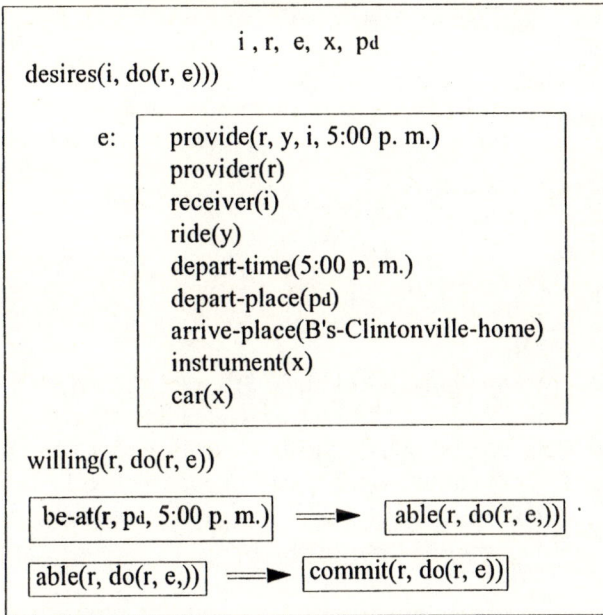

Figure 24.   The particularized B and M ride-request DRS

provide such rides had already been conceded, once M conceded that he would be at the talk, it would have been very difficult to turn B down for the precondition of the goal-state conditional was true. However, since there could have been some other reason for B's inquiry, it is reasonable that M go on to inquire as to whether B desired a ride, just as Debbie did in the baby-sitting case discussed earlier. However, unlike the none too polite Carl, B asks whether M is able to provide the ride after confirming that he needs one. I would argue that B's inquiry was no more needed transactionally in this case than in the baby-sitting example, and was uttered to mitigate the negative face-threat associated with the request.

Were B to have known in any particular case that M was going to the talk or faculty meeting, he could assume that M was both able to provide him with a ride (for the discourse condition "be-at(r, $p_d$, $t_d$)" would be true) and willing in principle to do so. This is the circumstance in which indirect speech acts are typically performed. Thus, in such a circumstance, B could have employed a form like *Could you give me a ride home today?* by way of initiating his ride-request.

As one last example of how DSAT interaction structures can be employed in DRT accounts of conversation, let us return to Donny's failed ride-request. I repeat this conversation (but in condensed form) for the convenience of the reader.

(16)   Schegloff (condensed)

> DONNY: Guess what.hh                                                     $T_1$
>
> MARCIA: What.                                                            $T_2$
>
> DONNY: .hh My ca: r is sta: : lled. (0.2)('n) I'm up here in
> the Glen?                                                                $T_3$
>
> MARCIA: Oh:                     :                 .                      $T_4$
>
> DONNY: (0.4) (.hhh) A: nd.hh (0.2) I don' know if it's
> po: ssible, but {.hhh/(0.2)} see I haveta open
> up the ba: nk.hha: t uh: (.) in Brentwood?hh=                            $T_5$
>
> MARCIA: (0.4)=Yeah: - en I know you want-(.) en I whoa-(.)
> en I would, but-except I've gotta leave in about
> five min(h)utes.[(hheh)                                                  $T_6$

In chapter 3, I argued that Marcia will hear, *My car is stalled*, as a "troubles telling," to which she would be expected either to provide a sympathetic ear or a solution. Since this call seems to have come early in the morning – both parties are on their way to work – only the latter interpretation is credible. This would not be the time to tell someone one's troubles.

I presume that we keep inventories of typical kinds of troubles and that these are indexed to the specific interaction structures to which they are relevant. Utterances as *L*-Meaning diverse as *My car is stalled, My car won't start,* and *My car battery's dead* would all point to "car trouble," which points to a variety of different types of interaction structures, in each of which the responder is expected to provide help of some sort – a ride, a tow, repair of the car, etc. Donny's inquiry in this case was interpreted as implicating that he wanted a ride from Marcia. The result is as in Figure 25. Marcia's recognition that Donny wanted her to give him a ride is the license to inject the ride-request DRS into the main DRS of their interaction. I would argue that this causes the initial assertion that he is in the Glen to be heard as an implicit question whether she is able to be at the Glen now (meaning "as soon as possible"), and therefore whether she is willing and able to provide him with a ride, represented in the DRS by (18).

d, m, x, p, t, l, f, g

Donny(d)
Marcia(m)

**Donny:** *.hh My ca:r is sta::lled.   (0.2)   ('n) I'm up here*
            *in the Glen?*

stalled(x)
car(x)
be-at(d, p, t)
Glen(p)
now(t)

i , r,  y, z, e,  $p_d$, $p_a$, $t_d$
i = d, r = m, z = x, $p_d$ = p, $t_d$ = t,  $p_a$ = l,  e = f
desires(i, do(r, e))

e:   provide(r, z, i, $t_d$)
     provider(r)
     receiver(i)
     ride(x)
     instrument(z)
     car(z)
     depart-time($t_d$)
     depart-place($p_d$)
     arrive-place ($p_a$)

possess(r, z)

| be-at(r, $p_d$, $t_d$)) | $\Longrightarrow$ | able(r, do(r, e)) |

| −inconvenient($p_a$, r) | $\Longrightarrow$ | willing(r, do(r, e)) |

| able(do(r, e)) willing(r, do(r, e)) | $\Longrightarrow$ | commit(r, do(r, e)) |

possible(able(r, do(r, e)) & willing(r, do(r, e))) = T v F

**Marcia:** *Oh::*

possible(−able(r, do(r, e)) V −willing(r, do(r, e)))

Figure 25.   The Donny and Marcia ride-request DRS

211

(17)   possible(able(r, do(r, e)) & willing(r, do(r, e))) = T v F

This is an implicit and therefore ignorable inquiry but any failure by the responder to provide some sort of positive response does implicate an inability or unwillingness to do what is wanted in such a case. Marcia's reply, *Oh: : .*, has the transactional effect of reducing Donny's confidence in her willingness and/or ability to provide the ride. At this point, DRS condition (18) is injected as an extension of the inner DRS.

(18)   possible(-able(r, do(r, e)) V -willing(r, do(r, e)))

Donny goes on to say, *A: nd.hh (0.2) I don' know if it's: po: ssible, but .hhh see I haveta open up the ba: nk.hh (0.3) a: t uh: (.) in Brentwood?hh=*. As I noted earlier, this is a transactionally very interesting utterance, which seems to have a meaning along the lines of (19).

(19)   And I don't know if it's possible (give me a ride), but see I (need a ride because I) have to open up the bank in Brentwood.

(19) is a representation of the *S*-Meaning of the utterance. However, in order to account for the oblique nature of this inquiry, it is necessary (cf. Figure 26, which should be read as an extension of Figure 25, rather than as a separate DRS) to posit a discourse referent "f," the significance of which is determined by the equation "e=f" in the inner ride-request DRS.[16] Notice that even after this utterance, Marcia could not felicitously reply with an utterance like, *I know you want one, but I can't,* for this utterance contains a pronoun linked to the discourse referent "y" of the inner DRS, which is inaccessible. Marcia's reply to this, *=Yeah: - en I know you want-(.) en I whoa-(.) en I would, but-except I've gotta leave in about five min(h)utes.=*, is similarly oblique. It too is represented by discourse conditions exploiting the

---

[16]   The DRS of Figures 25 and 26 represent instances in which background knowledge plays a critical role and much of the communication is indirect. The ride Donny wants, for instance, is never mentioned; Donny never explicitly requests a ride (i.e., never uses a colloquial request form); and Marcia never explicitly rejects it. I treat this distinction as one between inner and outer DRS as a way of distinguishing what is said from what is assumed and what is implicated. There are other ways of representing this distinction, e.g. including things that are believed, rather than said, under the intensional belief operator. I shall leave it to others to determine which is the better approach.

---

**Donny:** *(0.4) A:nd.hh (0.2) I don' know if it's: po:ssible, but .hhh see I haveta open up the ba:nk.hh (0.3) a:t uh: (.) in Brentwood?hh=*

–know(d, (able(m, do(m, f)))
cause(must(d, do(d, g)), need(d, do(m, f)))

g: | open(d, l)
| Brentwood-bank(l)

**Marcia:** *Yeah:- en I know you want-(.) en I whoa-(.) en I would, but- except I've gotta leave in about five min(h)utes*

know(m, desires(d, do(m, f)))
willing(m, do(m, f))
must(leave(m, t))

–able(m, be-at(m, p, t))

–able(m, do(m, e))

–commit(m, do(m, e))

---

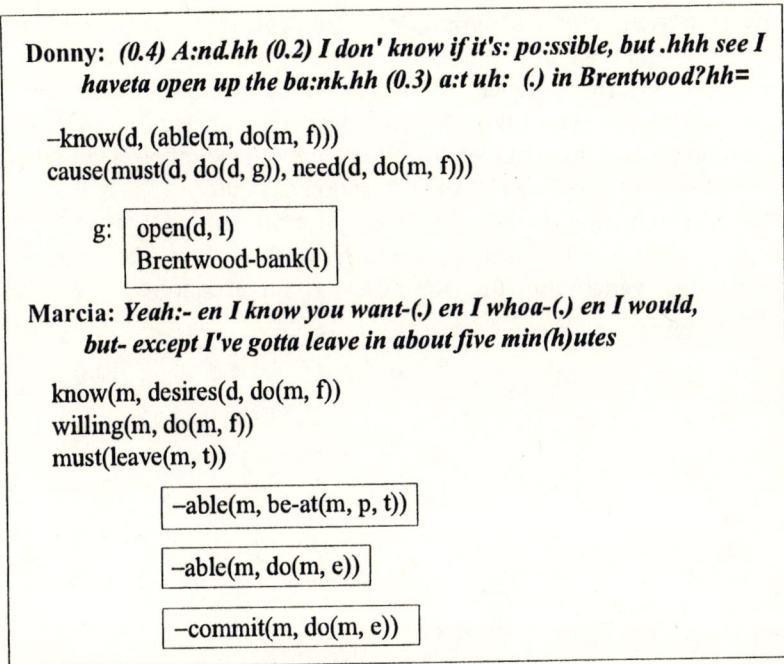

Figure 26.   The Donny and Marcia ride-request DRS, continued

discourse referent "f." Her saying, *I've gotta leave in about five min(h)utes*, is time-specific, and therefore will be interpreted as having a bearing on discourse conditions in which there is a temporal variable (namely, "be-at(r, $p_d$, $t_d$)"). This utterance therefore implicates that she will not be at the depart-place at the depart-time of the desired ride.[17] Since one of the preconditions on her ability to provide this ride is false, the ability condition cannot be satisfied, and since this is one of the preconditions on the goal state, the goal state cannot be achieved.

## Conclusion

The distinction between cognitive approaches to the treatment of discourse such as DSAT (whether implemented computationally or with DRT) and text-based approaches to discourse such as we find in

---

[17]   This DRS gives a representation for *but*, rather than *except*, which is much more complex. This has no bearing on the transactional side of the exchange. Rather, the switch to the stronger *except* has interactional significance, as we saw in chapter 4.

conversation analysis and in linguistics generally is a sharp one. The issue is whether we must make reference to notions like "adjacency pair" and "insertion sequence" in order to account for the apparent organization of conversation. My contention is that we do not – that the organization of conversation reflects various cognitive structures, not the least of which are DSAT interaction structures.

The conversation analytic approach to conversational structure is primarily concerned with utterance interpretation. It is when we turn to utterance generation, that the necessity for a cognitive approach becomes clear.

# 8

~~~⟫

# *Utterance generation*

## Introduction

In his early syntactic work, Chomsky (1965) made a distinction between the linguistic competence of speakers – the knowledge speakers have of their languages – and their linguistic performance – how speakers use their languages. In fact, of course, linguistic performance itself derives from another, much more complex competence than our linguistic competence, namely speakers' communicative competence. The question arises as to what the relationship is between our linguistic competence and our communicative competence.

Within the theoretical linguistic paradigm initiated by Chomsky's work, it is held that a speaker's linguistic competence is represented by a grammar of the language, a device that generates all and only the well-formed sentences of the language (to model the speaker's knowledge of what is and is not a sentence in the language) and associates one or more semantic interpretations with each sentence (to model the speaker's ability to associate meanings with sentences). The communicative competence of any normal speaker, on the other hand, presupposes (a) a quite general ability to construct communicative plans, including, in particular, conversational plans, in an attempt to achieve one's (normally) nonlinguistic goals and recognize and identify the plans and therefore the goals of others and (b) an ability to produce and to understand plan-relevant messages (including utterances, silences, and other verbal and nonverbal behaviors). Whether the communication is linguistic or not will depend on what operators are employed to put a given plan into action.

Viewed from the perspective of Searlean speech act theory, we might argue that his speech act structures constitute a species of communicative plans, with the essential condition specifying the goal of the communicative plan and the preparatory conditions specifying the preconditions on achieving the goal. If I need the salt and am willing and able to reach it, I might develop a noncommunicative plan to obtain the salt by employing the reaching-for-an-object operator. However, if I need the salt and am unwilling (because lazy) or unable (because it is too far away from me) to obtain it for myself and I believe that the person next to me is both willing and able to pass it to me, I might employ the request-an-object operator and say, *Could you pass the salt?*. As this example illustrates, plans are cognitive in nature, whereas operators (can) involve actions in the world.

Restricting our attention to oral communication in conversational interaction, we may say that the interaction structures associated with given interactions constitute goal-plan pairs, where the goals are the transactional and interactional effects of the interaction and the plan consists of the conditions on successful achievement of the goal relative to a specific domain. A speaker who has some transactional goal that can be achieved only through interaction with another person and who has certain interactional goals with respect to that person can be expected to choose to initiate that interaction which has the greatest chance for success in achieving the transactional goal at an acceptable interactional cost (in terms of its face-threats).

Let us refer to any device that can engage in communicative interactions with others in the respects just sketched as a conversation machine. A conversation machine differs from a grammar in many respects. A grammar (on one interpretation) accepts as input the symbol "S" and provides as output a labeled bracketing of a string of words, with a representation of its meaning and an abstract characterization of how it is to be pronounced. A conversation machine must do a variety of things, among them accepting either plans (in initiating an interaction) or others' utterances (during the course of interactions) and outputting utterances.[1] In the case of both a grammar and a conversation machine, therefore, linguistic expressions are central. However, in the case of utterance generation, the goal is not, of

---

[1] Obviously, a conversation machine must also output nonverbal behaviors as well. I ignore this to simplify the discussion.

course, simply to produce grammatical **sentences**, but, rather, contextually appropriate, plan-relevant **utterances** – utterances that advance the purposes of the talk exchange in which they occur (Grice 1975) and are consistent in style, politeness, register, and discourse with the context in which they occur. Such utterances may or may not be grammatical in the sense that they are generatable by a conventional grammar of a language. In fact, as we saw on page 82 of chapter 3, the perfectly intelligible utterances, (1) and (2), of the Donny and Marcia ride-request interaction, would ordinarily not be generatable by a grammar on their intended interpretations.

(1)  (0.4) (.hhh) A:nd.hh (0.2) I don' know if it's po:ssible, but {.hhh/(0.2)} see I haveta open up the ba:nk.hh a:t uh:(.) in Brentwood?hh=                                              $T_9$

(2)  =Yeah:- en I know you want-(.) en I whoa-(.) en I would, but- except I've gotta leave in about five min(h)utes.[(hheh)

A grammar could generate (1) only on an interpretation in which it meant something like "I don't know if it's possible for me to open the bank in Brentwood, but I have to open it." Simply relaxing conventional constraints on grammaticality will not lead to generation of this utterance ((2) either). A completely different conception of generation is required.

Utterance generation in fact must be pragmatically driven even if it employs both semantic and pragmatic data as input. I say this because the goal in producing any utterance is to construct an utterance that is not simply *L*-Meaning appropriate, which is all that a semantically driven utterance generation device can accomplish, but has the desired transactional and interactional significance, i.e., is *S*-Meaning appropriate. Such an approach is required, for instance, by examples like (1) and (2), the elliptical elements of which are recoverable only pragmatically by reference to conditions on interaction structures. Let us turn to consider some of the properties of a pragmatically driven conversation machine.

## Utterance planning

A conversation machine must contain (at least) a planner, which is the component primarily responsible for goal-achievement and goal-recognition and for constructing plan-relevant utterances and recognizing the transactional and interactional significance of others' utterances, a grammar, and some way of mapping the output of the planner into the grammar. We may assume that the output of the planner is a set of semantic and pragmatic features, that the device that mediates the relationship between the planner and the grammar maps semantic and pragmatic features into linguistic features, and that the grammar maps linguistic features into utterances.[2]

The mapping of planner output features into linguistic features must be capable of accounting both for those bits of utterances that are semantically compositional (semantic generation) and for those bits that involve conventions of use (pragmatic generation). I have argued that a pragmatic stratum along the lines sketched in chapter 6 can account for those bits of utterances that exhibit pragmatic conventionalization. I leave open how, exactly, the semantic side of utterance generation should be accounted for. However, it is clear that the pragmatic stratum and the semantic component, whatever it may be, must interact. In the case of a feature-driven theory like Head-Driven Phrase Structure Grammar (Pollard and Sag 1987, 1994), for instance, the syntactic, semantic, and pragmatic components constitute three co-equal, interconnected parts of an inheritance hierarchy. For such a theory, the planner would output both semantic and pragmatic features that would determine the form of an utterance.

Let me be more explicit about how utterance planning is done. In the case of any plan or subplan of a larger plan, there will be an initial state and a goal state. In the case of communicative plans, which normally form just a part of larger real-world domain plans, the initial state will consist of a desire to achieve a set of transactional and interactional goals. Thus, the initiator's initial state in a given case might consist of a desire (i) to cause the responder to commit to performing an action that benefits the initiator (ii) without unduly risking a face-threatening negative response and (iii) by sufficiently redressing the threat to the responder's negative face that no injury is done to the relationship. Such a set of goals would normally lead to an indirect approach to the interaction (e.g., initiating a ride-request with an utterance like *Are you going to the talk today?*) or a direct approach that is no-init-up, resp-up, and deferential in character (i.e., an

---

[2]  Just how the relationship between the planner and grammar is defined will depend, of course, on the nature of the grammar employed. The characterization in the text is one such definition.

utterance like *Could you take me home after work today?*). The final state of the communicative plan would, then, consist of this set of desired outcomes. In the example at hand, these would consist of the responder's committing himself to perform the desired action in a way that does not do injury to the initiator's positive face and did not injure the responder's negative face.[3]

In order to get from the initial state to the goal state, the machine must construct some plan, which will consist of an hierarchical array of subplans (abstract operators) and primitive operators that will carry the machine from the initial state to the goal state, the goal state being achievable only if all of the plan conditions are satisfied (true). Happily, we can normally take such a communicative plan "off the shelf" and employ an existing plan schema – the generalized ride-request interaction schema, perhaps, or, as B did in the B and M ride-request interactions, the particularized B and M ride-request interaction schema shared by B and M. When we cannot, we must devise some novel plan, perhaps one modeled on existing plan schemata. Thus, the first time one books a flight on an airline, one might combine elements of a more general event-booking schema learned from booking reservations in restaurants (which would have a bearing on the statuses and roles of participants and would contribute a domain predicate bearing on the size of the traveling party (from the size of the dining party) with the ride-request schema which would contribute domain predicates bearing on times and places of departures and arrivals.

In Searle's speech act theory, as noted, the essential condition identifies the goal state that may be achieved in executing the speech act, the sincerity condition is sometimes equivalent to the initial-state condition (requests) and sometimes not (conveying information), and the preparatory conditions are equivalent to plan conditions. The difficulty with this view for computational implementations is that his speech acts are treated as primitive operators. Within this framework, doing requesting in saying, *Can you pass the salt?*, is as primitive an action as reaching for the salt. In DSAT, interaction structures can be thought of as abstract plans, as opposed to primitive operators, for they link an initial state to a goal state and provide a set of plan

---

3    In fact, we must often revise our communicative plans during an interaction in order to achieve those goals that are achievable. Thus, in the Donny and Marcia conversation, Donny might have shifted from the goal of getting Marcia to rescue him to the goal of getting Marcia to suggest the name of someone who might be able to rescue him.

conditions, which are themselves subplans, on achievement of the goal state. It is this property that makes DSAT a better candidate than Searlean speech act theory for accounting for multiturn interactions.

## The context of situation

As noted, the planner is responsible for both goal-achievement (in which case the conversation machine is the initiator) and for goal-recognition (in which case the conversation machine is the responder) and for both utterance generation and utterance understanding. In order to do these things the planner must have access to various kinds of knowledge. Of special importance is knowledge of what context of situation (CoS) the conversation machine is in, where we understand a CoS to be defined by the event that brings people together (e.g., a dinner party, a class-room lecture, a business meeting, a retail service encounter, etc.), by who the participants are (including information about their statuses and roles and social power and distance relationships), and by the manner of interaction (e.g., telephone call, inter-person interaction, etc.).[4]

If a set of friends meet at a restaurant to have dinner together some evening (the event of the CoS), they can be expected to greet each other, negotiate with a restaurant employee for a table, engage with their waiter in the ordering of drinks and food, engage in conversation with each other (talk for talk's sake), engage in drinking and dining, possibly make plans for future get-togethers, engage in bill paying with the waiter, and engage in some sort of parting activity. Other things might go on. Some of the participants might engage in a business negotiation or request a ride home after dining or a ride to work the next day, and so on. It is quite unlikely, however, that one party will suddenly start giving a formal lecture, or start barking out signals for a football play, etc. In short, in any CoS, certain activities will be expected (e.g., food ordering, conversing, dining, bill paying, etc.); certain other activities are expectable (e.g., making future plans, making personal requests unrelated to the dinner party itself); and certain other activities will be quite unexpected (e.g., someone's giving a formal lecture or barking out football signals). These sorts of expectations play a critical role in goal recognition and language understanding. If in a classroom, one student says, *Do you have any*

---

[4]   These three elements correspond to what Halliday and Hasan (1989) call field, tenor, and mode.

*writing paper?*, to another, it will be understood that he wants a gift of a few sheets of writing paper, whereas, if uttered to a clerk in a retail store, it would be understood that he wants to buy a pad or two of paper.

The nature of the activity the participants of an event are engaged in in a particular CoS will determine the register of the interaction. Thus, if the responder is a travel agent and the initiator engages with the responder in requesting a booking on a flight, we can expect that the responder will employ the travel agent register, but should they turn to engage in some activity unrelated to the work of agents (say, discussing something in the news), we would not expect the agent to continue to employ this register.

The issue of who the participants are devolves into (at least) their statuses and roles in the activity in which they are engaged and any personal relationship they may have. Thus, travel agents who assist persons in their travel arrangements have the status of Agents, associated with which are certain roles (providing information, booking flights, etc.). The status of Agent is socially less powerful than that of Clients and the Agent-Client relationship involves considerable social distance (a distal as opposed to a familiar relationship). As a consequence, we would expect three things: the Agent will employ forms characteristic of the Agent-Client register while the Client may or may not do so; the Agent will employ relatively polite forms, whereas the Client may or may not do so; and the style of the conversation will normally be moderately formal unless some sort of personal relationship exists. On the other hand, if the initiator and the responder are ordinary people, and the initiator asks the responder to arrange a ride for the initiator to a party and the responder complies, the responder does not thereby become an Agent though she is in some sense doing precisely what an Agent does. Instead, we have a simple Provider-Receiver relationship. We would not expect language characteristic of the Agent-Client register; there may be no social power difference between the parties; and the social distance relationship could be distal or familiar.

I am assuming that the institutionally defined status of participants determines their power relationship, whereas any personal history between them will have a bearing on how familiar or distant they may be socially. We may expect that both the social power and social distance relationships among participants will have a significant bearing on what sorts of activities (including what sorts of interactions) they engage each other in, how they redress face-threatening acts, and what style levels they employ.

The third element of a CoS concerns the manner of interaction. The interaction might be oral or written, and if oral, it might be a face-to-face interaction or a telephone interaction, and if written, it might be done via letters or e-mail, etc. We would expect that the details of how any interaction will play out will depend on the manner of the interaction.

The theory of conversational competence cannot now be, and may never be, a predictive theory in the sense that it is able to predict why a given person might choose to try to achieve a given goal by engaging in any one interaction as opposed to another. Similarly, we cannot expect to be able to predict why a given speaker makes the style and politeness choices he makes on a given occasion. However, we can imagine trying to simulate what people do computationally by devising a conversation machine that makes choices that are appropriate in a given context. In what follows in this chapter, I shall discuss certain features of utterance generation and utterance understanding and of goal-recognition that seem sufficiently tractable to be implemented computationally. In the case of utterance generation, what I shall have to say is a modification and elaboration of what was said in Patten, Geis, and Becker (1992).

### Participant knowledge

Obviously, what a speaker says at any given point will reflect what this speaker believes is true at the time. If the initiator wants a hot chocolate and does not know whether the responder has hot chocolate, she might employ the value-requesting, domain-oriented utterance, *Do you have hot chocolate?* She will surely not employ the value-positing, thing-specific form, *I'll have a hot chocolate,* for doing that would presuppose the very information she does not have. Utterance choice depends, however, not just on what the initiator knows about the CoS, but also on what the initiator believes the responder knows. Recall conversation (6) on page 124 of chapter 5, in which the initiator initiated a request sequence in saying, *Do you have the blackberry jam?* We cannot account for the presence of *the* in this utterance unless we assume that the initiator believes that there was some sort of prior exchange between the initiator and the responder in which reference was made to a certain kind of blackberry jam, believes that the responder believes that such reference was made, and believes that the responder believes that the initiator believes that such reference was made. That is, the initiator must assume that there is mutual or common knowledge of this prior reference to blackberry jam. We might expect then that a representation of this mutual knowledge, usually called the "common ground" (Stalnaker 1978), would contain a discourse referent "x" with an associated condition "blackberry jam(x)."

In fact, of course, the notion of a common ground is a fiction, as I noted in chapter 7, for if we assume that all CoS-specific knowledge relevant to utterance generation and understanding is shared we shall be quite unable to account for certain kinds of errors. I will argue, instead, that each participant in an interaction maintains two representations – a representation of that participant's knowledge of the CoS, which would include a knowledge of what interaction is being interacted and the respects in which the interaction structure associated with that act has been instantiated, among many other things, and a representation of the common ground as that participant **believes** it to be. These assumptions are critical to an account of utterance production, for what each speaker says reflects what that speaker believes is and is not in the common ground. In what follows, I propose to develop this point.

## Utterance generation

Let us suppose that a person, Sandy, has been dining out with a number of friends and the group is about to break up. At this point, Sandy is faced with the problem of getting home and she must therefore devise some plan that will cause her to achieve this goal. Some possible options are:

- She might drive herself home.
- She might take a taxi.
- She might request a ride from someone else.

Associated with each of these plans is a set of preconditions that must be satisfied if she is to carry out her plan. If she is to drive herself home, she must have her car with her. If she is going to take a taxi, she must have some means of summoning a taxi and must have the funds to pay the fare. If she is to request a ride from some person, she must

enjoy the sort of social relationship with this person that is consistent
with such a request and this person must herself have a car with her
and otherwise be able to provide this ride and she must also be willing
to provide this ride. Which plan Sandy will carry out will reflect some
sort of cost-benefit analysis of those plans whose preconditions are
satisfied (or can be satisfied through negotiation).

There are, then, two basic considerations that influence selection
of a particular plan in any given circumstance: transactional considerations and interactional considerations. The transactional considerations are that the plan have as its transactional effect the desired goal
state, and that the satisfaction conditions either are met or can be met.
The interactional considerations involve whether or not the relationship of the initiator to the responder is consistent with the interactional
effects of the plan.

Brown and Levinson (1987: 81) suggest that there could be a
calculus of the "weightiness" of a face-threatening action which
employs function (3), where "$W_x$" is the weightiness of the face-
threatening act (FTA) "x," "D" is the social distance of speaker (S)
and hearer (H), "P" is a measure of the power H has over S, and "R"
is a measure of the relative degree to which x threatens face in the
culture at hand.

(3)   $W_x = D(S,H) + P(H,S) + R_x$

Function (3) would be relevant in planning to the question of what
interaction an initiator might choose to engage the responder in to
achieve some goal and, in circumstances in which the responder must
provide a dispreferred response, what sort of dispreferred response the
responder might choose (whether he will decline directly or indirectly
and whether the declination will be ability-based or willingness-based).
However, function (3) cannot decide what choice any given speaker
will actually make on any given occasion, for there are factors other
than the degree of face-threat associated with interactions that have a
bearing on choosing between them, including social costs. Someone
might choose not to steal money from another person because of the
possibility of getting caught.

Transactional and interactional considerations will also influence
how any abstract plan is actualized as a concrete plan-in-action. Let
us suppose that Sandy has chosen to request a ride from someone she
was dining with. She has a number of options available to her. She has

choices as to which interaction structure condition to attack. She may choose to attack the initial-state condition or the ability or willingness condition. A second pair of options concerns whether she will attack a given condition directly or indirectly. Finally, she must choose a particular linguistic form – more precisely a set of pragmatic features reflecting how she chooses to redress any face-threats associated with the act and what style level she believes to be appropriate. Let us begin by considering the first two choices together.

### Direct and indirect communication

I shall take the position here that a speaker is communicating directly when he employs utterances that instantiate primary conditions of interaction structures and is communicating indirectly when he employs utterances instantiating preconditions of primary conditions. On this view, the utterances of (4) are direct and those of (5) are indirect.

(4)  a.  I need a ride home.
     b.  Can you give me a ride home?
     c.  Give me a ride home.

(5)  a.  My car is stalled.
     b.  Do you have a car?
     c.  Do you live near Henderson and High?

According to Searle, however, an utterance like (4c) is a direct request form, whereas all of the other forms are indirect. In the taxonomy of Lycan, discussed in chapter 5, the forms of (5) are instances of Type 1 indirect speech acts and (4a) and (4b) are instances of Type 2 indirect speech acts.

I assume that Searle's reason for saying that (4c) is direct and the others are indirect is that it utilizes a sentence form (the imperative form) believed to be dedicated in some way to requests, whereas (4a) and (4b) manifestly do not. However, imperatives can be used for a wide array of acts which have as legitimate a claim to the imperative form as do requests, including orders, warnings (*Watch out for that bull!*), suggestions (*Brush with Crest!*), etc, so this is not a particularly compelling reason to see (4c) as being a direct **request** form.

225

The distinction I am making corresponds much more closely than does Searle's to what we intuitively perceive as being direct and indirect, for the illocutionary points of each of the utterances in (4) are immediately recognizable.[5] This would not necessarily be true of utterances like those of (5) that instantiate preconditions of primary conditions, which are often consistent with other interpretations. Thus, someone who asks another whether she has her car may want her to carry some heavy object from one place to another, not give the responder a ride. A second reason to prefer the DSAT view of directness and indirectness in communication is that in being based on the distinction between utterances that instantiate primary interaction structure conditions and those that instantiate preconditions on same, the DSAT distinction has a sounder theoretical basis than does Searle's, which is based on the notional sentence type in a not fully explicit way, and is precise and has genuine cross-linguistic utility in that it is not tied to details of a language's syntax.

## Orientation and directness choices

At the outset of initiation of some particular communicative interaction, the state of the conversation machine must be the same as the initial state of the interaction structure. At that point, the machine must determine whether or not the satisfaction conditions associated with that sort of interaction are satisfied by examining its representation of the common ground. In the case of a thing-request, this would mean that the machine believes the precondition that the responder possesses what is desired is satisfied. In the case of a ride-request, it would mean that the machine believes that the responder will not find the destination inconvenient, that the responder possesses a car, and that the responder is able to be at the point of departure at the time of departure; and so forth. If they are satisfied, the machine **must** employ a value-positing utterance that (a) instantiates the initial-state condition of the interaction structure associated with that interaction (i.e., communicates what it is that is desired) and (b) instantiates the most critical domain predicates – the "object" predicate of thing-requests or the "action" predicate of action-requests, for instance. In a frozen yoghurt store, an utterance like, *I'd like a large pineapple*, would meet these conditions. There might be further domain-oriented talk –

---

5 Recall Good's (MS) point that the illocutionary forces of many indirect speech acts "are so transparent that to call them 'indirect' seems perverse" (p. 6).

226

perhaps, about whether the initiator wants the yoghurt in a cup or cone and whether he wants any toppings.

I have taken the position that any init-centric or resp-centric utterance can, in principle, can be used either directly to posit the value "true" for the initial-state condition or to implicate that the value of this condition is "true." The init-oriented, init-centric forms (*I want/would like/need a large pineapple*) directly instantiate the initial-state condition, as do the thing-specific, init-centric forms, *I'll take/have a large pineapple*, for the latter branch off the feature "init-centric." The various resp-centric forms (*Give me a large pineapple*, a nondeferential, resp-willingness form, *You can give me a large pineapple*, a nondeferential, resp-ability form, *Can you give me a large pineapple?*, a deferential, no-resp-up, ability form, and *Would you give me a large pineapple?*, a deferential, resp-willingness form) all can be used to implicate a true value for the initial-state condition, where the implicature is directly computed, rather than "calculated" in Grice's sense of the term.[6] This is in fact what is going on in the DSAT account of so-called "indirect speech act" utterances.

Interrogative init-centric and resp-centric forms can also, of course, be used to request values for conditions. An utterance like, *Can I have my yoghurt in a sugar cone?*, can be used to inquire whether having yoghurt in a sugar cone is an option (i.e., is selectable) and *Could you give me the yoghurt in a sugar cone?* can be used to inquire as to whether the responder is willing (perhaps permitted) to serve yoghurt in a sugar cone. An interesting speech-act-theoretic ambiguity results, as was noted in chapter 6. The standard position of speech act theorists is that a sentence like (6) can be taken either as an information question or as an indirect request.

(6) Can you give me a ride home?

However, within DSAT, three readings of this sentence are available. There is first the (often contextually implausible) "pure" information request reading. And, there are two request-specific readings. In cases in which the ability of the responder to satisfy the request has not been established and the initiator employs an interrogative utterance like this, the responder cannot know (unless the intonation makes it clear)

---

[6] The principle is that if the initiator of an interaction employs an utterance that specifies a satisfaction condition on achievement of the goal state, this immediately implicates that the initial-state condition is true.

whether the initiator is employing a deferential, value-positing utterance or a nondeferential, value-requesting utterance that directly
specifies the ability condition and indirectly specifies the initial-state
condition. The first reading is the "indirect speech act" reading. The
second reading, though value-requesting in nature, is not the same as
the "pure" information question reading for it, unlike the information
question reading, has action implications (i.e., implicates that the
initial-state condition of the ride-request interaction structure is true).

Interestingly, this latter "ambiguity" has no transactional consequences, for if the responder says, *Yes*, to an utterance like (6) on the
assumption that it was intended to be a deferential, value-positing
utterance (*vis-à-vis* the initial-state condition), he will take himself to
have committed himself to performing the desired action directly, but
if the responder says, *Yes*, on the assumption that the utterance was
intended to be a value-requesting, resp-ability utterance, then the
responder will have implicated a commitment to perform the action
(i.e., implicated the value "true" for the initial-state condition), thanks
to the effect of the axiom of commitment. This "ambiguity" makes
these forms particularly useful for they can be taken as polite,
redressive forms, however they may have been intended.

I shall assume that the orientation features (i.e., init-oriented, thing-
specific, resp-ability, and resp-willingness) and the politeness features
(i.e., (no-)deference, (no-)init-up, and (no-)resp-up) are primitive
operators, for they have effects on the forms of utterances. The
problem is how does the planner make choices from among these
features and what criteria govern the choices the planner makes.

To some degree the choices a planner makes will be based on social
norms. However, there seems also to be an important personal
dimension to these choices. In Geis and Harlow (forthcoming), we
report on an experiment on how English-speaking and French-
speaking subjects do requesting in an informal, puzzle-solving task
and found that there was substantial variation among subjects. This
may be because the experiment was not sufficiently controlled to give
more uniform results. However, all one has to do is listen to people
order frozen yoghurt to confirm that in this transactionally simple and
interactionally straightforward context, a relatively wide variety of
forms are used.

One thing does seem clear and this is that for any given speaker
only a small range of forms will seem appropriate in any given
circumstance. I find that I use forms like *I'll have a large pineapple*,

*I'd like a large pineapple,* and (much less frequently) *Couldja gimme a large pineapple?* in retail stores in which I am certain that what I wish is available. Certain other forms strike me as too "pushy" (i.e., too much emphasize my greater social power in the context), namely, *I want a large pineapple, I'll take a large pineapple, You can gimme a large pineapple, Can you gimme a large pineapple?,* and *Gimme a large pineapple,* but I suspect that they may be used by others. Some other choices seem overly deferential, such as *I need a large pineapple, Can I have a large pineapple?,* or *Would you gimme a large pineapple?* These observations suggest to me that we set switches for the binary options in particular types of CoS that restrict the class of utterance types that will be available and that discourse considerations will dictate which choice is made. Since I seem to restrict myself in a frozen yoghurt store to forms like *I'll have a large pineapple, I'd like a large pineapple,* and *Couldja gimme a large pineapple?,* it appears that I must set the resp-up/no-resp-up switch to resp-up. Then, if I choose an init-centric form, it must be init-oriented and init-up or thing-specific and no-init-up, and if I choose a resp-centric form, it must be a resp-ability, deferential form. We might represent this set of options as in (7).

(7)  resp-up ∧ (((init-centric form ⊃ (init-oriented ∧ init-up) ∨ (thing-specific ∧ no-init-up)) ∨ (resp-centric ⊃ (resp-ability ∧ deference)))

Why I might choose one of these three forms over another is difficult to say, but I suspect that my choices may vary with discourse position. I tend to initiate interactions with *I'll have a large pineapple,* use *I'd like a large pineapple* after specifically being asked what I would like and say *Couldja gimme a large pineapple?* after a clerk says something on the order of *Can I help you?.* However, my intuitions about these facts should be taken with a box of salt. I trouble to say these things to illustrate a possible computational approach to fine-tuning utterance choices.

### Direct and indirect attacks on conditions

Let us suppose that we have an interaction in which the initiator does not know whether or not the responder is either willing or able to assist her as might be true of Sandy, who in the scenario sketched above needed a ride after dining with friends in a restaurant. Sandy might choose to be direct and employ an utterance that instantiates any one of the three major conditions with a value-positing utterance. However, there is substantial risk in initiating something like a ride-request with an unambiguous attack on the initial-state condition (e.g., saying something like *Say, Terry, I need a ride home*), for not only does the request itself threaten the responder's negative face, one may be embarrassed to discover that the contextual presuppositions of such a move – that the responder is willing and able to provide the desired ride – are false. As a consequence, we tend to employ this tactic only when we are reasonably confident that the responder is able and willing (at least in principle) to provide the ride.

A direct attack on the two satisfaction conditions is less problematic if the utterances are deferential (*Say, Terry, could you give me a ride home?* or *Say, Terry, would you give me a ride home?*) and can therefore be heard as nonpresumptuous resp-centric value-requesting forms. When speakers choose this tack, they tend to opt for a resp-ability form, for such a form poses less potential threat to the initiator's positive face in that ability-based rejections are less threatening than willingness-based rejections.

Alternatively, the initiator might choose to attack one of the conditions indirectly. She might, for instance, attack the initial-state condition indirectly by employing an utterance that provides the reason why the initiator has initiated the interaction, as Donny did when he initiated his ride-request with the utterance, *My car is stalled.* Such a tactic mitigates the face-threat to the responder in virtue of its indirectness. It is framed as a plea for help without specifying precisely what sort of help is desired, and thus gives the responder more options than would an unambiguous attack on the initial-state condition, and does not presume either the willingness or the ability of the responder to help.

When the initiator is less powerful than the responder or the initiator and responder do not enjoy a close personal relationship, an unambiguous attack on the initial-state condition is unlikely. Such persons will normally attack this condition indirectly if they are to attack it at all. On the other hand, superiors or intimates may choose to attack this condition indirectly, rather than directly, by way of displaying spontaneous politeness.

A second indirect approach would be to attack the ability condition indirectly through an utterance like, *Do you have a car?* or *Are you going to the talk today?*, that specifies a precondition on the ability condition. This tactic seems to be available to anyone whose relationship to the responder is consistent with the FTA involved. A third indirect approach is to attack the willingness condition indirectly, as would be the case if someone wanting a ride were to say, *Do you live anywhere near Henderson and High?* If the responder says, *Not really*, the initiator may terminate the exchange. If the responder says, *Pretty close*, she will feel encouraged to continue.

Now, which of the above tactics is adopted in a particular case will depend on what is known and on the social relationship of the initiator to the responder. If the initiator is superior to or an intimate of the responder, she may feel free to attack the initial-state condition in certain circumstances with an init-centric utterance even when she does not know if the responder is willing or able to perform the desired action. Superiors may choose this option when the interaction is contextually legitimate, as in the case of legitimate work-related impositions, as I have argued earlier, for such interactions are not configured as FTA. And intimates can choose this option in some cases for the same reason. Requesting a ride from a friend may not be configured as an FTA; requesting a large loan very well might be. Inferiors and what we might call "mere acquaintances" must either attack the initial-state condition indirectly or attack the ability or willingness conditions. In the latter case, I suspect that such persons will attack the conditions indirectly.

## Conclusion

The computational implementation of utterance generation of Patten, Geis and Becker (1992) did establish that pragmatic generation of utterances was feasible for one type of interaction in one context. However, this implementation, though it did allow for a modest amount of stylistic variation, did not allow at all for politeness variation. The pragmatic stratum·discussed in chapter 6 is intended to remedy this defect.[7] The problem lies in taking the next step – to devise a planner for a given machine that is capable of engaging in a number of different interactions with a number of different persons with whom the machine enjoys very different social power and

---

[7]   This pragmatic stratum has been tested computationally in a somewhat different form employing a systemic grammar. The present version was modified to allow reference to more familiar grammatical notions.

distance relationships. Such a planner would be forced to select different orientation and directness options and to vary other politeness choices from interaction to interaction. We can expect that this may be difficult to do, primarily because we lack the social knowledge required. Thus, an important next step is to do research into the linguistic choices people actually make and determine what social parameters govern these choices.

# References

Allen, J. 1983. Recognizing Intentions from Natural Language Utterances. In M. Brady and R. C. Berwick, eds., *Computational Models of Discourse*, 107–66. Cambridge, MA: MIT Press.

Asher, N. 1993. *Reference to Abstract Objects in Discourse*. Dordrecht, Boston, London: Kluwer Academic Publishers.

Atkinson, J. M. and Drew, P. 1979. *Order in Court*. London: Macmillan.

Atkinson, J. M. and Heritage, J. 1984. *Structures of Social Action: Studies in Conversational Analysis*, 57–101. Cambridge University Press.

Austin, J. L. 1962. *How to Do Things with Words*. Oxford University Press.

Bach, K. and Harnish, R. M. 1979. *Linguistic Communication and Speech Acts*. Cambridge, MA: MIT Press.

Bilmes, J. 1988. The Concept of Preference in Conversation Analysis. *Language in Society*, 17 (2): 161–82.

Boër, S. and Lycan, W. G. 1976. *The Myth of Semantic Presupposition*. Bloomington, IN: Indiana University Linguistics Club.

Brewer, W. F. 1975. Memory for Ideas: Synonym Substitution. *Memory and Cognition*, 3 (4): 458–64.

1977. Memory for the pragmatic implications of sentences. *Memory and Cognition*, 5 (6): 673–78.

Brewer, W. F. and Lichtenstein, E. H. 1975. Recall of Logical and

Pragmatic Implications in Sentences with Dichotomous Continuous Antonyms. *Memory and Cognition*, 3: 315–18.

Brown, P. and Levinson, S. C. 1987. *Politeness: Some Universals in Language Usage*. Cambridge University Press.

Cheepen, C. 1988. *The Predictability of Informal Conversation*. London: Pinter Publishers.

Cohen, P. R. and Perrault, C. R. 1986. Elements of a Plan-based Theory of Speech Acts. In G. Groszy *et al.*, eds., *Readings in Natural Language Processing Tasks*, 423–30. Los Altos, CA: Morgan Kaufman.

Coulthard, M. and Barzil, D. 1979. Exchange structure. In M. Coulthard and M. Montgomery, eds., *Studies in Discourse Analysis*, 82–106. London: Routledge and Kegan Paul.

Davidson, D. 1967a. The Logical Form of Action Sentences. In N. Rescher, ed., *The Logic of Decision and Action*. Pittsburgh: University of Pittsburgh Press.

1967b. Truth and Meaning. *Synthese*, 17 (3): 304–23.

Davidson, J. 1984. Subsequent Versions of Invitations, Offers, Requests, and Proposals Dealing with Potential or Actual Rejection. In J. M. Atkinson and J. Heritage, eds., *Structures of Social Action: Studies in Conversational Analysis*, 102–28. Cambridge University Press.

Drew, P. 1984. Pursuing a Response. In J. M. Atkinson and J. Heritage, eds., *Structures of Social Action: Studies in Conversational Analysis*, 129–51. Cambridge University Press.

Edmondson, W. 1981. *Spoken Discourse: A Model for Analysis*. London: Longman.

Engdahl, E. 1986. *Constituent Questions*. Dordrecht: D. Reidel Publishing Co.

Fraser, B. and Nolen, F. 1981. The Association of Deference with Linguistic Form. *International Journal of the Sociology of Language*, 27: 93–109.

Gavioli, L. and Mansfield, G. 1990. *The Pixi Corpora*. Bologna: Cooperativa Libraria Universitaria Editrice. Computer-readable version (from the Oxford University Text Archives) edited by Guy Aston. Ancona: CISeL.

Geis, M. L. 1989. A New Theory of Speech Acts. *Proceedings of the Sixth Annual Meeting of the Eastern States Conference on Linguistics*. Columbus: Department of Linguistics.

Geis, M. L. and Harlow, L. Forthcoming. Politeness Strategies in

French and English: Implications for second language acquisition. In S. Gass and J. Neu, eds. *Speech Acts Across Cultures*. Berlin: Mouton de Gruyter.

Geis, M. L. and Lycan, W. L. 1995. Nonconditional Conditionals. *Philosophical Topics*.

Goffman, E. 1967. *Interaction Ritual: Essays on Face to Face Behavior*. Garden City, New York.

Good, D. MS. The Psychology of Requests: The Illocutionary Assumption. Unpublished MS, University of Cambridge. (Contact: DG25@phx.cam.ac.uk)

Gordon, D. and Lakoff, G. 1971. Conversational Postulates. *Papers from the Seventh Regional Meeting of the Chicago Linguistic Society*, 63–84. Chicago: Department of Linguistics, University of Chicago.

Green, G. M. 1975. How to Get People to Do Things with Words: The Whimperative Question. In P. Cole and J. Morgan, eds., *Syntax and Semantics*, vol. 3: *Speech Acts*, 107–42. New York: Academic Press.

Grice, H. P. 1957. Meaning. *Philosophical Review*, 67. Reprinted in numerous anthologies including J. F. Rosenberk and C. Travis, eds., *Readings in the Philosophy of Language* (pp. 436–44). Englewood Cliffs, NJ: Prentice-Hall, Inc.

   1975. Logic and Conversation. In P. Cole and J. L. Morgan, eds., *Syntax and Semantics*, vol. 3: *Speech Acts*, 41–58. New York: Academic Press.

Halliday, M. A. K. 1985. *An Introduction to Functional Grammar*. London: Edward Arnold.

Halliday, M. A. K. and Hasan, R. 1989. *Language, Context, and Text: Aspects of Language in a Social-semiotic Perspective*. Oxford University Press.

Harris, R. J. 1974. Memory and Comprehension of Implications and Inferences of Complex Sentences. *Journal of Verbal Learning and Verbal Behavior*, 13: 626–37.

Harris, R. J. and Monaco, G. E. 1978. Psychology of Pragmatic Implication: Information Processing Between the Lines. *Journal of Experimental Psychology, Gen.*, 107: 1–22.

Heritage, J. 1984. *Garfinkel and Ethnomethodology*. Cambridge: Polity Press, in conjunction with Basil Blackwell, Oxford.

Houghton, G. and Isard, S. 1987. Why to Speak, What to Say and How to Say It: Modelling Language Production in Discourse. In P. Morris, ed., *Modelling Cognition*. London: John Wiley & Sons.

Hymes, D. 1967. Models of the Interaction of Language and Social Setting. *Journal of Social Issues*, 23.

Isaacs, E. A. and Clark, H. H. 1990. Ostensible Invitations. *Language in Society*, 19 (4): 493–509.

Jacobs, S. and Jackson, S. 1983a. Speech Act Structure in Conversation: Rational Aspects of Pragmatic Coherence. In R. T. Craig and K. Tracy, eds., *Conversational Coherence: Form, Structure, and Strategy*, 47–66. Beverly Hills: Sage Publications.

1983b. Strategy and Structure in Conversational Influence Attempts. *Communications Monographs*, 50: 285–304. Cambridge University Press.

Kadmon, N. 1987. On Unique and Non-unique Reference and Asymmetric Quantification. Ph. D. Dissertation. UMass at Amherst.

1990. Uniqueness. *Linguistics and Philosophy*, 13: 273–324.

Kamp, H. and Reyle, U. 1993. *From Discourse to Logic: Introduction to Modeltheoretic Semantics of Natural Language, Formal Logic and Discourse Representation Theory*. Dordrecht: The Netherlands.

Kratzer, A. 1979. What *must* and *can* Must and Can Mean. *Linguistics and Philosophy* 1: 337–55.

Labov, W. 1972. Rules for Ritual Insults. In D. Sudnow, ed., *Studies in Social Interaction*, 122–69. New York: Free Press.

Labov, W. and Fanshel, D. 1977. *Therapeutic Discourse: Psychotherapy as Conversation*. New York: Academic Press.

Lakoff, R. 1968. *Abstract Syntax and Latin Complementation*. Cambridge, MA: MIT Press.

1973. The Logic of Politeness: Or Minding Your P's and Q's. In C. Corum, T. C. Smith-Stark, and A. Weiser, eds., *Papers from the Ninth Regional Meeting of the Chicago Linguistic Society*, 292–305. Chicago: Chicago Linguistic Society.

Levinson, S. C. 1981. The Essential Inadequacies of Speech Act Models of Dialogue. In H. Parret, M. Sbis‘a, and J. Verschueren, eds., *Possibilities and Limitations of Pragmatics. Proceedings of the Conference on Pragmatics, Urbino, July 8–14, 1979*. Amsterdam: John Benjamins.

1983. *Pragmatics*. Cambridge University Press.

Litman, D. J. and Allen, J. A. 1987. A Plan Recognition Model for Subdialogues in Conversations. *Cognitive Science*, 11: 163–200.

Longacre, R. E. 1967. *An Anatomy of Speech Notions*. Lisse: Peter de Ridder Press.

Loosen, F. 1981. Memory for the Gist of Sentences. *Journal of Psycholinguistics*, 10: 17–25.

Lycan, W. G. 1984. *Logical Form in Natural Language*. Cambridge, MA: MIT Press.

Lyons, J. 1977. *Semantics*, vol. 1. Cambridge University Press.

Mandelbaum, J. and Pomerantz, A. 1991. What Drives Social Action? In K. Tracy, *Understanding Face-to-face Interaction: Issues Linking Goals and Discourse*. Hillsdale, NJ: Lawrence Erlbaum Associates, Publishers.

Merritt, M. 1976. On Questions Following Questions (in Service Encounters). *Language in Society*, 5.3: 315–57.

Morgan, J. L. 1978. Two Types of Convention in Indirect Speech Acts. *Syntax and Semantics*, vol. 9: *Pragmatics*, 261–80. New York: Academic Press.

Patten, T., Geis, M., and Becker, B. 1992. Toward a Theory of Compilation for Natural-Language Generation. *Computational Intelligence*, 8 (1): 77–101.

Peirce, C. S. 1955. *Philosophical Writings of Peirce*, selected and edited with an introduction by Justus Buchler. New York: Dover.

Perrault, C. R. and Allen, J. F. 1980. A Plan-based Analysis of Indirect Speech Acts. *American Journal of Computational Linguistics*, 6.3–4: 167–82.

Pollard, C. and Sag, I. 1987. *Information-Based Syntax and Semantics*, vol. 1 *Fundamentals*. CSLI Lecture Notes no. 13. Stanford: CSLI Publications. Distributed by University of Chicago Press.

    1994. *Head-Driven Phrase Structure Grammar*. University of Chicago Press, and CSLI, Palo Alto, CA.

Pomerantz, A. 1984. Agreeing and Disagreeing with Assessments: Some Features of Preferred/Dispreferred Turn Shapes. In J. M. Atkinson and J. Heritage, eds., *Structures of Social Action*: Studies in Conversational Analysis, 57–101. Cambridge University Press.

Recanati, F. 1987. *Meaning and Force: The Pragmatics of Performative Sentences*. Cambridge University Press.

Roberts, C. MS. Uniqueness Presuppositions in Definite Noun Phrases.

Ross, J. R. 1970. On Declarative Sentences. In Jacobs, R. A. and Rosenbaum, P. S., eds., *Readings in English Transformational Grammar*. Waltham: Ginn.

Sacks, H. and Schegloff, E. 1979. Two Preferences in the Organization of Reference to Persons in Conversation and Their

Interaction. In G. Psathas, ed., *Everyday Language: Studies in Ethnomethodology.* New York: Irvington.

Sadock, J. M. 1970. Whimperatives. In J. Sadock and A. Vanek, eds., *Studies Presented to Robert B. Lees by His Students*, 223–38. Edmonton, Alberta: Linguistic Research, Inc.

1972. Speech Act Idioms. In P. M. Peranteau, J. N. Levi, and G. C. Phares, eds., *Papers from the Eighth Regional Meeting of the Chicago Linguistic Society*, 329–39. Chicago: Chicago Linguistic Society.

1974. *Toward a Linguistic Theory of Speech Acts.* New York: Academic Press.

Sadock, J. M. and Zwicky, A. M. 1985. Speech Act Distinctions in Syntax. In T. Shopen, ed., *Language Typology and Syntactic Description: Clause Structure.* Cambridge University Press.

Schegloff, E. A. 1972a. Notes on a Conversational Practice: Formulating Place. In D. Sudnow, ed., *Studies in Social Interaction.* New York: Free Press.

1972b. Sequencing in Conversational Openings. In J. Gumperz and D. Hymes, eds., *Directions in Sociolinguistics*, 346–80. New York: Holt, Rinehart & Winston.

1984. On Questions and Ambiguities in Conversation. In J. M. Atkinson and J. Heritage, eds., *Structures of Social Action: Studies in Conversational Analysis*, 28–52. Cambridge University Press.

1988. Presequences and Indirection: Applying Speech Act Theory to Ordinary Conversation. *Journal of Pragmatics*, 12: 55–62.

1991. Reflections on Talk and Social Structure. In D. B. and D. H. Zimmerman, eds., *Talk and Social Structure: Studies in Ethnomethodology and Conversation Analysis.* Cambridge: Polity Press.

Schegloff, E. A. and Sacks, H. 1973. Opening up Closings. *Semiotica*, 7.4: 289–387.

Schiffrin, D. 1987. *Discourse Markers.* Cambridge University Press.

Searle, J. R. 1969. *Speech Acts: An Essay in the Philosophy of Language.* Cambridge University Press.

1975. Indirect Speech Acts. In P. Cole and J. Morgan, eds., *Syntax and Semantics*, vol. 3: *Speech Acts.* New York: Academic Press.

1979. *Expression and Meaning.* Cambridge University Press.

1992. Conversation. In J. R. Searle *et al.*, eds., *(On) Searle on Conversation*, 7–29. Amsterdam and Philadelphia: John Benjamins.

Searle, J. R. and Vanderveken, D. 1985. *Foundations of Illocutionary Logic.* Cambridge University Press.

Sinclair, J. M. and Coulthard, R. M. 1975. *Towards an Analysis of Discourse: the English Used by Teachers and Pupils.* London: Oxford University Press.

Sperber, D. and Wilson, D. 1986. *Relevance: Communication and Cognition.* Oxford: Blackwell.

Stalnaker, R. 1978. In P. Cole, ed., *Syntax and Semantics,* vol. 9: *Pragmatics,* 315–32. New York: Academic Press.

Stampe, D. W. 1975. Meaning and Truth in the Theory of Speech Acts. In P. Cole and J. Morgan, eds., *Syntax and Semantics,* vol. 3: *Speech Acts.* New York: Academic Press.

Tarski, A. 1956. The Concept of Truth in Formalized Languages. *Logic, Semantics, Metamathematics,* 152–278. Oxford: Clarendon Press.

Tsui, A. B. M. 1989. Beyond the Adjacency Pair. *Language and Society,* 18: 545–64.

Van Dijk, T. A. 1972. *Some Aspects of Text Grammars.* The Hague: Mouton.

Welker, K. 1994. Plans in the Common Ground: Toward a Generative Account of Conversational Implicature. Unpublished Ohio State University Ph. D. Dissertation.

Zwicky, A. M. and Zwicky, A. D. 1982. Register as a Dimension of Linguistic Variation. In R. Kittredge and J. Lehrberger, eds., *Sublanguage: Studies of Language in Restricted Semantic Domains.* Berlin: Walter de Gruyter.

# Index